IMAGES
of America

TERRE HAUTE
FARRINGTON'S GROVE

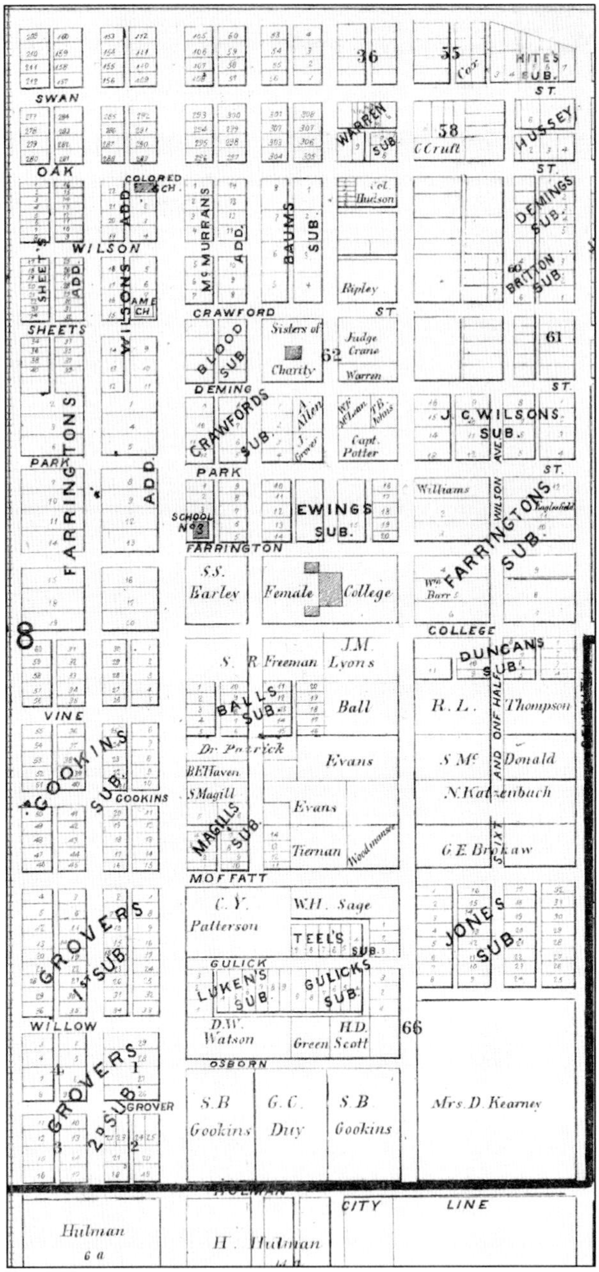

This 1874 map shows the area of Farrington's Grove Historic District; names of homeowners are visible. The north boundary is Poplar Street, and Hulman Street at the bottom was the city limit then. South Seventh Street is the east boundary. The west boundary is South Fourth Street, just west of the Terre Haute Female College on the map. (Vigo County Historical Society.)

On the Cover: Crowds flocked to the opening of Oakley Drug Store at the southwest corner of Seventh and Hulman Streets in 1941. As the first super drugstore in the city, it offered a wide assortment of products compared to neighborhood pharmacies. Wartime price controls soon affected even items on the lunch counter menu. (Oakley Corporation.)

IMAGES
of America

TERRE HAUTE FARRINGTON'S GROVE

Donna Gisolo Christenberry on behalf of
Farrington's Grove Historical District Inc.

ARCADIA
PUBLISHING

ISBN 978-0-7385-8319-8

Published by Arcadia Publishing
Charleston, South Carolina

Printed in the United States of America

Library of Congress Control Number: 2011928975

For all general information, please contact Arcadia Publishing:
Telephone 843-853-2070
Fax 843-853-0044
E-mail sales@arcadiapublishing.com
For customer service and orders:
Toll-Free 1-888-313-2665

Visit us on the Internet at www.arcadiapublishing.com

To the unsung heroes in libraries and museums
who keep history from disappearing.

Contents

ACKNOWLEDGMENTS

So many fascinating stories lie within Farrington's Grove. The challenge was finding photographs to accompany them. Special thanks go to Marylee Hagan and Barbara Carney at the Vigo County Historical Museum, who shared a treasure trove of materials and truly made this book possible. My thanks also go to David Lewis, a font of knowledge of everything Farrington's Grove, who pointed me toward information in the Vigo County Public Library and linked me with people who had stories to tell and pictures to share.

Thanks also to Vigo County historian Mike McCormick for suggestions, tips, and guidance. Your enthusiasm for local history and your reportorial skills in tracking down details make history come alive in your articles.

I would like to express my gratitude to Farrington's Grove Historical District board for their support, especially Marie Pontius, who gave me an early start with historical information she had, and Geoff Wayton, who assisted with obtaining photographs from the Indiana State University archives.

In addition, thanks to J. Richard Becker Jr., another history buff, for providing many photographs and historic materials, and to Martin Plascak, who rescued photographs from radio station WBOW's former home before the building fell to the wrecking ball.

Many people, too many to name in this acknowledgment, sat with me and shared their family stories and pictures. Beyond the dry facts in books, newspapers, and city directories, these personal stories added a human touch. Please know that the credit lines for your photographs are expressions of my thanks.

To my husband, Albert, and son Daniel, thank you for your patience while I worked on this book.

Abbreviations are given in the credit lines for frequently used sources: Vigo County Historical Society (VCHS), Vigo County Public Library Community Archives (VCPL), Indiana State University Archives (ISU), *Terre Haute Tribune-Star* (Tribune-Star), and Rose-Hulman Institute of Technology (Rose-Hulman).

Introduction

This book is not a chronological journey. Rather, it is a story of connections.

With the passage of decades, some of the history of Farrington's Grove has faded from people's memories. Digging into that history is like playing a game of Six Degrees of Kevin Bacon, except with a Terre Haute twist. It is hard to find someone of local note who does not have some connection to the Grove.

Some, such as Farrington's Grove residents Col. Richard W. Thompson, Col. William E. McLean, and Sen. Daniel Voorhees, were among a group known as Terre Haute's Big Five in the 1800s because of their political and financial influence. Others were less famous but still have stories to tell.

This book covers a period from the mid-1800s to the 1960s. The address system for Terre Haute as a whole—and sometimes for individual structures—has changed during that period. As much as possible, I have tried to use the addresses currently visible on houses so that people can visit the neighborhood and find the buildings described. The colors are gorgeous, and the gingerbread designs on the smaller homes are wonderful. Take a tour.

Farrington's Grove Historic District officially extends from South Fourth to South Seventh Streets and from Poplar to Hulman Streets. It contains nearly 1,000 homes, schools, offices, and other buildings. In 1986, the entire district became the first Terre Haute neighborhood to be listed in the National Register of Historic Places; regrettably, this book can show only a small percentage of the structures here.

In 1816, the year Indiana became a state, the village of Terre Haute was established. Near the riverfront was a settlement of the Wea tribe, but the Europeans who came gave the area a French name—Terre Haute, meaning "high land." Dependent on the Wabash River for travel and trade, the early settlers lived along the riverfront and then expanded businesses beyond the riverfront to the public square and the muddy Main Street, which later was renamed Wabash Avenue.

Thomas Bullitt and his brother Cuthbert were among the five men who, as the Terre Haute Company, originally platted the village of Terre Haute. Bullitt owned the land in the area known today as Farrington's Grove. Most of the land within today's historic district was sold to two men: James Farrington and Samuel Gookins, law partners and good friends.

Farrington bought much of the land in the northern half of the district. In 1831, he bought 47.76 acres and "other lands" from one of Thomas Bullitt's heirs. Boundaries of the 47.76 acres would today consist of South Third and South Seventh Streets to the west and east, and Deming Street and College Avenue to the north and south. Another smaller section was bounded by Crawford, Deming, South Third, and South Sixth Streets.

Farrington built his house, named Woodlawn, on the east side of South Fifth Street between Park and Farrington Streets. "Mr. Farrington's Grove," as his farm was known, was a wooded area in the country in 1841. It became a gathering place for neighbors attending picnics, celebrations, and political events. A fire nearly destroyed Woodlawn in 1855; Farrington restored it at about half its original size, less grand, at 920 South Fifth Street.

In 1847, Gookins bought a tract at the southern edge of the district from a different Bullitt heir, smaller than Farrington's acreage. The boundaries were Third and Sixth Streets and Osborne and Hulman Streets. On it, he built a large mansion known as Strawberry Hill. In 1854, the Vigo County Fair, one of the county's first, took place near his home.

Among notable speakers at the Farrington property and at a grove near the Gookins property were Sen. Stephen A. Douglas, who ran against Abraham Lincoln for US president; abolitionist Sen. Cassius Clay, who spoke in 1860; and Oliver Morton, later elected governor of Indiana in 1850.

From the 1840s to 1860s, the wealthier members of the community built large, two-story homes on Fifth, Sixth, Center, and Seventh Streets. The homes were within easy walking distance of their offices downtown. Initially, several businesses were based around meatpacking and pork exporting. Farrington was a partner with H.D. Williams in pork exporting, a profitable local industry. In 1848, a total of 54,750 hogs were packed in Terre Haute; the number grew to 108,791 in 1852. In the stream of time, the cattle industry overlapped the pork industry. Beef packing by businessmen, such as Farrington's Grove resident Charles Ehrmann, continued into the early 1900s; even at that time, residents sometimes had to evade the cattle herded through the streets.

Although tutors were available for those who could afford it, private schools began to make their appearance in Terre Haute in the mid-1800s; an advertisement for one in an 1860 city directory noted the city had "no public schools." The Terre Haute Female College opened in 1858 to pomp and circumstance by local business leaders; it was also called Covert College after its founder John Covert. Sold in 1863, it became St. Agnes Academy, also known as St. Agnes Hall. Jane Coates, of Greencastle, purchased the former Gookins home and created Coates College for Women, which opened in 1885 and closed in 1897. Once legal objections to tax-supported education in Indiana were out of the way, Terre Haute established public schools. In Farrington's Grove, the Second District School opened in 1867.

Among early residents of Farrington's Grove were members of the Crawford, Deming, and Fairbanks families, prominent in the early business life of Terre Haute. Some of their elaborate homes closer to the downtown area no longer exist today. By the late 1880s and early 1900s, smaller houses were built in Farrington's Grove, particularly along South Fourth Street, for workers and their families.

In the heart of Farrington's Grove was St. Anthony's Hospital. It moved into the Grove in 1884 and became Terre Haute's first permanent hospital through the philanthropy of Herman Hulman Sr. and the wishes of his wife, Antonia, who died in 1883.

Among newspaper publishers who lived in Farrington's Grove were W.C. Ball, Col. Robert Hudson, and Donald Nixon, founder of the *Saturday Spectator*. Nixon had honed his reporting skills in New York, and his crusading journalism earned him an attack with brass knuckles when he angered officials of the Terre Haute, Indianapolis & Eastern Traction Company (THI&E), who hired a union strikebreaker to intimidate him.

Farrington's Grove also has been home to its share of artists. Among them is James Farrington Gookins, son of Samuel Gookins, who won fame for his fanciful landscapes and was instrumental in pushing to make the Chicago lakefront a park and place for museums. John Rogers Cox grew up in the Grove, became the first director of Terre Haute's Swope Art Museum, and went on to teach at the Art Institute of Chicago. In the early 1900s and until his death, Max Ehrmann brought a quiet philosophy to his poetry and writings, winning honor as Terre Haute's poet laureate.

In the 1950s and 1960s, fraternities from Indiana State Teachers College and Rose Polytechnic moved into the neighborhood, using older houses with plenty of room for students. Today, that trend has been reversing, as fraternities have been moving out and private owners have been renovating historic properties.

One

A Poet, Politicians, and Educators

Farrington's Grove has been home to movers and shakers in the fields of both education and politics. It also was the home of Terre Haute's poet laureate Max Ehrmann.

Though Ehrmann was a Harvard-trained lawyer and initially worked in that profession, he had the heart of a poet and gave full rein to his writing from 1912 onward. He often sat on a bench at Seventh Street and Wabash Avenue in downtown Terre Haute, taking notes and reflecting on the sea of humanity swirling by. Though his poem "Desiderata" is his best-known work, Ehrmann produced a collection of thoughtful writings, including 20 books and pamphlets as well as many essays and poems.

In the political arena, Sen. Daniel Voorhees helped establish the Library of Congress as it exists today by pushing for funding of the building. After the Copyright Law of 1870, applicants had to send the library two copies of their work; materials quickly overflowed the Capitol storage space for Congress's research library. Virginia Jenckes made history with her election to Congress in 1932 as Indiana's first female representative; she campaigned because as secretary of the Wabash-Maumee Improvement Association, she knew the need for improved flood control on the Wabash River. Socialist candidate for US president and labor leader Eugene V. Debs was a frequent visitor and speaker at the Red House. Col. Richard W. Thompson served as secretary of the Navy and stumped the state so that tax-supported public schools would be available to everyone.

Within the boundaries of Farrington's Grove have been several private schools, especially in Terre Haute's early days before public education existed. Among them have been Terre Haute Female College, opened in 1858; Coates College, opened in 1885; and King Classical School, founded in 1906. Once the constitutional issue of public-supported schools was settled, public schools were built in the Farrington's Grove area. Second District School, later renamed Hulman School, opened in 1867. The first Crawford School, originally the Third District School, opened in 1872 and its successor in 1961. Fairbanks School opened in 1906.

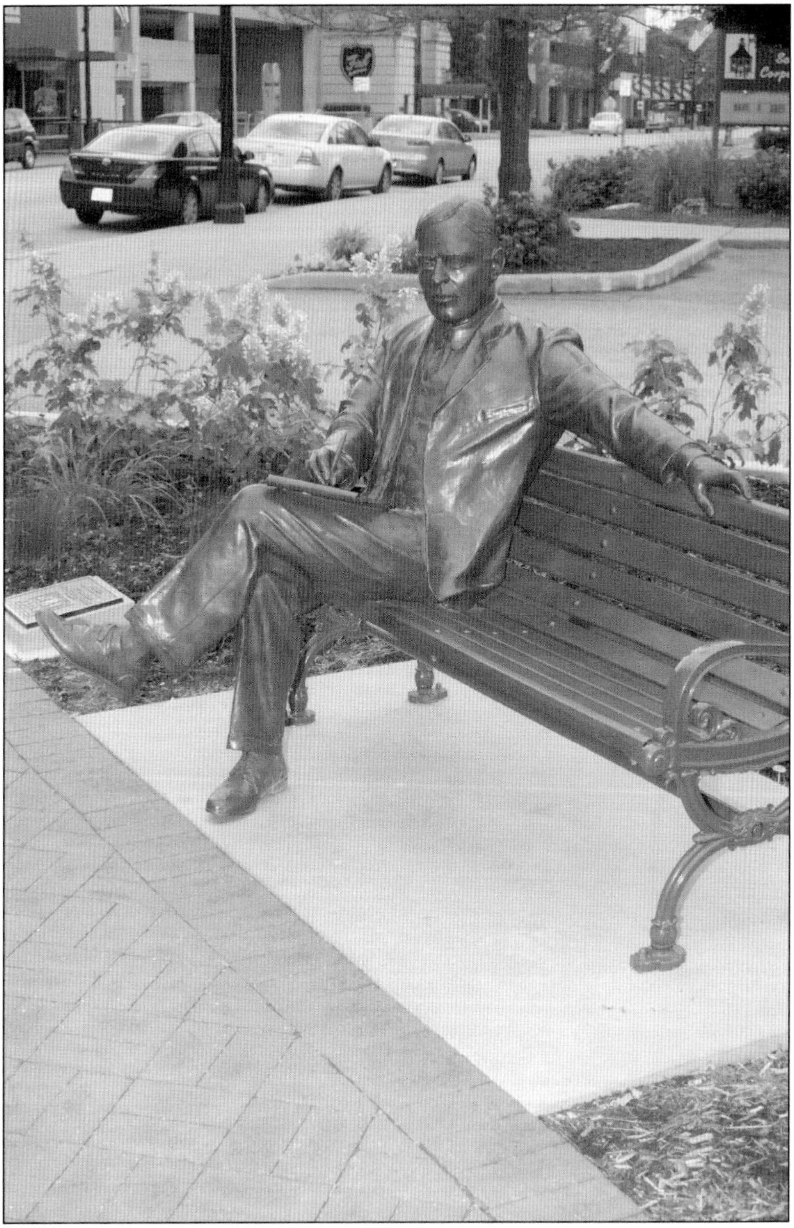

Best known for his poem "Desiderata," Max Ehrmann has inspired people worldwide to "go placidly amid the noise and haste" and to "remember that you are a child of the universe; no less than the trees and stars, you have a right to be here." He published the poem in 1927, but for many years, it was mistakenly attributed to a Boston church before Ehrmann reclaimed his authorship. A recording of his poem by Les Crane won a Grammy in 1971, and ambassador Adlai Stevenson had it by his bedside when he died. The Harvard-trained Ehrmann served as deputy state's attorney and then worked on legal matters for his brother Charles Ehrmann's businesses. Living with his brothers at 805 South Fifth Street gave Ehrmann the opportunity to work on his writing. From age 40 onward, he devoted himself exclusively to writing. Terre Haute's poet laureate is depicted in bronze at Seventh Street and Wabash Avenue. Terre Haute artist Bill Wolfe created the sculpture.

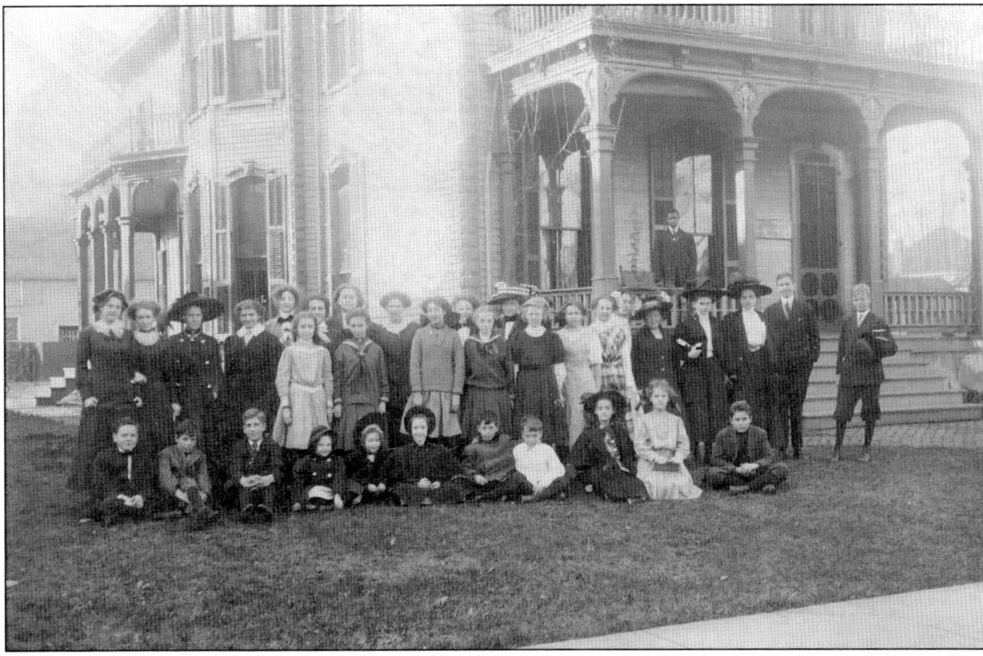

Poet Max Ehrmann married longtime companion Bertha Pratt King in King Classical School at 901 South Sixth Street on June 3, 1945. King was a Smith College graduate, suffragette, and Chautauqua lecturer; she cofounded the school in September 1906. This photograph of the school's faculty and students is from about 1920. Stricken with a cerebral hemorrhage here, Ehrmann died in nearby St. Anthony's Hospital on September 9, 1945. (VCHS.)

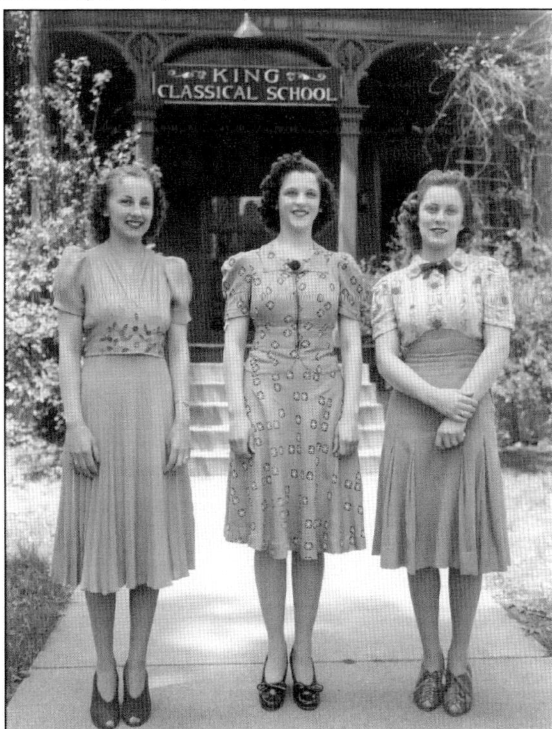

From left to right, Marcella McCann, Rose Jenkins, and Ann Monninger comprise the 1940 graduating class of King Classical School at 901 South Sixth Street. The private school accepted boys and girls from kindergarten through junior high school, but only girls for high school and college preparation. Graduates attended Vassar, Radcliffe, and other prestigious colleges, and did not have to take examinations to enter certain midwestern colleges. (Photograph by Martin's Photo Shop; VCHS.)

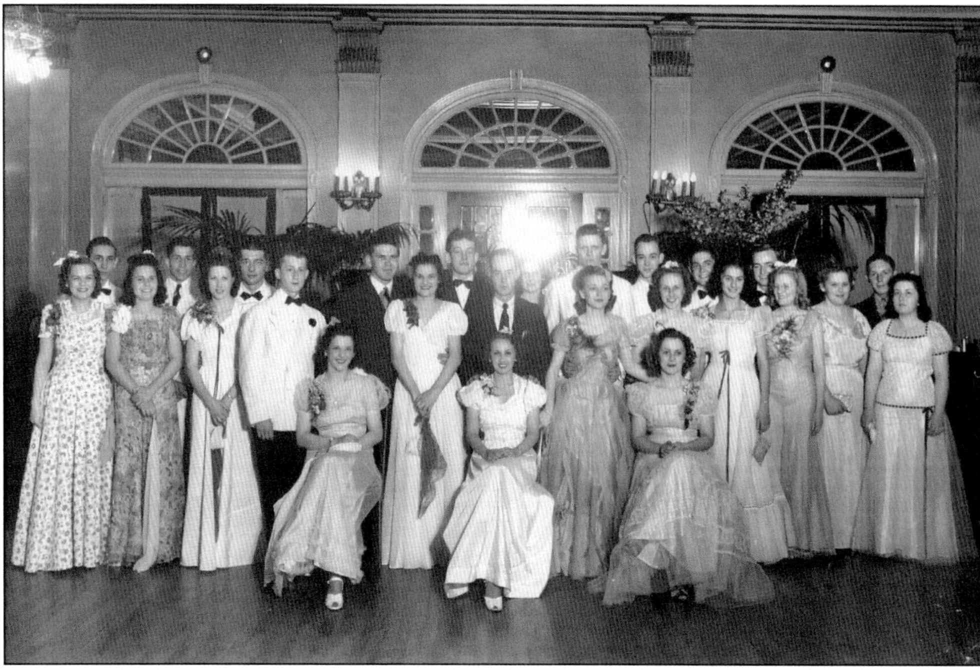

At the 1940 formal graduation dance in the Deming Hotel, King Classical School students practiced social niceties. Daily work at the school comprised four hours in the morning. The school originally was in the 600 block of Oak Street. It was a community asset; businessmen purchased 901 South Sixth Street in 1920, creating a stock company and entrusting school management to Bertha Pratt King. (Photograph by Martin's Photo Shop; VCHS.)

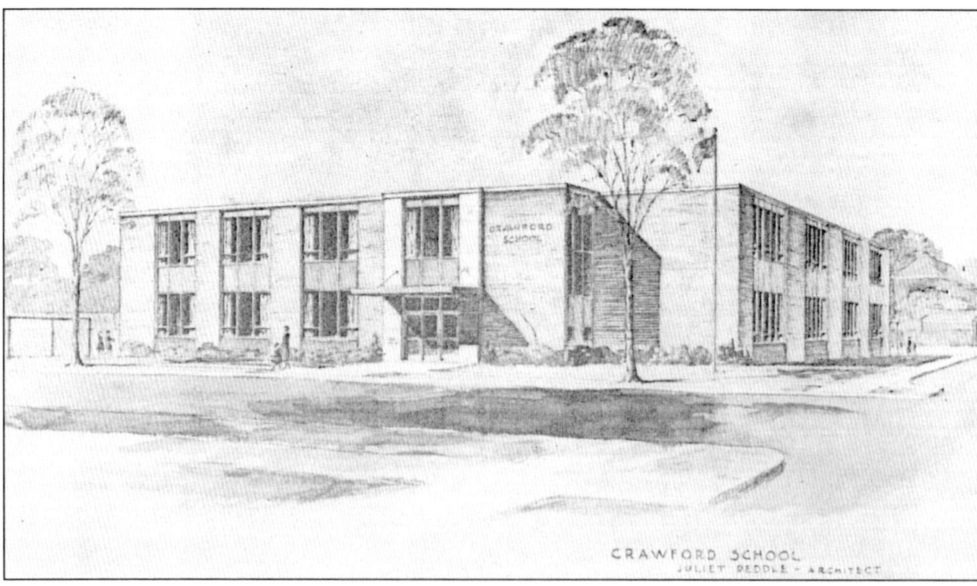

Juliet Peddle, a King Classical School graduate, was the first female registered architect in Indiana. Among her Terre Haute works are the Community Theatre and the new Crawford School at 701 South Fifth Street, shown here. It opened October 30, 1961. The $475,212 structure contained a multipurpose room, office suite, teachers' workroom, and lounge. Classrooms were wired for television reception. It closed in 2002. (Educational Heritage Association of Vigo County.)

These kindergarteners await pickup at Crawford School in October 1962. Their parents drove them in from Prairieton because the school there did not have kindergarten classes. They are, from left to right, Julie Francis, Robin Hawkins, James Drake, Hal Johnston (who grew up to become an attorney), and Brian Francis. (Brian Francis.)

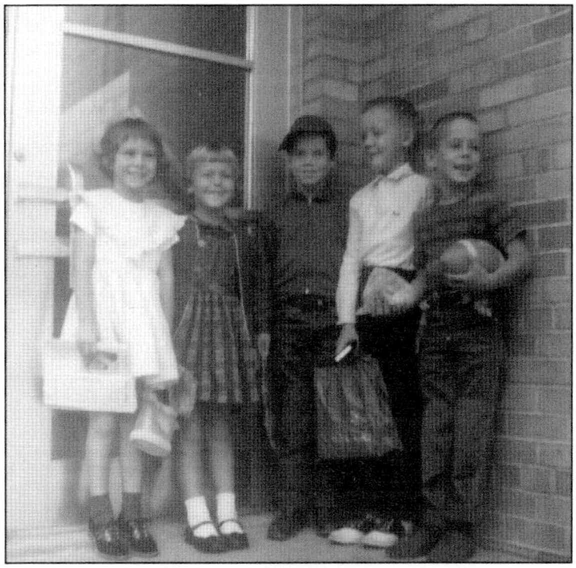

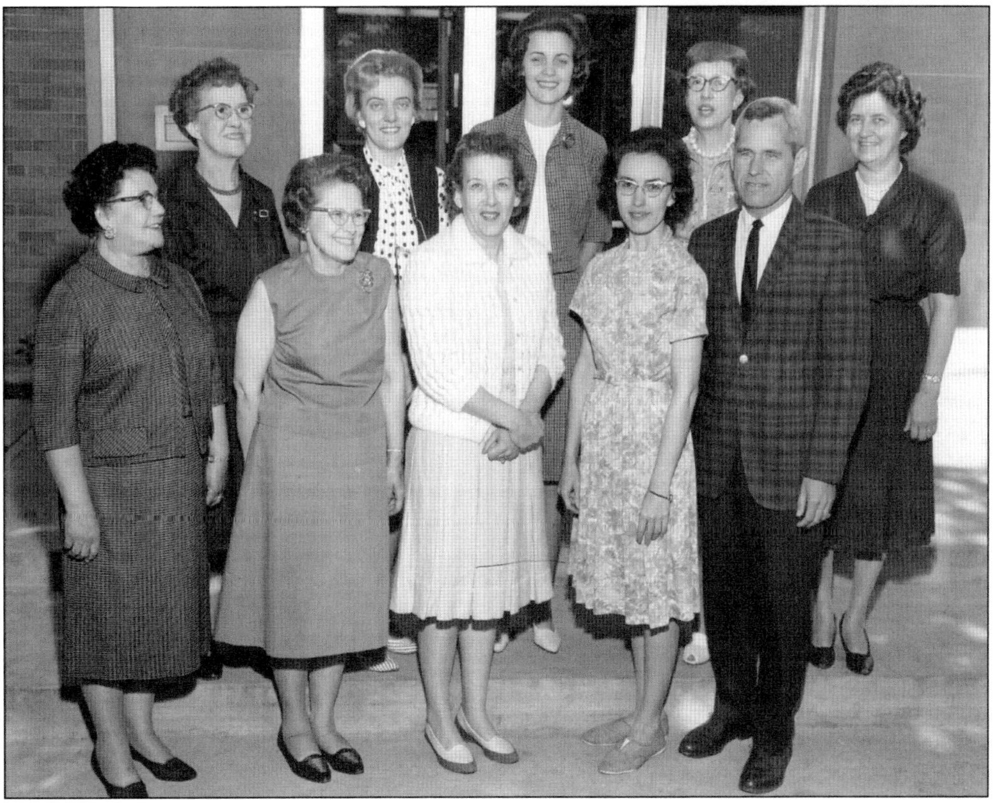

Crawford School at 701 South Fifth Street was designed with synchronized clocks and automatic day-night control of a forced warm air system. The 1964–1965 faculty are, from left to right, (first row) principal Ruth Laxen, Irene McDonough, Ruth Jonas, Ladonna Strahla, and Herman Neckar; (second row) Jean Archibald, Gerri Black, Mary Lou Woods, Margaret Gantner, and Thelma Chatman. (Photograph by Richard H. Bruce; Educational Heritage Association of Vigo County.)

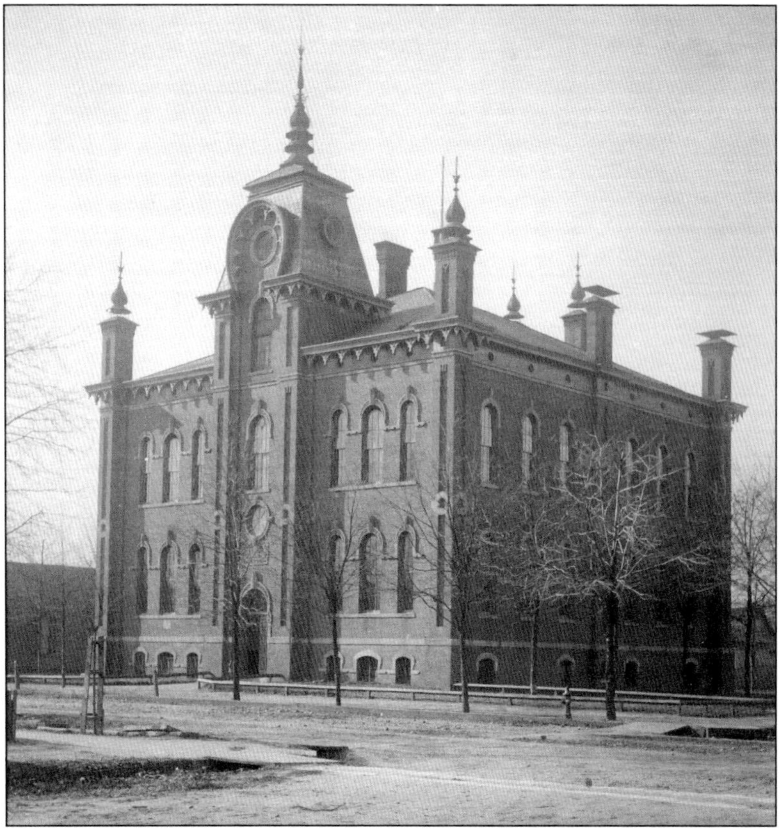

The old Crawford School at 930 South Third Street, originally called the Third District School, was completed in 1872. Principal John Donaldson earned $800 a year as principal and for teaching eighth grade. The 10 classrooms had no indoor plumbing. Coal stoves heated the basement, and a central warm air system heated the rest. Added in 1905 were indoor plumbing and a new furnace for a hot water system. (VCHS.)

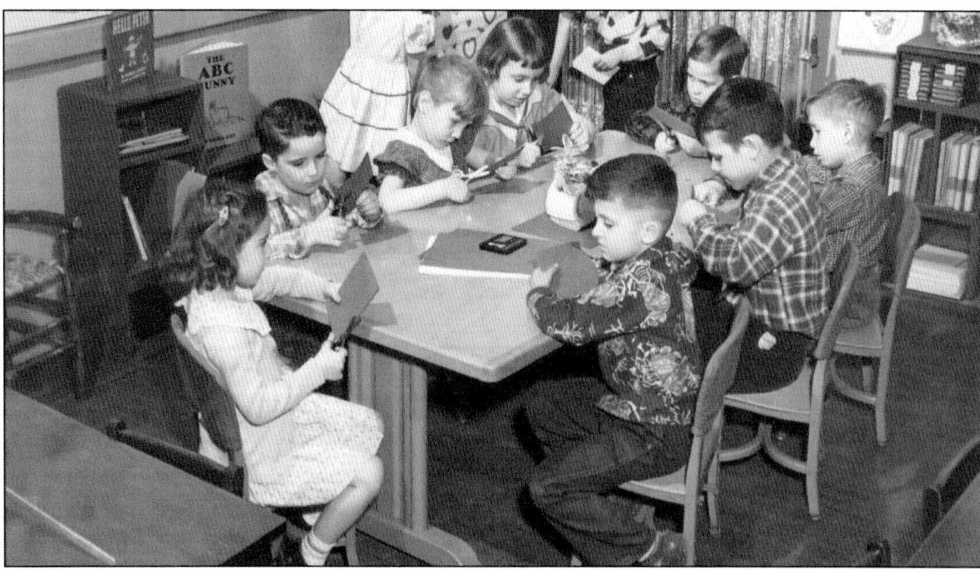

A group of first graders work on a construction paper project in the old Crawford School at 930 South Third Street in this 1954 photograph. Times had changed since 1872, when Katherine Lamb earned $320 a year to teach two first-grade classes and one second-grade class. When the Third District School was renamed Crawford in 1906, Clara Graff served as its first principal. (Photograph by Martin's Photo Shop; VCHS.)

Col. Richard W. Thompson campaigned for tax-supported public schools, was president of the board of Terre Haute Female College in 1859, and was later trustee for Indiana State Normal. His father married into George Washington's family; as a boy in Virginia, Thompson saw Thomas Jefferson, James Madison, James Monroe, and the Marquis de Lafayette. He served in Indiana's General Assembly, in Congress, and as secretary of the Navy under Pres. Rutherford Hayes. (Tribune-Star.)

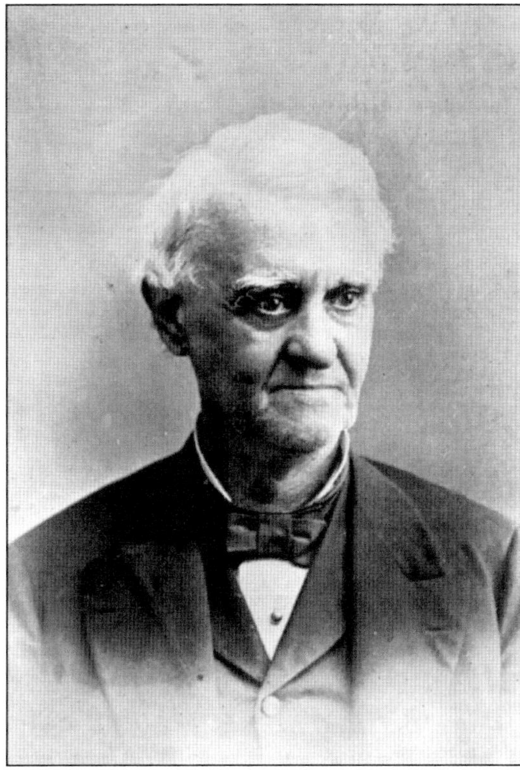

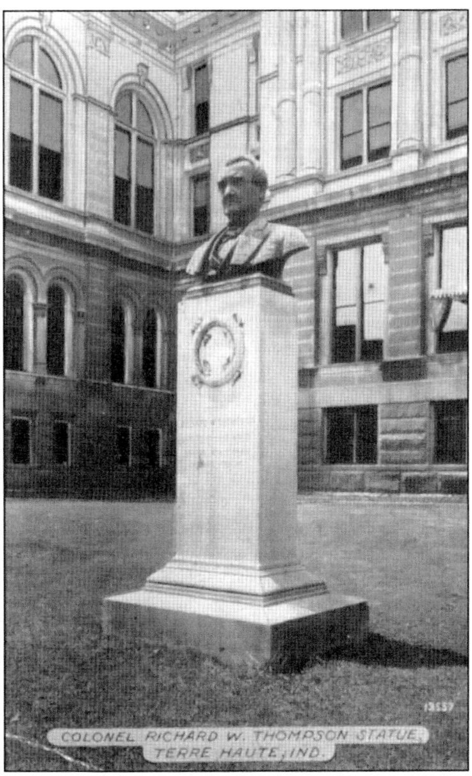

Colonel Thompson was highly respected by friends and opponents, and his life was commemorated by this bust on the northeast side of the Vigo County Courthouse lawn in 1902, two years after his death. Col. W.E. McLean, like Thompson one of Terre Haute's Big Five, delivered the address. Family friend E.H. Bindley, who owned a wholesale pharmacy in town, unveiled the statue. (Ray Thomas.)

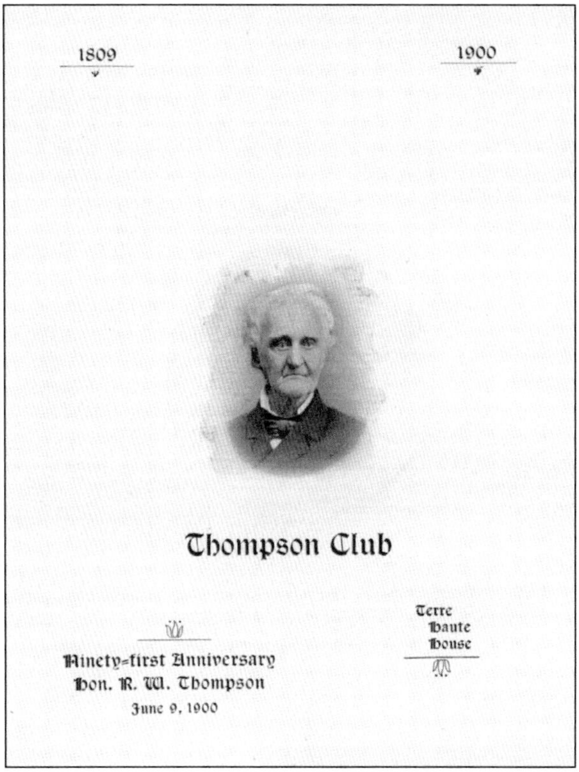
1809

1900

Thompson Club

Terre
Haute
House

Ninety-first Anniversary
Hon. R. W. Thompson
June 9, 1900

John Volkers, husband of Alice Yeakle Volkers, received this invitation to the second annual meeting of the Thompson Club on June 9, 1900. He worked with Col. Richard W. Thompson in the Revenue Collection Service. The meeting on the 91st anniversary of Thompson's birth was a posthumous honor to Terre Haute's elder statesman, who died in February 1900. It lasted until 2:00 a.m. George O. Dix was president. (Vivian S. Bath.)

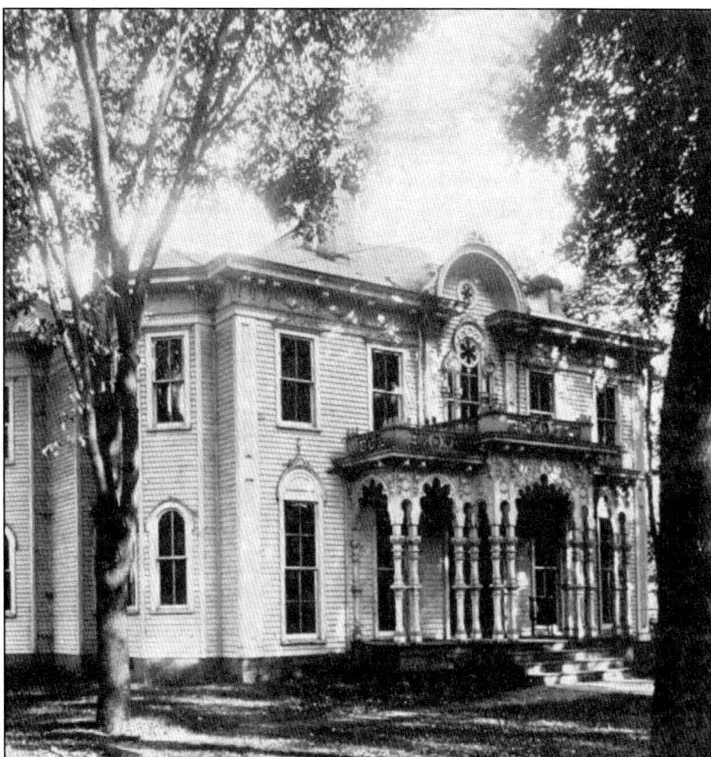

In 1877, Colonel Thompson purchased this house, no longer extant, at 1200 South Sixth Street. He and the two preceding owners brought respectability to the house once known as "Rowdy Hall." Wealthy young Samuel McDonald had reveled in the name of Rowdy Hall and gained notoriety for his expensive coaches and hunting dogs, wild parties, fancy Baltimore ladies, and chariot races down Sixth Street. (Anne Burkett.)

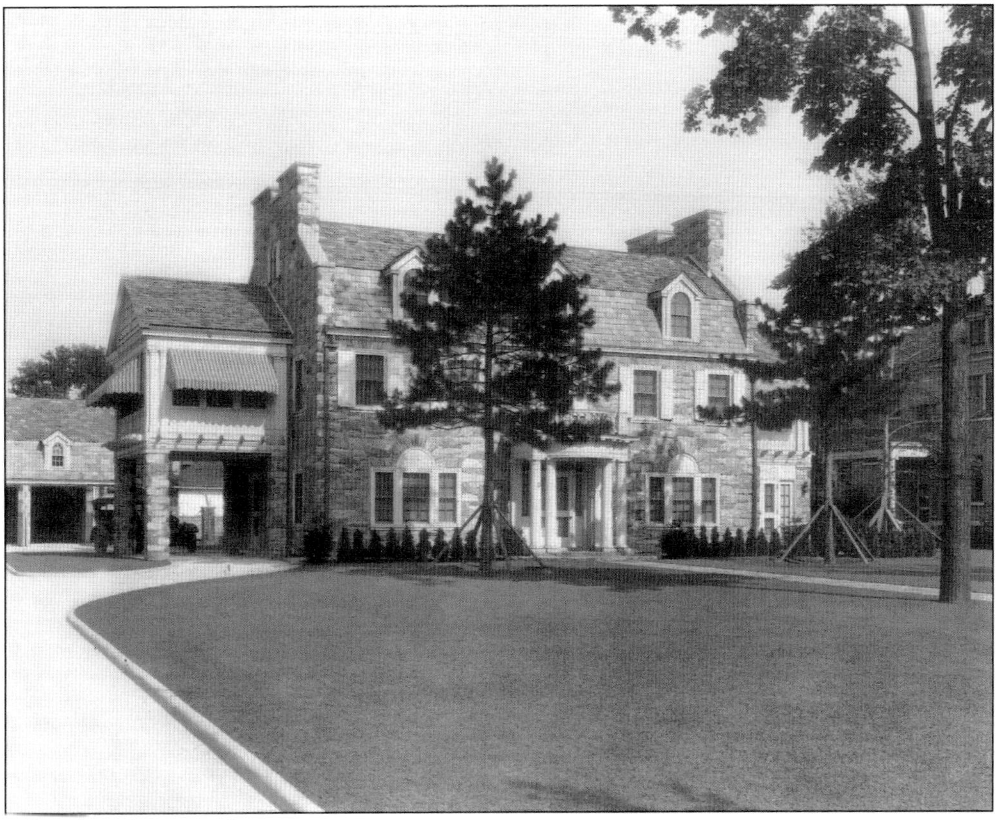

After the Thompson house was demolished, parts were salvaged for two other houses in Farrington's Grove. In 1928, Homer and Carrie Talley built this Georgian–Colonial Revival house of handpicked Pennsylvania fieldstone on part of the Thompson property at 1200 South Sixth Street. Homer and his brothers Walter and John ran the Talley Coal Company. He died in 1935 while returning from South Africa. (Steve and Marie Pontius.)

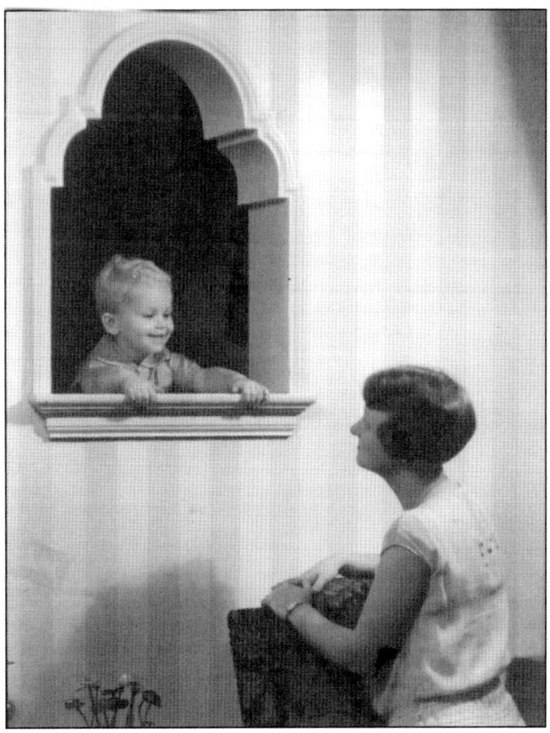

John Talley Edmonds, age two, peeks through an interior window toward his mother, Mary Alice Talley Edmonds, in the living room of the house at 1200 South Sixth Street in this photograph from about 1930. Mary Alice was the daughter of Homer Talley. The Talleys sold the home to Lambda Chi Alpha fraternity in 1965. It returned to private ownership in 2002. (Steve and Marie Pontius.)

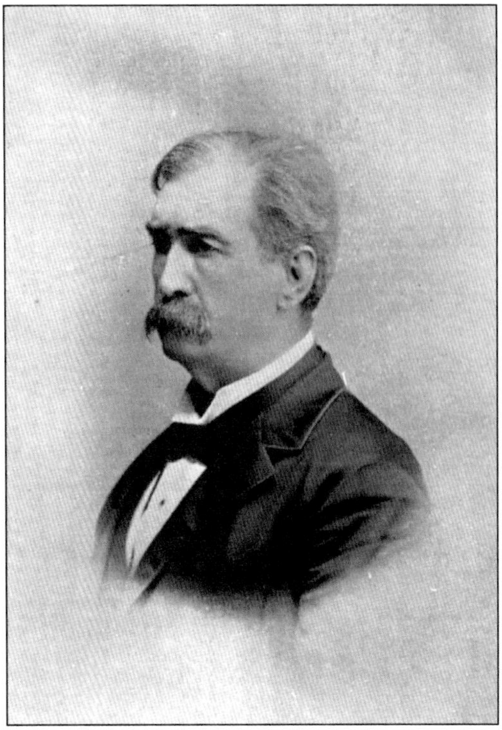

Sen. Daniel Voorhees sometimes clashed politically with Col. Richard Thompson, yet each respected the other. In 1859, Voorhees gained national fame for defending the Indiana governor's brother-in-law, co-conspirator of abolitionist John Brown at Harper's Ferry. The Library of Congress credits Voorhees for its creation; he championed a $6.5 million appropriation to build a home for the library, which had been overspilling congressional research shelves in the Capitol. (J. Richard Becker Jr.)

Senator Voorhees was known as the "Tall Sycamore of the Wabash" for his height. His funeral on April 15, 1897, attracted many dignitaries—a procession of 36 carriages, 20 buggies, and 511 marching men accompanied the flag-draped coffin from downtown to Highland Lawn Cemetery. Honorary pallbearers included Col. Richard Thompson, Herman Hulman Sr., Indiana governor James Mount, and ex-governor Claude Matthews. (VCHS.)

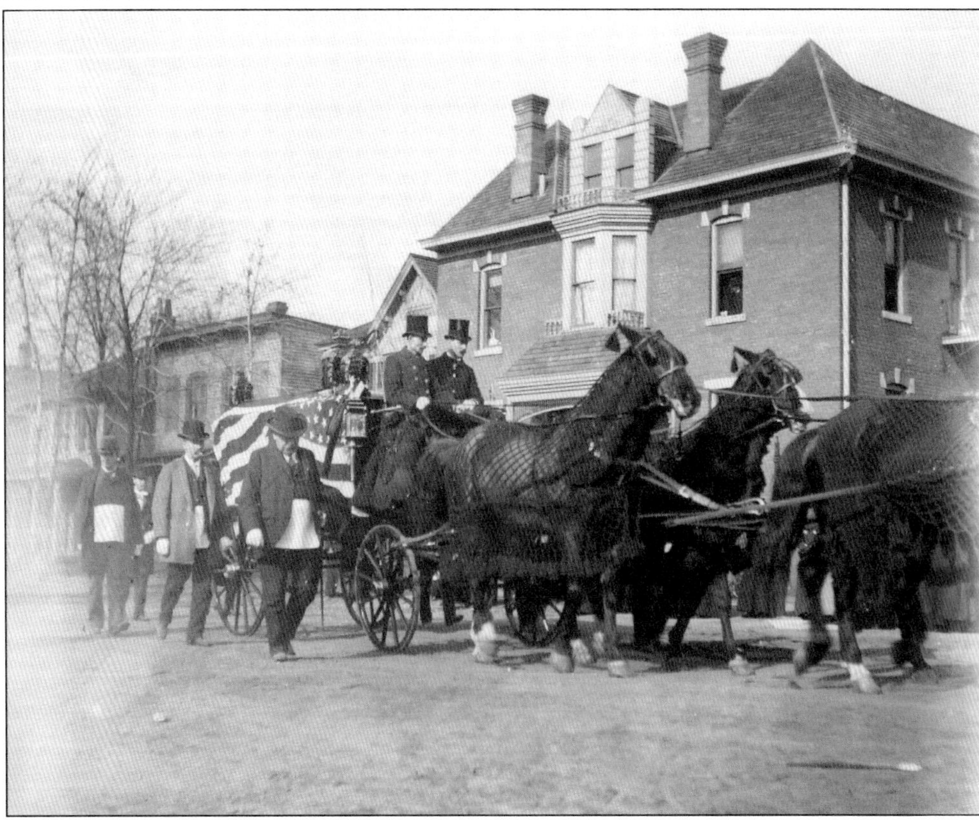

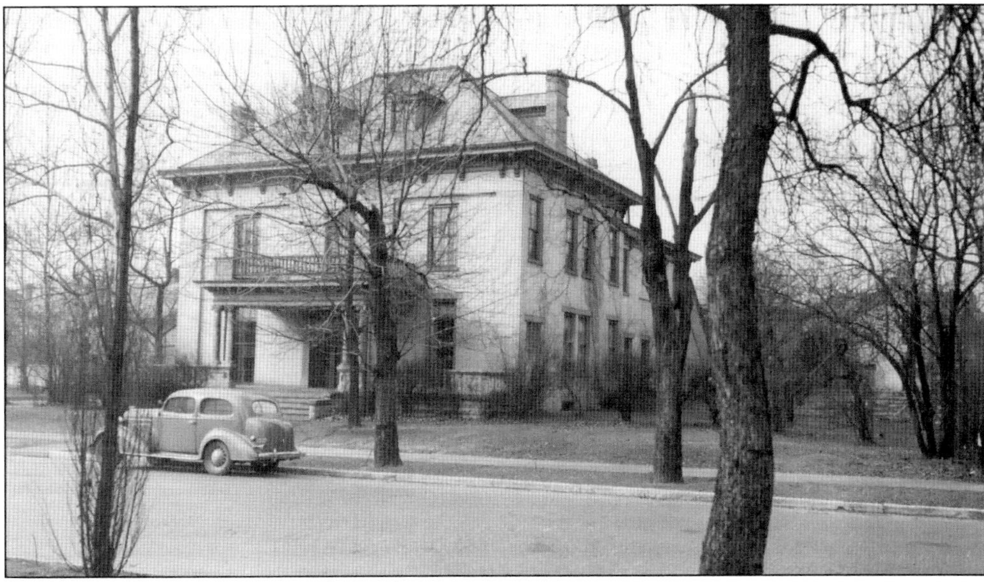

Senator Voorhees and his family lived at 625 South Sixth Street during the Civil War; the Italianate-style brick house was built in the early 1850s. This house later served as the home of Virginia Jenckes, another legislator. In 1932, Jenckes was the first woman elected to Congress from Indiana—after suffrage became the law of the land. She ousted two incumbents. (Photograph by Juliet Peddle; VCHS.)

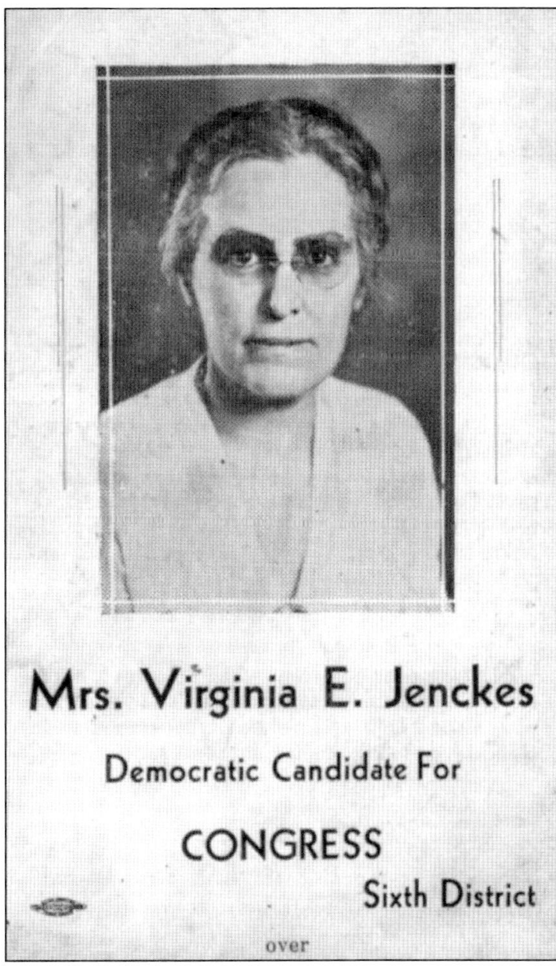

The back of this Virginia Jenckes campaign card says she was campaigning to aid farmers, laborers, and businessmen and to repeal the 18th Amendment to end bootlegging. However, the card clarifies that Jenckes "never drinks intoxicating liquors." Running the family farm after her husband Ray died, Jenckes witnessed Prohibition's effect on law and order and saw the need for Wabash River flood control. (VCPL.)

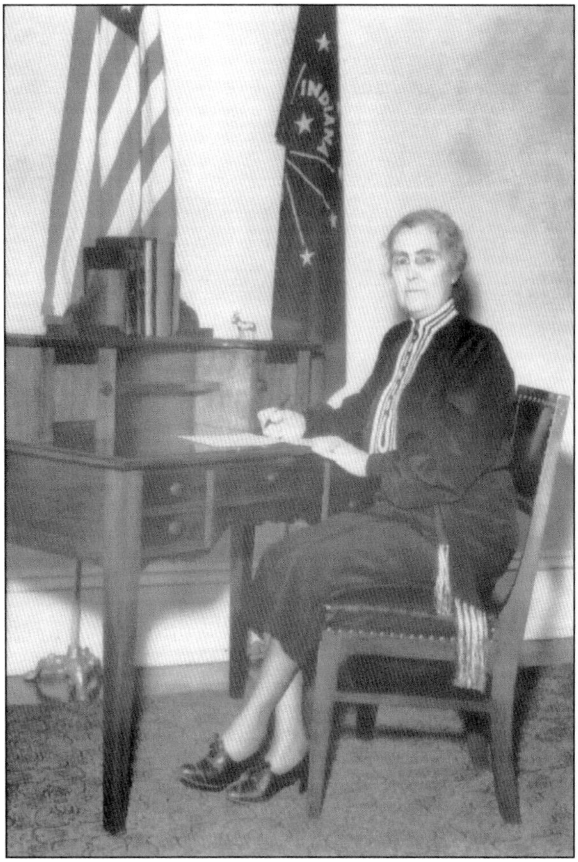

Politicians who gave the public a dirty deal felt the sting of Rep. Virginia Jenckes's sharp wit. During the New Deal era, she clashed with Eleanor Roosevelt and worried that the Works Progress Administration (WPA) would compete with local businesses. She also worried about Russia's growing power and stood by in support as the capital's fire chief burned a Russian flag hoisted on the Supreme Court flagpole. (VCHS.)

Introduced to President Kennedy as "America's James Bond," CIA agent William Harvey plotted the Berlin Tunnel to wiretap East German communications and personally met JFK in Chicago with evidence of Soviet missiles in Cuba. The Cuban Missile Crisis began two days later. Harvey lived here at 654 Oak Street during high school; his mother taught at Indiana State Normal. Terre Haute attorney Benjamin Small mentored Harvey's intellectual talents. (Photograph by Albert Christenberry.)

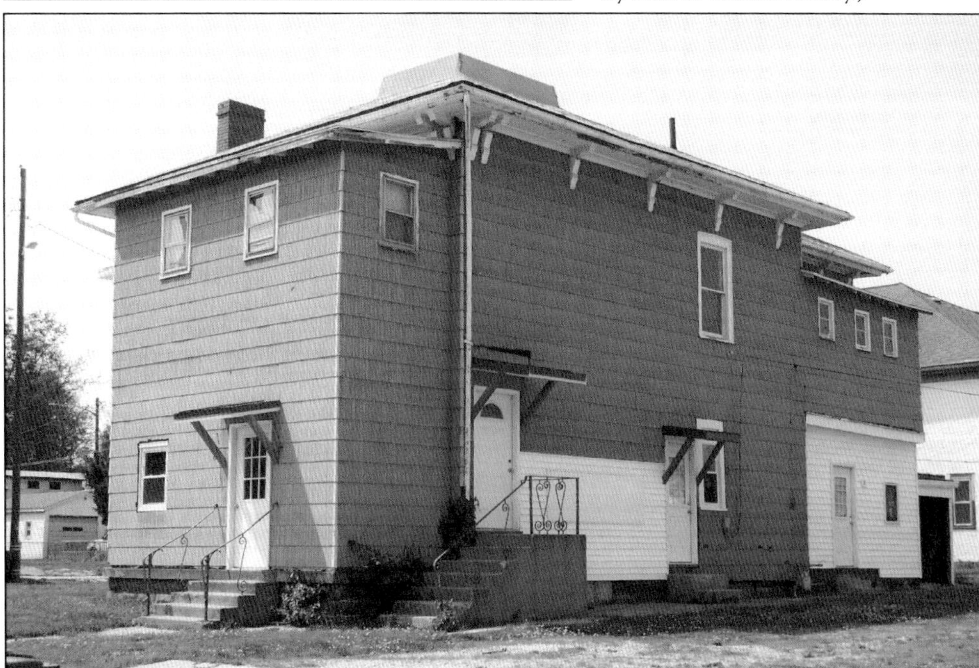

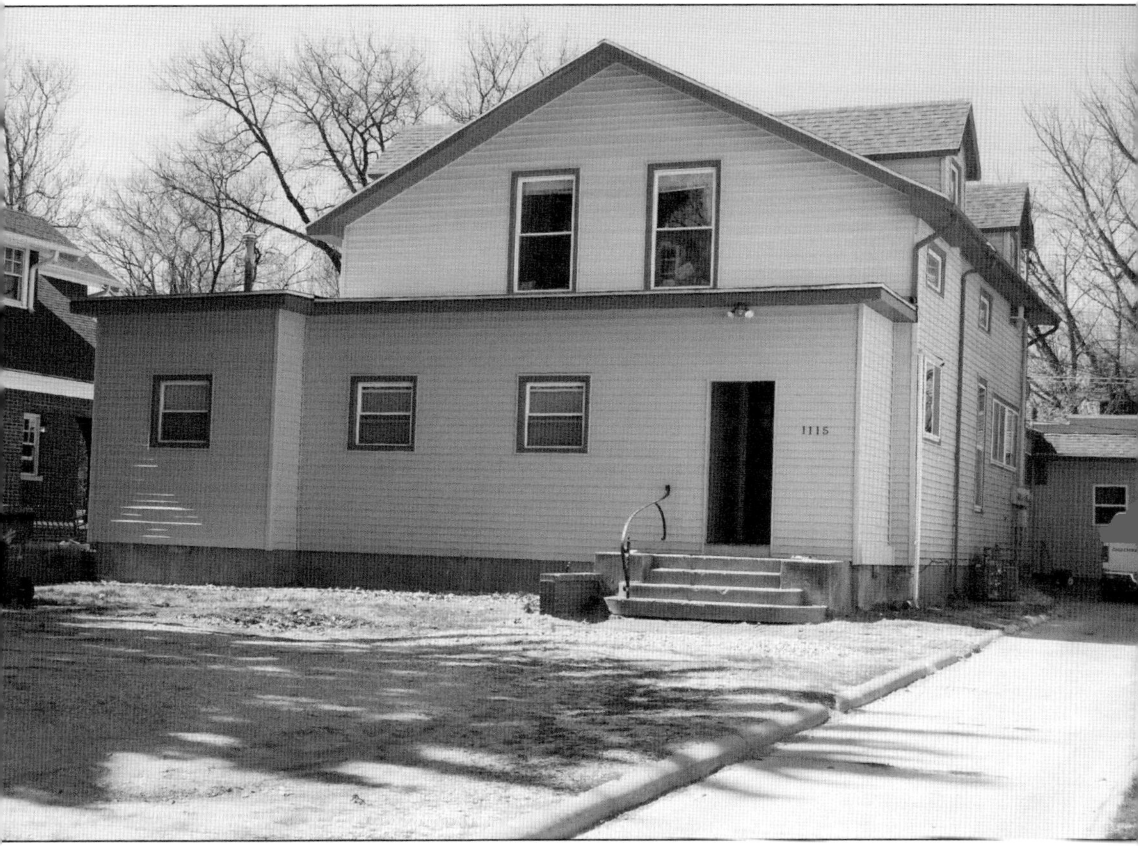

Attorney Stephen Reynolds and his wife, Jessie, purchased this house at 1115 South Sixth Street in 1890, later painting the exterior a bright red. From that paint job, it gained the nickname the "Red House." The Reynolds family became friends and supporters of Eugene V. Debs, labor organizer and Socialist candidate for president. Debs would sometimes ride over on his bicycle and cook a meal for the couple. The Reynoldses provided a three-month literacy course for workingmen and farmers, teaching more than 500 students in eight years in the Red House. As hosts of the Co-Operative Dinner Club, they opened their home to guest lecturers, such as defense attorney Clarence Darrow, American photographer Clarence White, and Walt Whitman biographer Horace Traubel. When they moved from Terre Haute in 1915, they sold the house to the Seventh-Day Adventists. Today, it is an apartment house, and the fountain formerly in the front yard is gone.

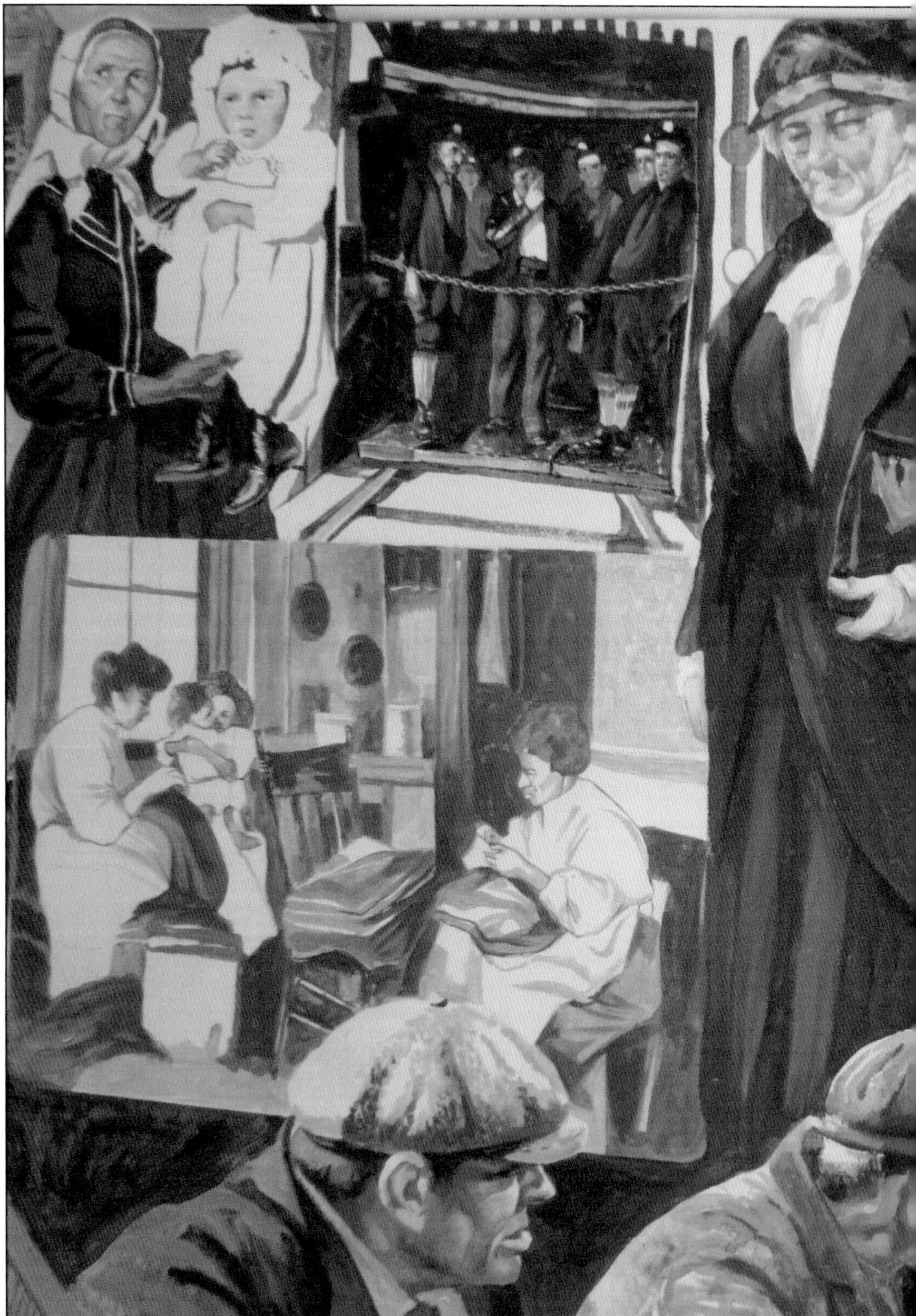

In this mural by Terre Haute artist John Laska, labor leader Mother Jones (center) and labor organizer and fedora-wearing Terre Haute native Eugene V. Debs (right) take center stage. Coal miners are visible in a mining shaft elevator. When Jones came to town, she and Debs met with coal miners at the Red House at 1115 South Sixth Street to discuss an ongoing coal strike. Tobacco-chewing, coal-dust-dirty miners filled the home. At the Red House, everyone was welcome to discuss the

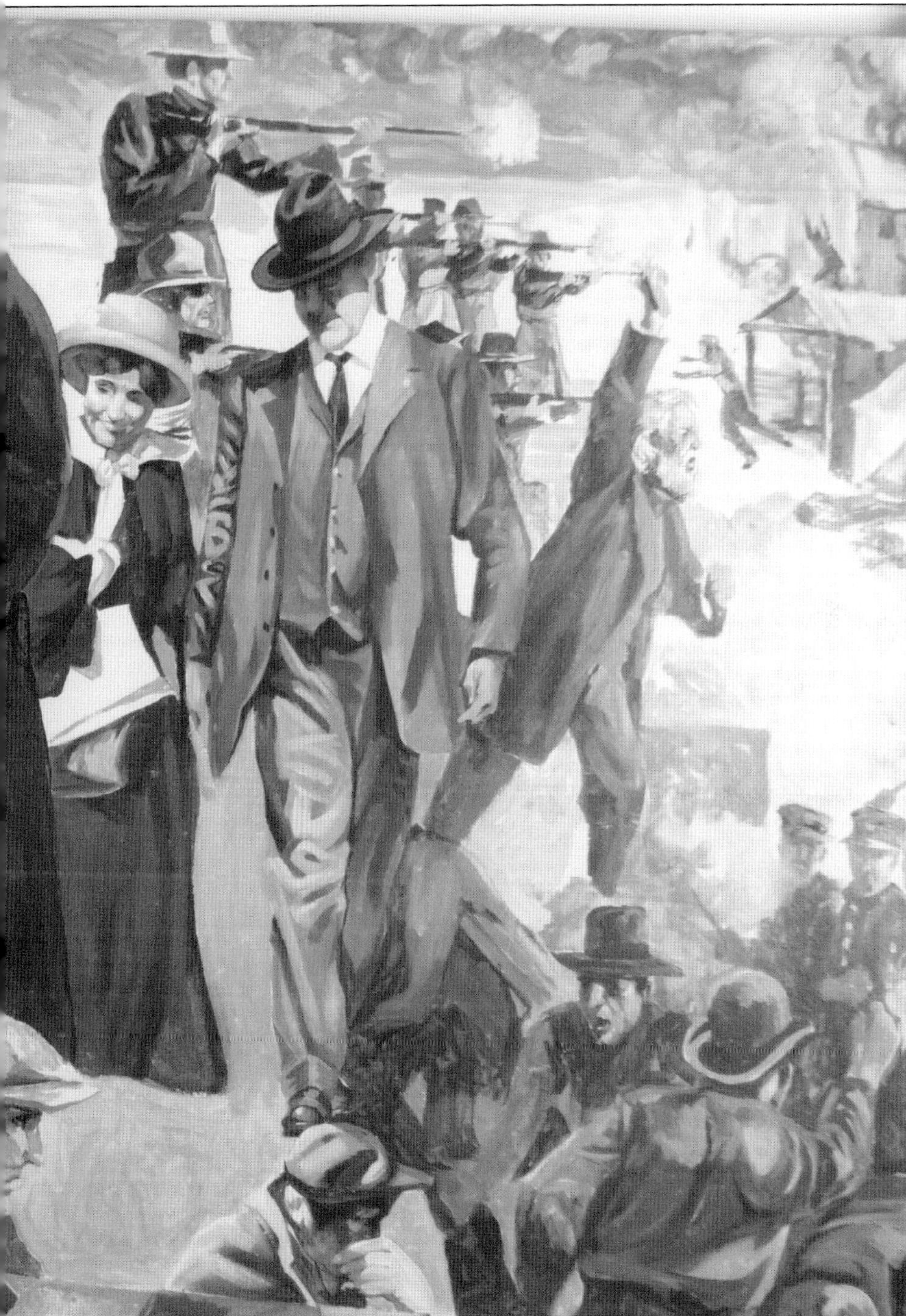

issues. In his youth, Debs worked for wholesaler Herman Hulman Sr. as a clerk. He also worked for the railroads and became a national officer of the Brotherhood of Locomotive Firemen and editor of its publication, the *Locomotive Firemen's Magazine*. Debs ran as Socialist candidate for US president in 1900, 1904, 1908, 1912, and 1920. (Eugene V. Debs Museum.)

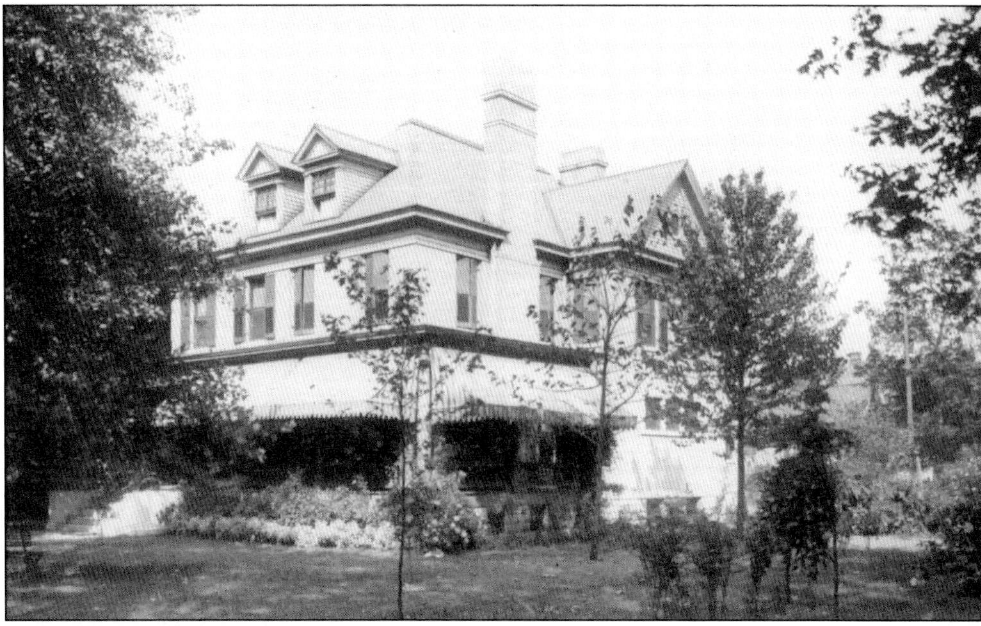

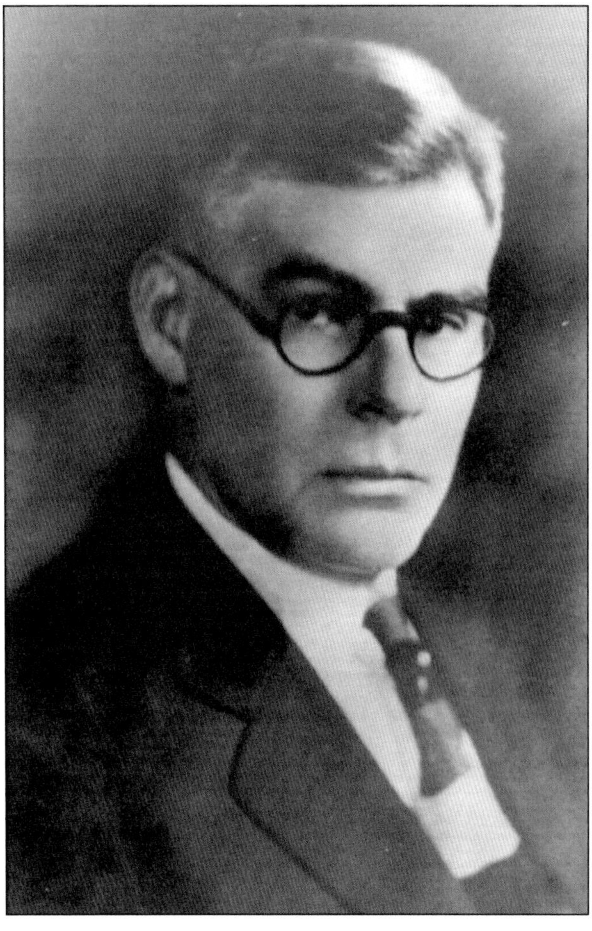

Emil Froeb, of Froeb Brothers Saddlery, lived at 1114 South Sixth Street in the early 1900s; it no longer exists. Ida Husted Harper frequently visited her sister—Froeb's wife. Eugene V. Debs hired newspaper columnist Harper to write a woman's column for *Locomotive Firemen's Magazine*. Harper helped found the Indiana Suffragette Society in 1887. She worked with Susan B. Anthony and became her official biographer. (J. Richard Becker Jr.)

Crusader Donald Nixon founded the *Saturday Spectator* and purchased other newspapers—groundwork for Nixon Newspapers. Officials targeted him for aggressively reporting THI&E Traction Company's shoddy streetcar service in 1913; strikebreaker Jack Martin assaulted Nixon with brass knuckles. Fellow strikebreaker David "Bat" Masterson, of Indianapolis (not the famous frontier lawman), testified to the plot. Nixon's house formerly stood at 916 South Center Street. (Wabash Plain Dealer.)

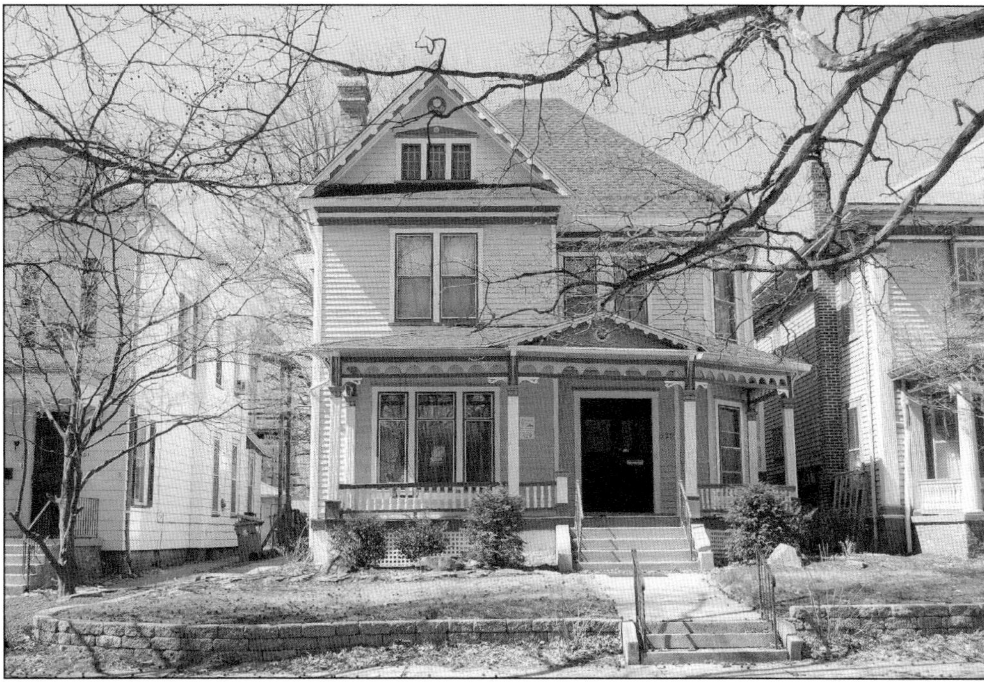

Arthur Cunningham, of 529 South Center Street, contributed to literary life in Terre Haute. Indiana State Normal president William W. Parsons invited him to be college librarian after a fire destroyed the library in 1888. Cunningham catalogued 5,000 new books before the fall semester in 1890. He served until 1928; the catalog grew to 100,000 books. Cunningham helped plan the library built on the quadrangle in 1910.

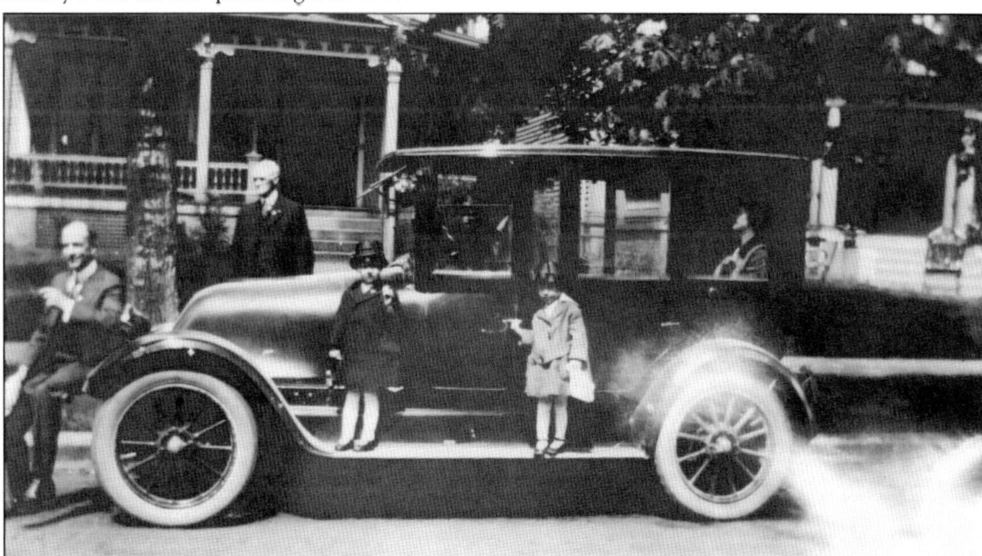

Arthur Cunningham, one of the first in town to own a car, shows off his latest model at 529 South Center Street in 1918. When it rained, he would walk to work rather than get it wet. Indiana State University named Cunningham Memorial Library in his honor in 1973. From left to right are Arthur Cunningham, his father-in-law James Rippeth, and his daughters Jane and Mary Alice Cunningham. (Peggy Apgar.)

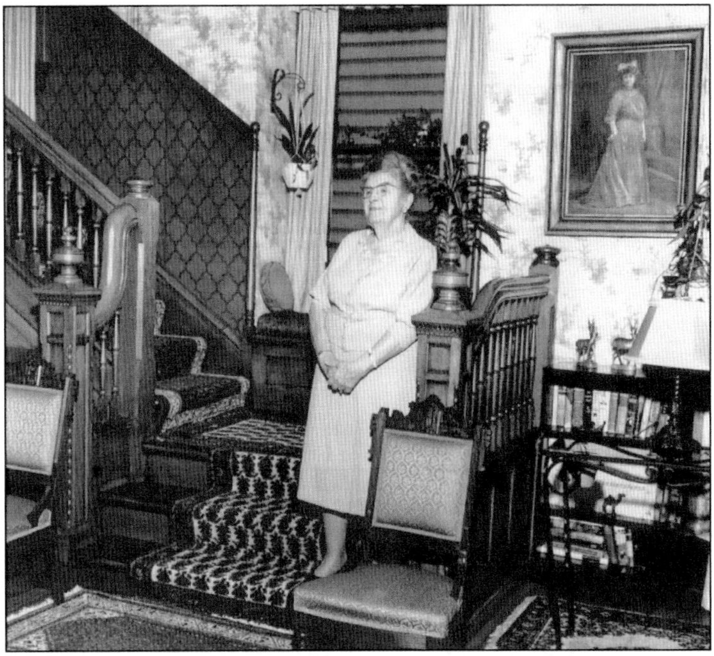

Arthur Cunningham's wife, Bess Rippeth Cunningham, stands at the foot of the stairway in their home at 529 South Center Street in this 1965 photograph. Son-in-law Kenneth Hazledine did the painting on the wall behind her for use in a Community Theatre production. It replicates her high school graduation photograph. Interested in the arts, Cunningham hosted a table at the luncheon after the new Terre Haute Symphony's first performance. (Peggy Apgar.)

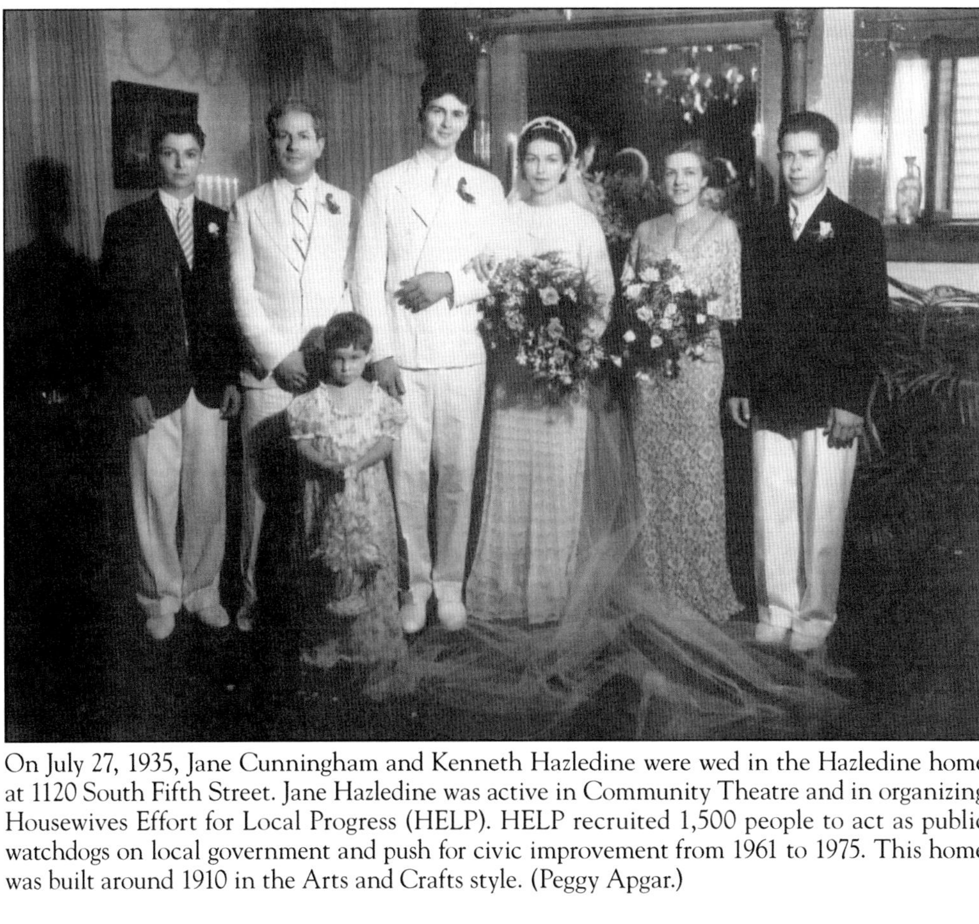

On July 27, 1935, Jane Cunningham and Kenneth Hazledine were wed in the Hazledine home at 1120 South Fifth Street. Jane Hazledine was active in Community Theatre and in organizing Housewives Effort for Local Progress (HELP). HELP recruited 1,500 people to act as public watchdogs on local government and push for civic improvement from 1961 to 1975. This home was built around 1910 in the Arts and Crafts style. (Peggy Apgar.)

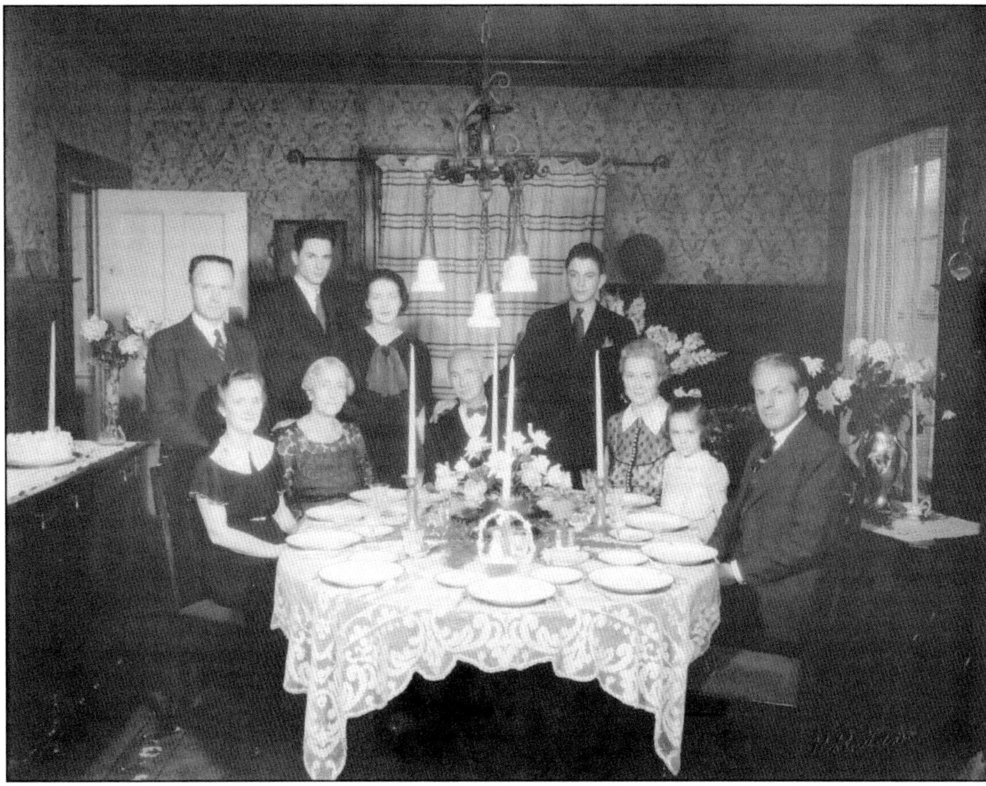

Edward Thomas Hazledine sits at the head of the table; his wife, Gertrude, sits at left during a family gathering at 1120 South Fifth Street. Directly behind Gertrude are her son Kenneth Hazledine and his wife, Jane. Edward owned Machine and Architectural Iron Works, which created the ornate entrance gate at Highland Lawn Cemetery. Kenneth later ran the family business. (Peggy Apgar.)

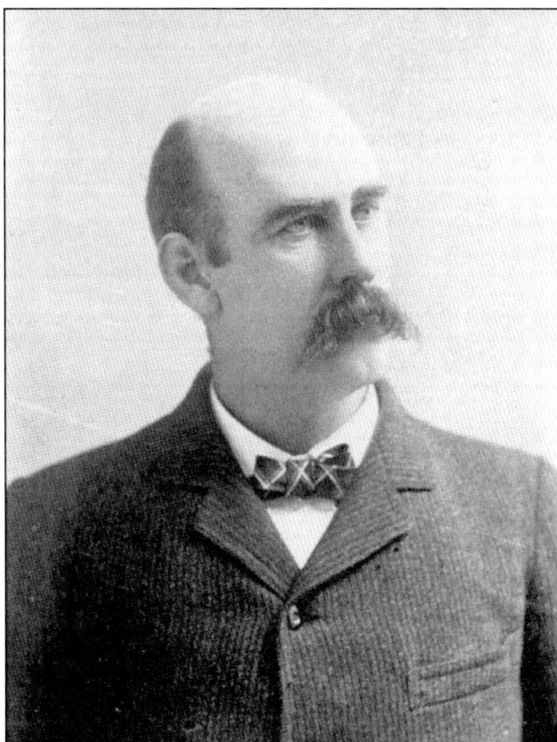

William W. Parsons, who persuaded Arthur Cunningham to become librarian at Indiana State Normal (ISN) rather than a Kentucky college president, served as ISN president from 1885 to 1921. Parsons kept the school open after the fire of 1888. Born in Farrington's Grove at 602 South Seventh Street, he died at 1444 South Center Street. He was in the first class that entered Indiana State Normal in 1870. (J. Richard Becker Jr.)

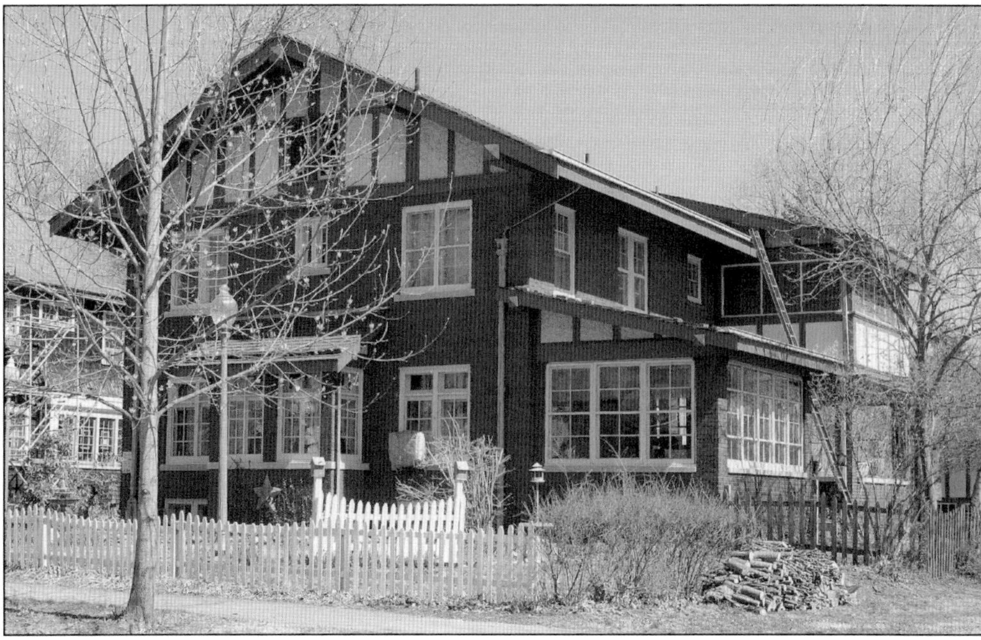

Indiana State Normal president William W. Parsons told the contractor what he wanted, went on vacation, and turned him loose to construct this Arts and Crafts–style home at 1444 South Center Street in 1915. The photograph above shows the summer sleeping porch on the second floor, providing a cool night's sleep on sultry nights. Parsons loved to have company, and the home had several guestrooms. The photograph below shows the double stairway in the house and the dividing wall. The stairway at the left led upstairs from the entryway to the guest quarters. The separate stairway at right led upstairs to the servant's rooms and downstairs to the kitchen. (Photographs by Albert Christenberry.)

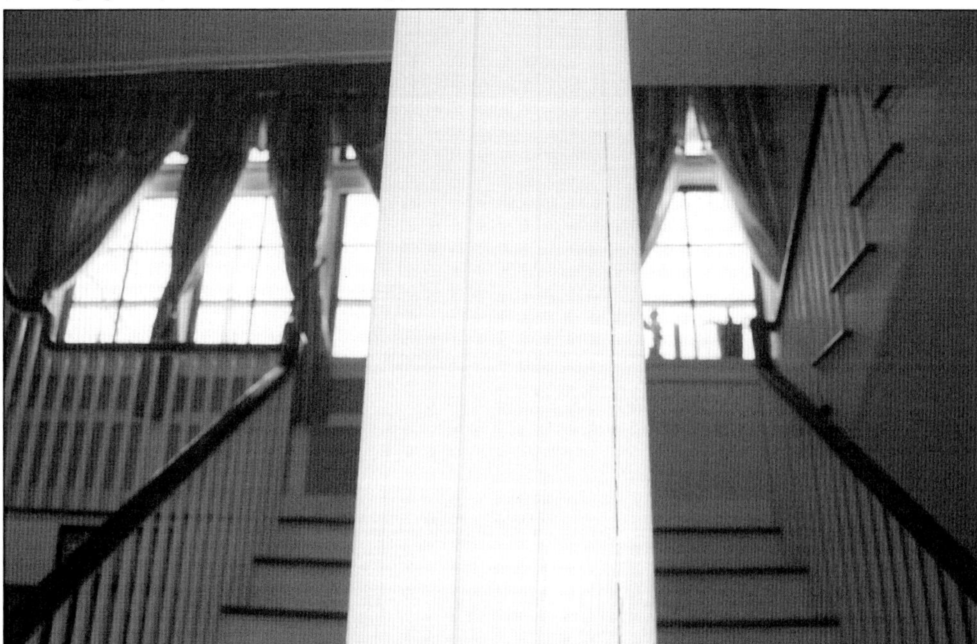

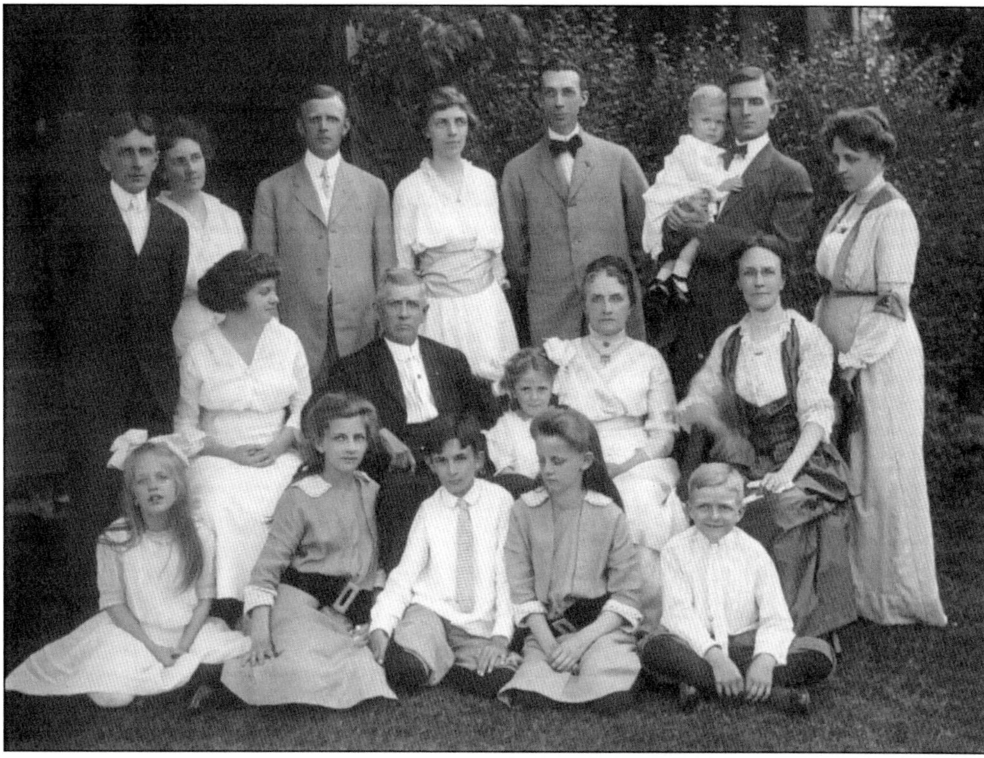

After Parsons, attorney George Oscar Dix owned 1444 South Center Street. He jokingly put out a doormat with the phrase, "This is the house of G.O.D." Dix served on the Thompson Club board and was its president in 1900. His wife, Helen Layman Dix, worked for Arthur Cunningham as second assistant librarian at Indiana State Normal before her marriage. They are in the back row, fourth and fifth from left. (Glenn Cass.)

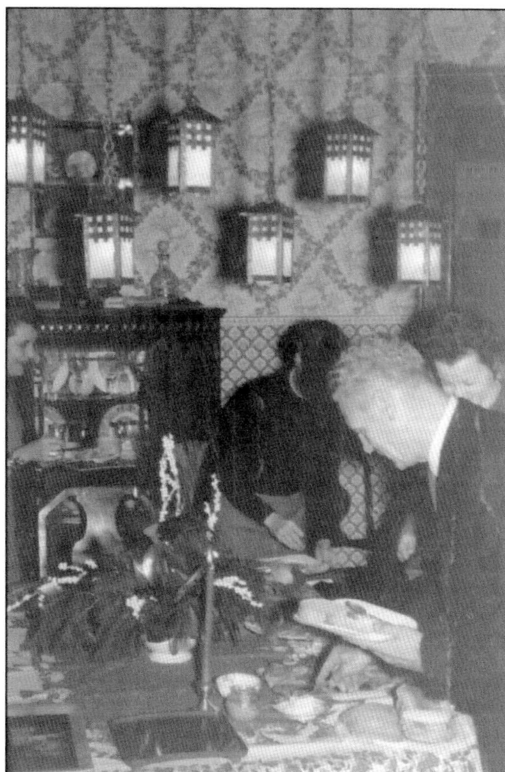

Duane and Mary Alice Klueh host Indiana State Teachers College (ISTC) coaches at 1000 South Center in 1960. Walter Marks, right, samples the food; Marks Field is named for him. Duane was MVP in the 1948 National Association of Intercollegiate Athletics (NAIA) tournament, played professional basketball, and taught at ISTC, where as basketball and tennis coach he amassed the most wins in the college's history. The college retired his jersey. Previous homeowner Omar Mewhinney, a confectioner, created the light fixtures from a metal bathtub next door. (Duane and Mary Alice Klueh.)

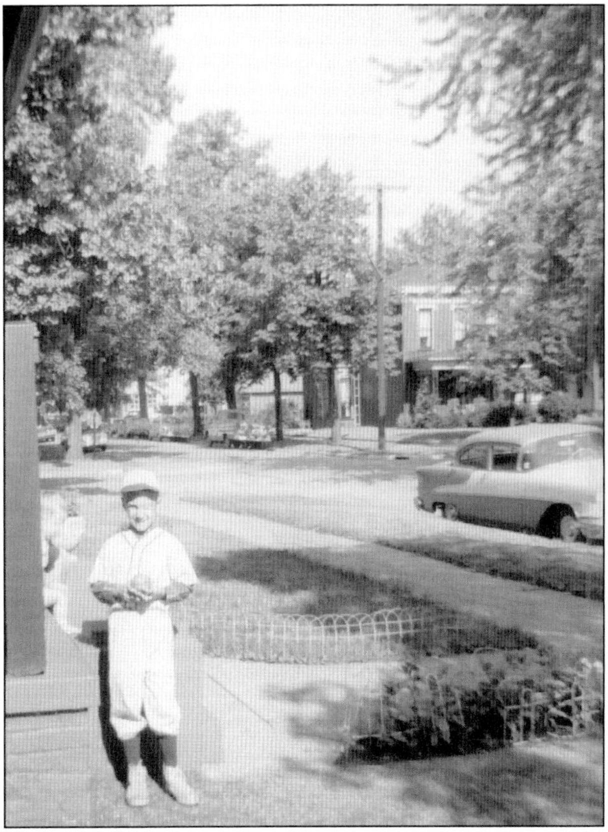

Though Duane Klueh was a gifted athlete, his son Michael Klueh, shown in his baseball uniform in 1964, was the only one of the three children interested in sports. Michael's younger brother James sits on the steps of their home at 1000 South Center Street, looking to the northwest to the home at 935 South Center. (Duane and Mary Alice Klueh.)

Wiley High School teacher Rebecca Torner willed the city $12,000 in 1929 for a park; Torner Park was purchased in 1937. The Torner House at the southwest corner of College Avenue and South Fourth Street hosted the Girls Club from 1945 to 1983. It no longer stands. Torner helped develop the Woman's Department Club. In 1899, she was first president of the Terre Haute section of National Council of Jewish Women. (Photograph by Jesse Smith; VCPL.)

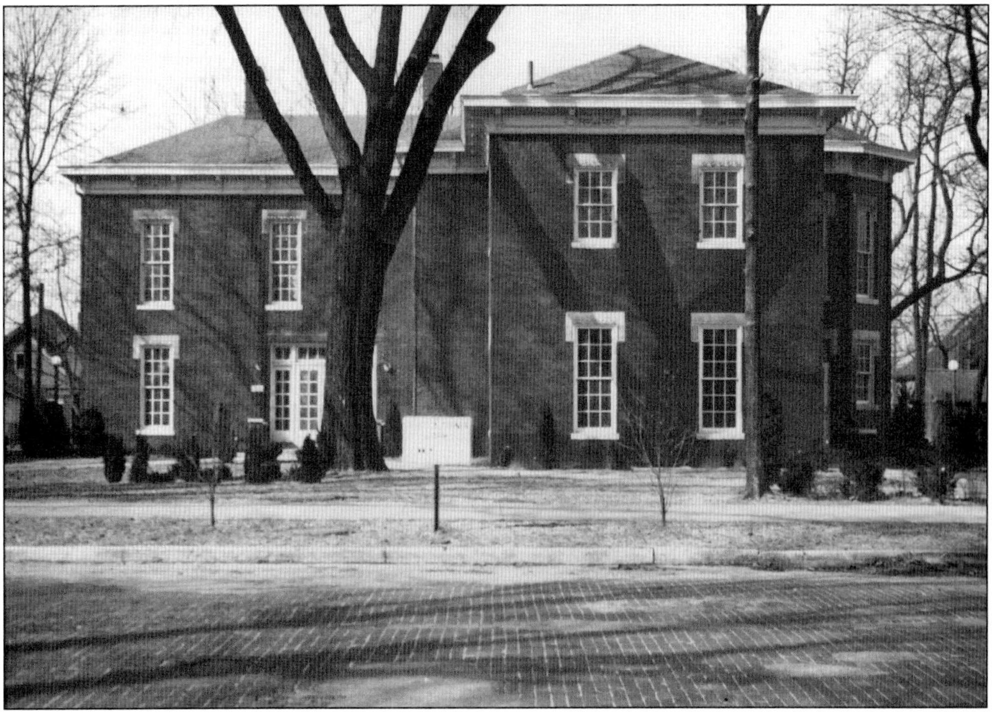

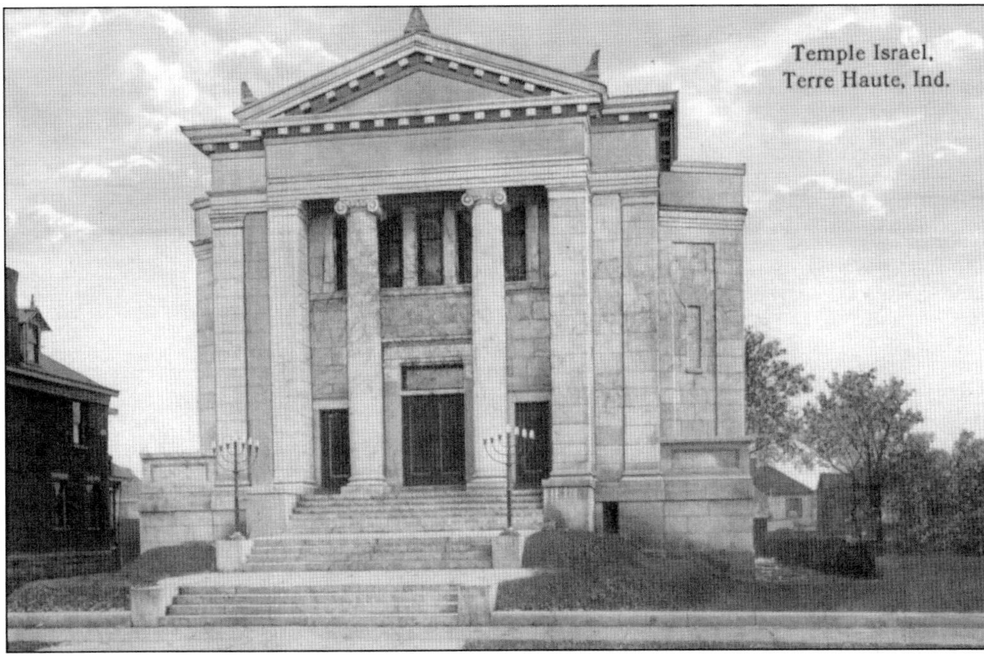

In 1935, Temple Israel, the Reform Congregation, and B'Nai Abraham, the Orthodox Congregation, merged into United Hebrew Congregation. It was the first such successful merger in the United States. Temple Israel was built here at 540 South Sixth Street in 1911, replacing the former 420 South Fourth Street building purchased in 1890 from the German Evangelical Lutheran congregation. The local Jewish community began in 1849 with a burial society. (Ray Thomas.)

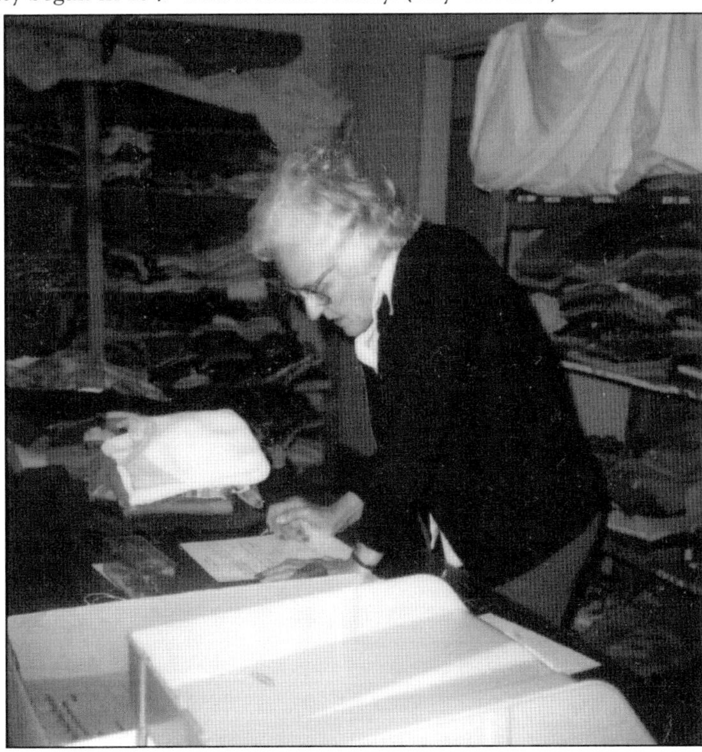

Carolyn Gurman fills orders at the Clothes Closet. The Terre Haute Federation of Jewish Women collected good used clothing for needy schoolchildren and sorted, mended, washed, and pressed clothes for 28 years. Sometimes, when the need was acute, their husbands' shoes and shirts disappeared. In 1990, the League of Terre Haute took over the Clothes Closet project. Women at the temple conducted many service projects over the years. (Temple Sisterhood.)

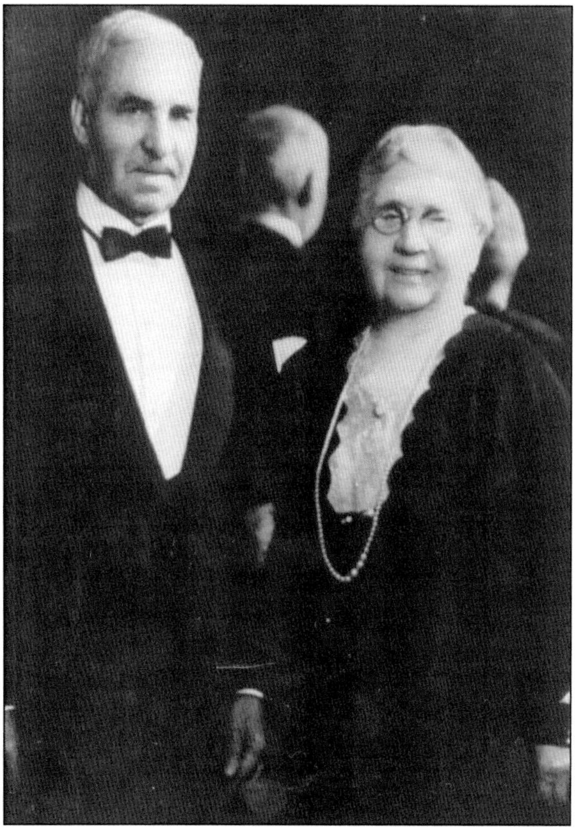

Max and Theresa Blumberg came to the United States from Russia in 1887, arriving in Terre Haute soon thereafter. Max Blumberg was a jeweler, went into real estate, and then founded Security Loan Company, eventually having loan offices in Indiana, Illinois, Iowa, and Ohio. He was known for contributions to Temple Israel, B'nai B'rith, and the Terre Haute community. By 1949, a total of 41 Jewish businesses existed on Wabash Avenue. (Gay Ann Weaver.)

Max and Theresa Blumberg bought 328 South Fifth Street and lived here from 1916 to 1934. In 1939, the Blumbergs' son Benjamin and his wife, Fannie, gave the home to the Public Health Nursing Association, later the Visiting Nurse Association of the Wabash Valley. The home contains original oak woodwork and pocket doors and has an interior in Victorian style. (Gay Ann Weaver.)

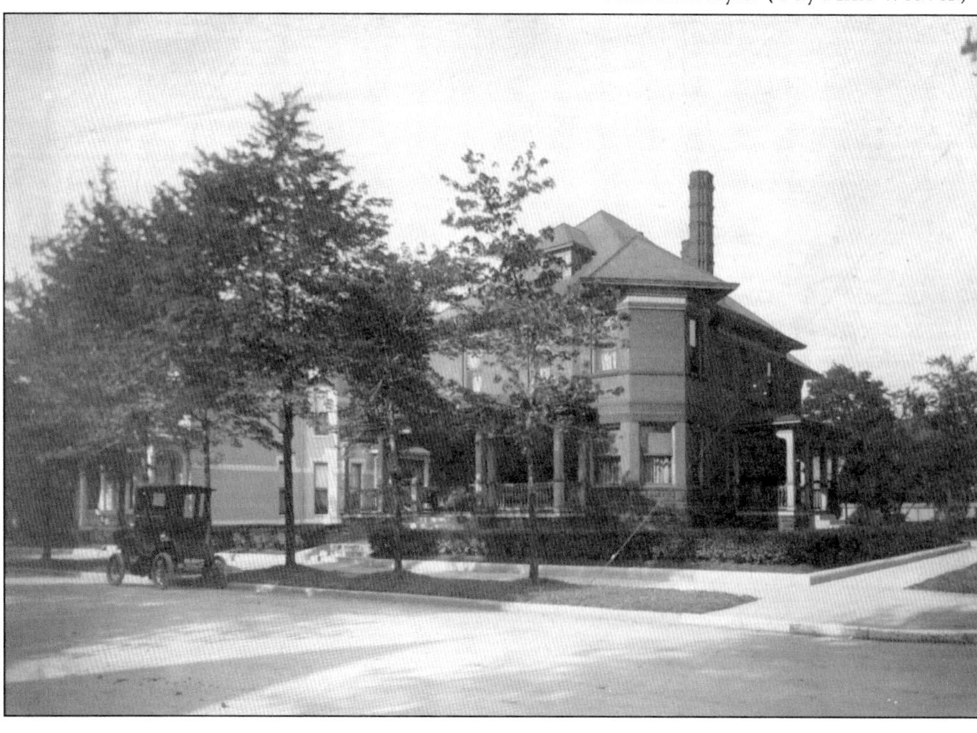

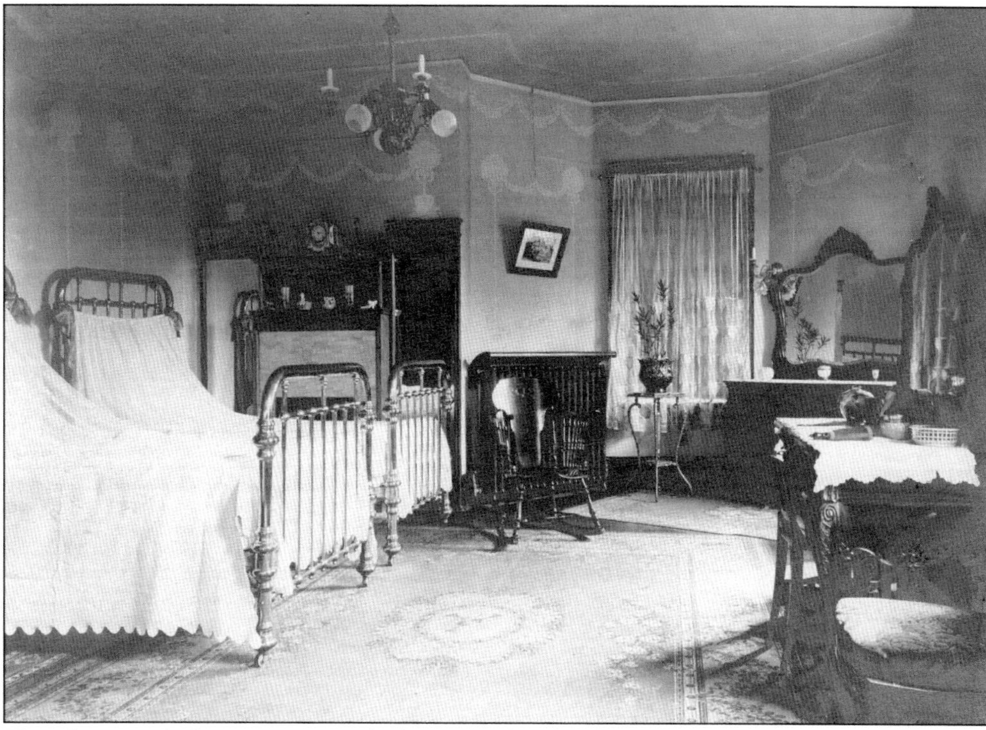

This photograph shows an upstairs bedroom in the Blumberg home at 328 South Fifth Street in the early 1900s. Ornate patterns are visible on the wallpaper. Businessman Robert Cox built the home in the mid-1890s. The Romanesque Revival–style house has two hexagonal towers and several ceramic tile fireplaces. (Gay Ann Weaver.)

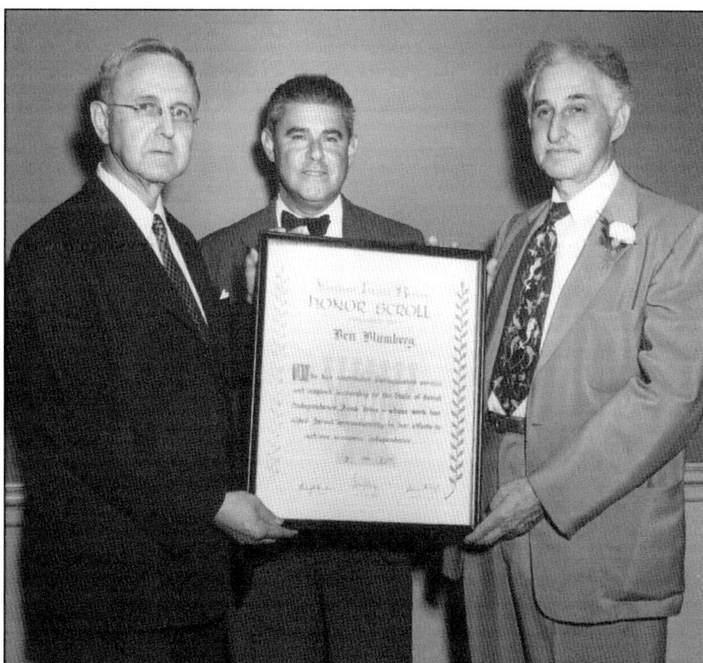

Benjamin Blumberg, at right, is honored at a 1953 Bonds for Israel dinner. Blumberg was elected the first president of the United Hebrew Congregation in January 1936 after the Reform and Orthodox Congregations merged. Previously, he was president of Temple Israel. His wife, Fannie Burgheim Blumberg, was an author, artist, and donor to Indiana State Teachers College; the college named Blumberg Hall for her. (Photograph by Martin's Photo Shop; VCPL.)

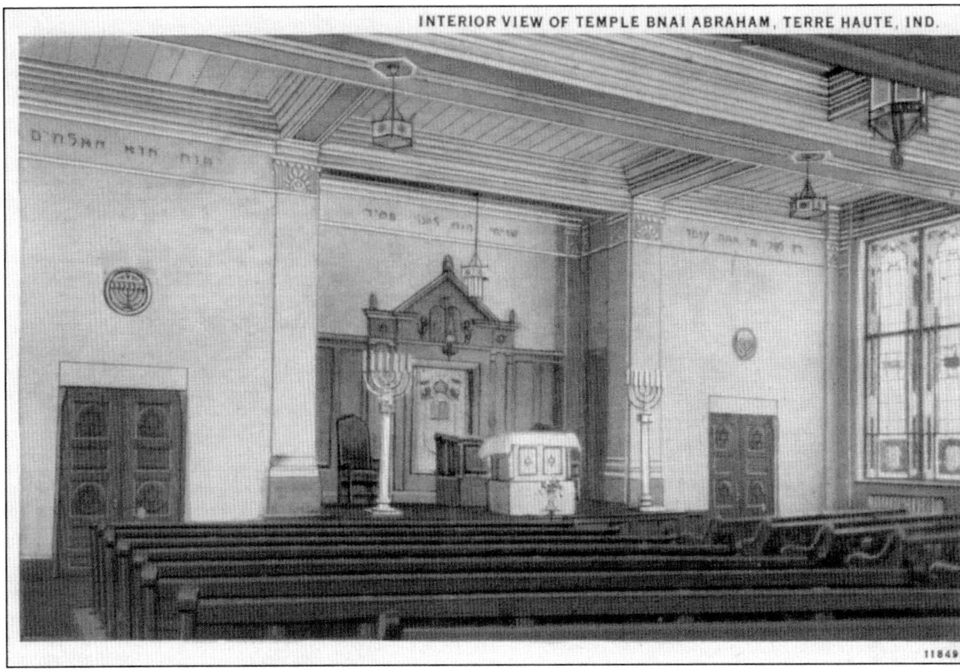

This postcard is a rare item that shows the interior of Temple B'Nai Abraham at 300 South Fifth Street. The temple's name honored the father of the four Levin brothers—Morris, Max, Isaac, and Meyer—who owned Levin Brothers dry goods wholesalers above Terre Haute Savings Bank downtown. Some of the Levin brothers lived on Washington Avenue in Farrington's Grove. (Ray Thomas.)

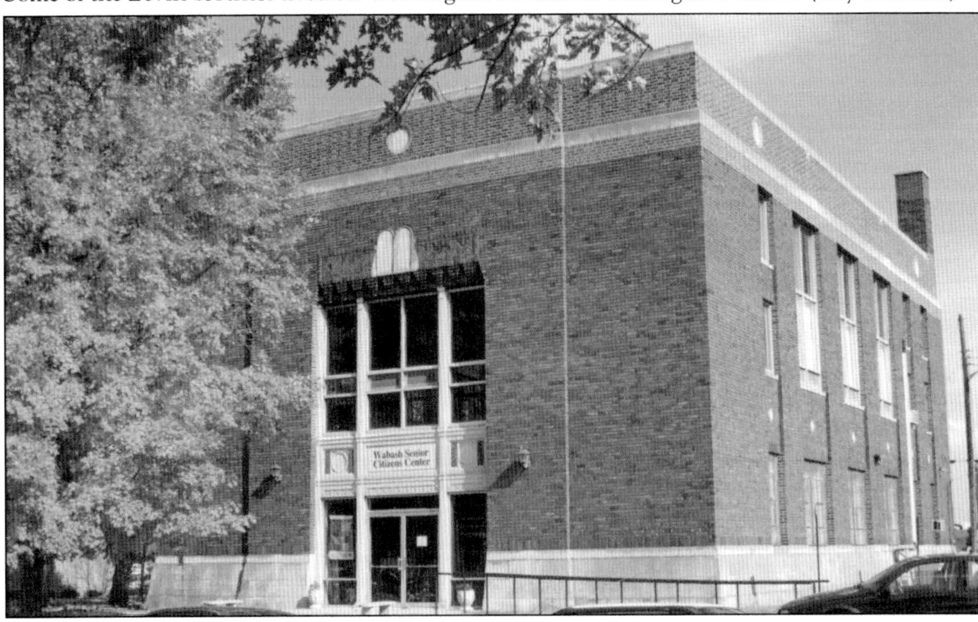

The B'Nai Abraham Orthodox Jewish Congregation formed in 1886, grew, met in various places, built a synagogue at 12th and Mulberry Streets, then built this new synagogue at 300 South Fifth Street, dedicating it in 1927. After the building became the Wabash Senior Citizens Center, the stained glass was removed in 1971, and two—of a candelabra and the Star of David—were framed and transferred to Temple Israel. (Photograph by J. Richard Becker Jr.)

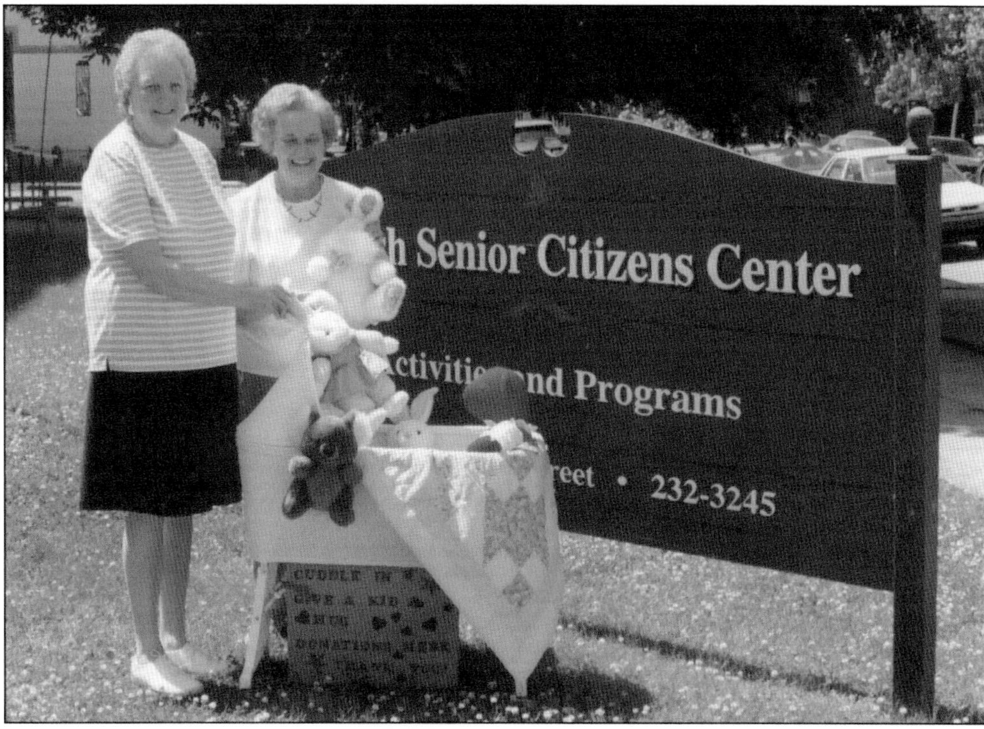

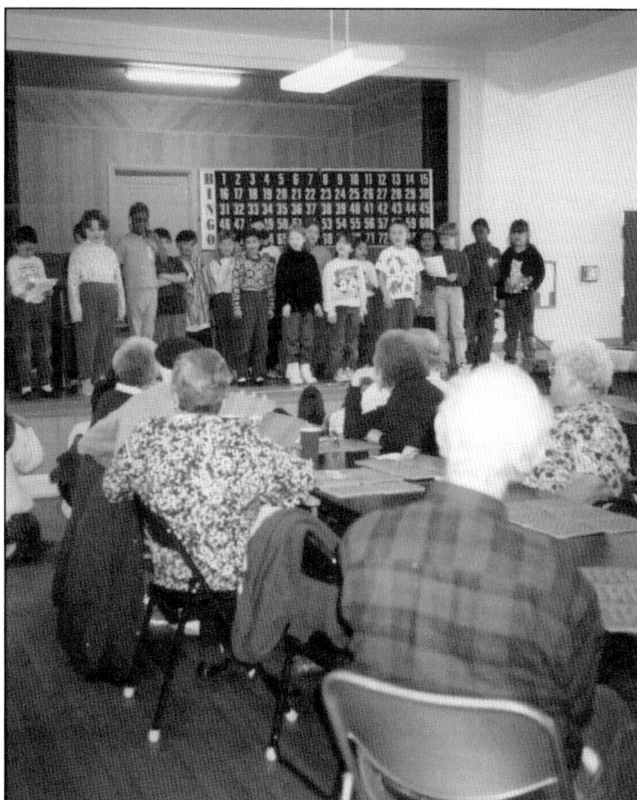

In the photograph above, two Wabash Senior Citizens Center members display stuffed animals collected for the Give a Kid a Hug program for hospitalized children. In the photograph on the right, Crawford School second and third graders perform a play for members in the former sanctuary of Temple B'Nai Abraham. Crawford School had a buddy relationship with the senior center. The center began in 1965 when Benjamin Blumberg bought Temple B'Nai Abraham at 300 South Fifth Street from the United Hebrew Congregation. He then provided it to the Wabash Senior Citizens Group for a dollar and gave the group $50,000 for two years' operating costs. He strongly supported programs on aging. (Wabash Senior Citizens Center.)

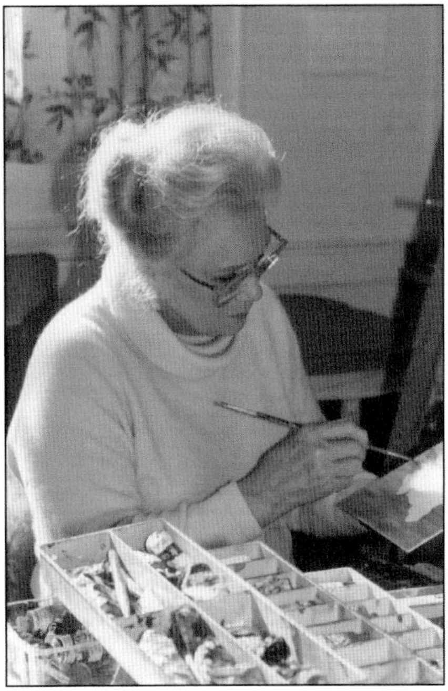

Since it began in 1965, the Wabash Valley Senior Citizens Center at 300 South Fifth Street has offered a variety of programs for those 55 and older. At left, a member takes part in a painting class. Many paintings adorn the walls of the center, and sales of artwork contribute to fundraising efforts. Bimonthly dances, like the one in the photograph below, draw other community members in addition to senior citizens. Other programs include exercise classes, music classes, health checkups, and billiards. United Hebrew Congregation member Sidney Levin, who established Corner Furniture Store, was the first president of the Wabash Senior Citizens Center in 1965. Gov. Otis Bowen appointed him commissioner-at-large for the Indiana Commission on the Aging and Aged. (Both, Wabash Senior Citizens Center.)

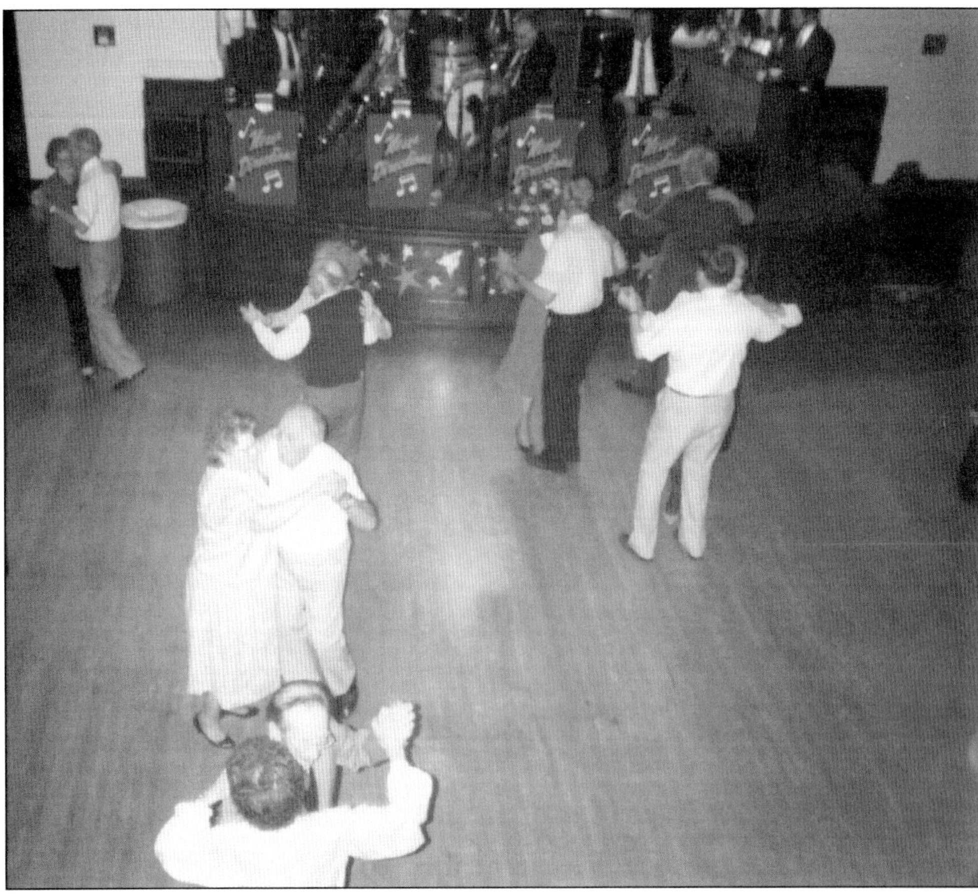

Two

Hulmans, a Hospital, and a Symphony

The Hulman name has been associated with Terre Haute since 1850, and several members of the Hulman family have lived in Farrington's Grove. From their profitable wholesale business, they have given back to the community.

For example, Rose-Hulman Institute of Technology (originally Rose Polytechnic Institute) moved from its original location at Thirteenth and Locust Streets to the east of Terre Haute on 123 acres formerly owned by the Hulmans. The municipal airport east of town, originally named Hulman Field, got its start with a $100,000 donation from Anton Hulman Jr. He also purchased the Indianapolis Motor Speedway, restored it, and made the Indianapolis 500-mile race a Memorial Day weekend event. With the blessing of his father, Anton Hulman Sr., he oversaw a nationwide advertising campaign that made Clabber Girl Baking Powder the best-selling baking powder in the United States.

St. Anthony's Hospital was not the first hospital in town, but it was the first permanent one by the time it moved into Farrington's Grove in 1884. Herman Hulman Sr. established it and let the nuns run it, putting doctors on notice not to give them a hard time. Besides the usual medical needs, the hospital dealt with victims from the tornado of 1913 and the injured from coal mine and plant disasters. Its School of Nursing was established during World War I.

The Woman's Department Club, which moved into 507 South Sixth Street in 1932, has focused on the arts, literature, and gardening. When the newly reorganized Terre Haute Symphony gave its first performance in 1926 in the Indiana Theater, it was done under the auspices of the club's Music Section. A previous version of the symphony started in 1903 but lasted only a few years.

Radio station WBOW 1230 on the AM dial moved to the southwest corner of Sixth and Poplar Streets in 1938 and stayed there until the 1960s. During those years, the station changed from an NBC affiliate carrying radio shows to a Top 40 station. WBOW was famous for various promotions and gimmicks to entice listener interest.

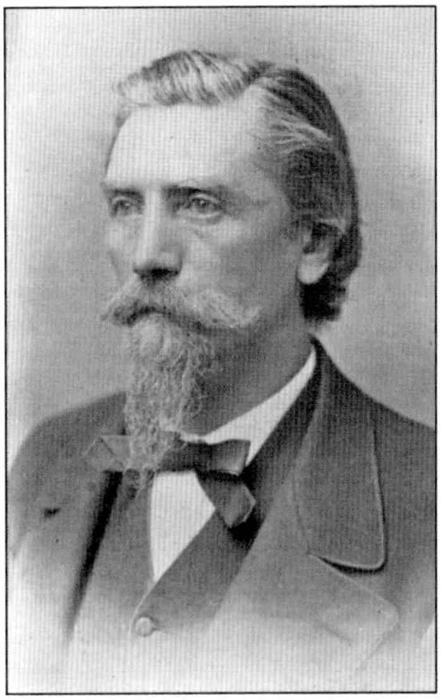

Herman Hulman Sr. came to Terre Haute from Germany at his brother Francis's request; after Francis's death at sea in 1858, Herman managed his wholesale business. Francis and partner John Ludowici founded Ludowici and Hulman in 1850 with $2,100; they parted in 1853. The Hulman firm later merged with R.S. Cox and Son to form Hulman and Cox, which later became Hulman and Company. (J. Richard Becker Jr.)

Francis Hulman's partner John Ludowici built this Italianate house at 1000 South Sixth Street in 1873 for $11,000. He sold his interest in Ludowici and Hulman in 1853 to Hulman, starting his own grocery business, but later selling out and building the National Hotel downtown. He built 1003 South Center Street directly behind this house as a wedding gift for his daughter. Ludowici came from Prussia in 1831. (VCPL.)

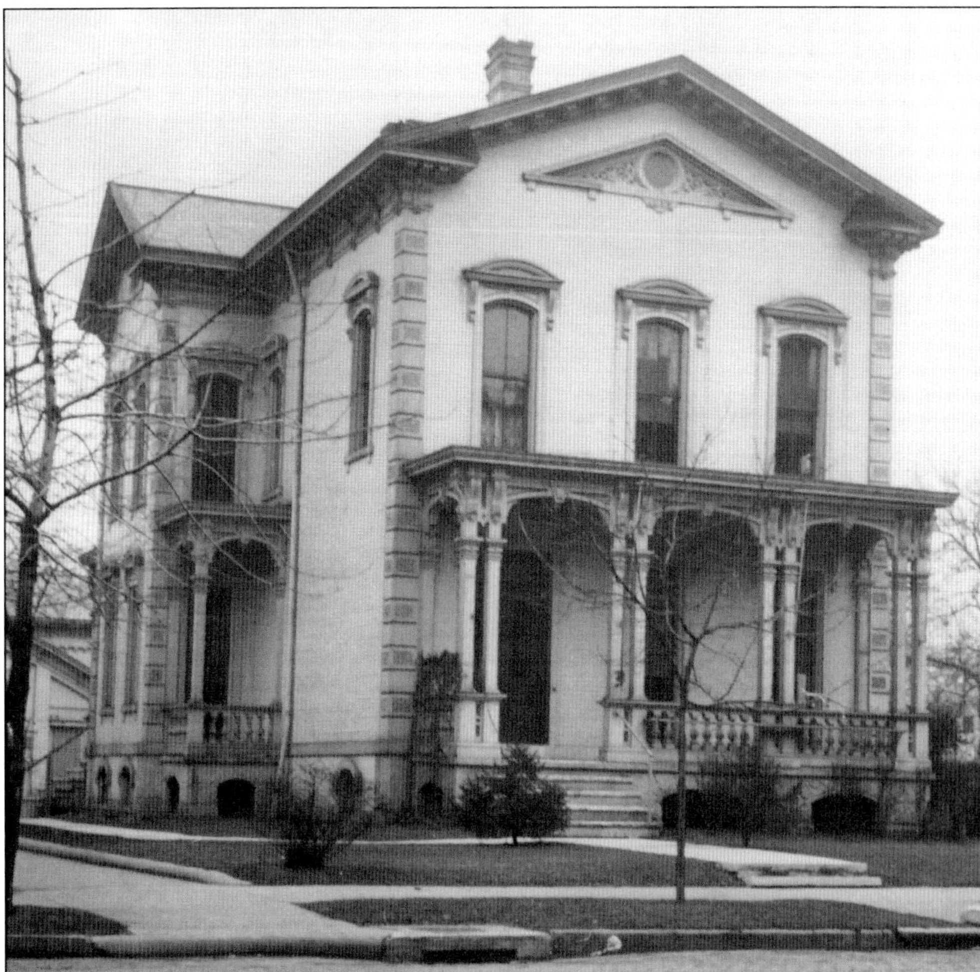

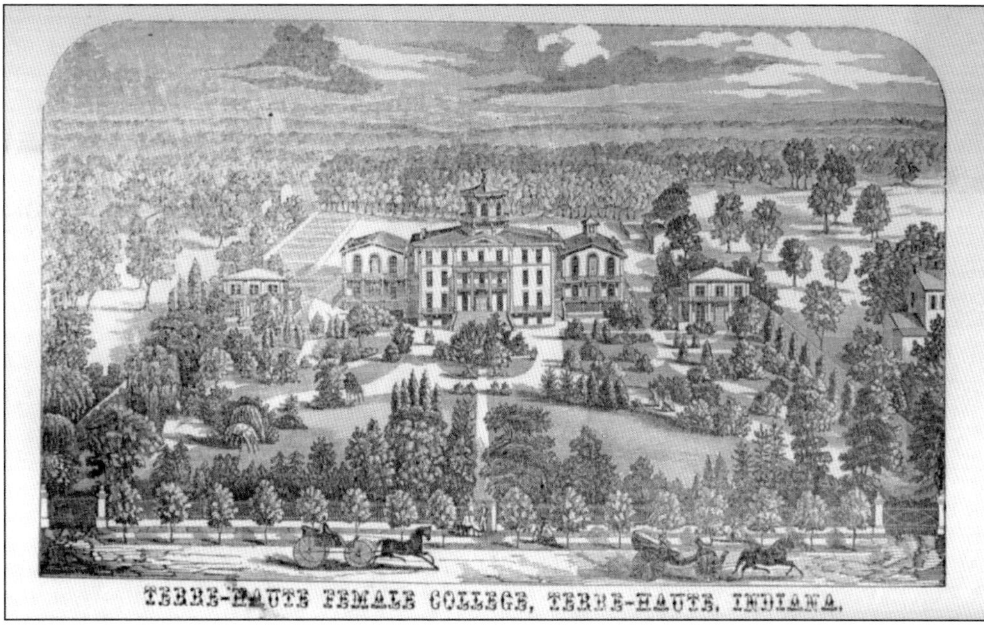

Before Herman Hulman Sr. turned it into St. Anthony's Hospital, this was Terre Haute Female College. This first catalog from 1858–1859 shows buildings and college grounds of eight and a half acres. The daily schedule was regulated from rising at 5:00 a.m. until retiring at 9:30 p.m. Col. Richard Thompson was board president, and James Farrington was a board member. It later became St. Agnes Academy. (John R. Becker III.)

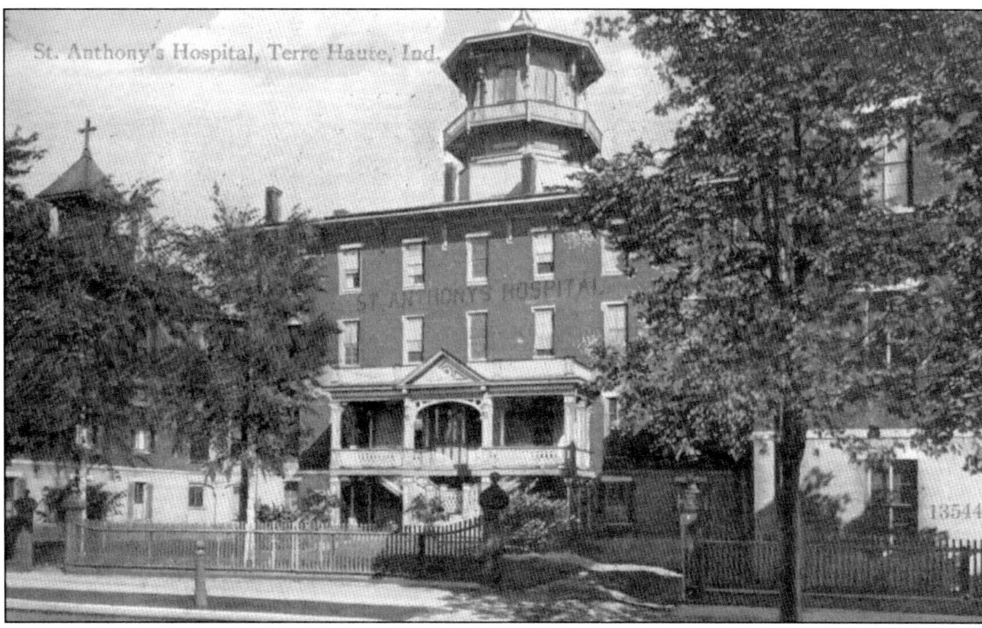

Herman Hulman Sr. founded St. Anthony's Hospital at the urging of his wife, Antonia, in 1882 and moved it January 1, 1884, into the former Terre Haute Female College and St. Agnes Academy in the 1000 block of South Sixth Street. The Sisters of St. Francis ran the hospital, the city's first permanent one. Herman gave the nuns firing authority "if any physician becomes obnoxious to them." (John R. Becker III.)

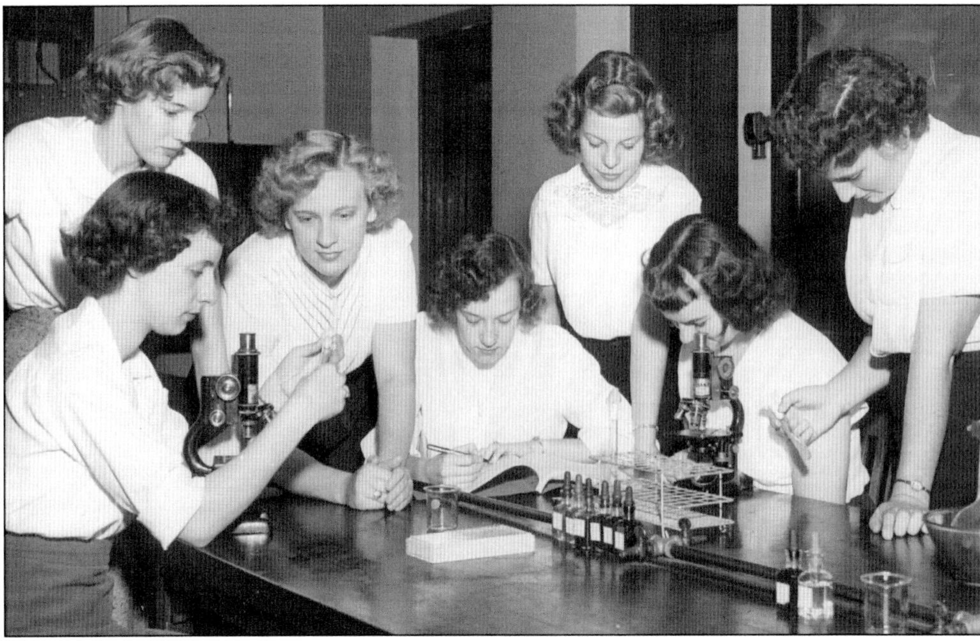

Student nurses study in the laboratory at St. Anthony's Hospital in the photograph above. During World War I, the US government requested more nursing schools to open, and the St. Anthony's School of Nursing opened January 14, 1918. The photograph below shows the graduating class of 1932. From its beginnings, St. Anthony's Hospital had a reputation for good care. During Buffalo Bill Cody's Wild West Show performance in the 1890s, gunslinger James Myerly nearly blew his hand off. Buffalo Bill donated a "roll of money" to the hospital in appreciation of the care his performer received. (Both photographs by Martin's Photo Shop; VCHS.)

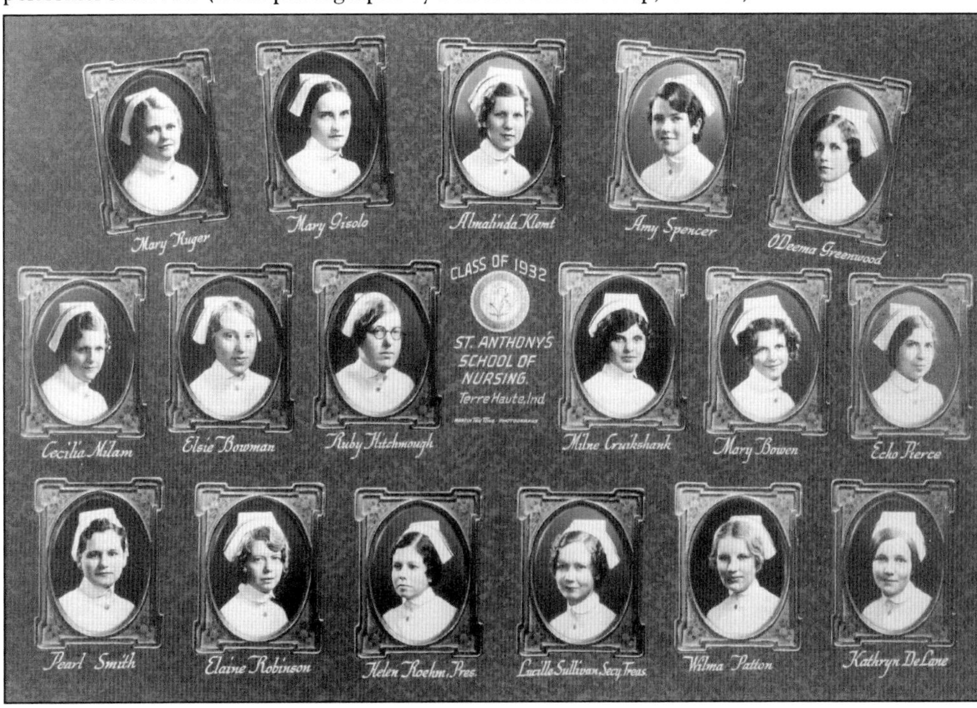

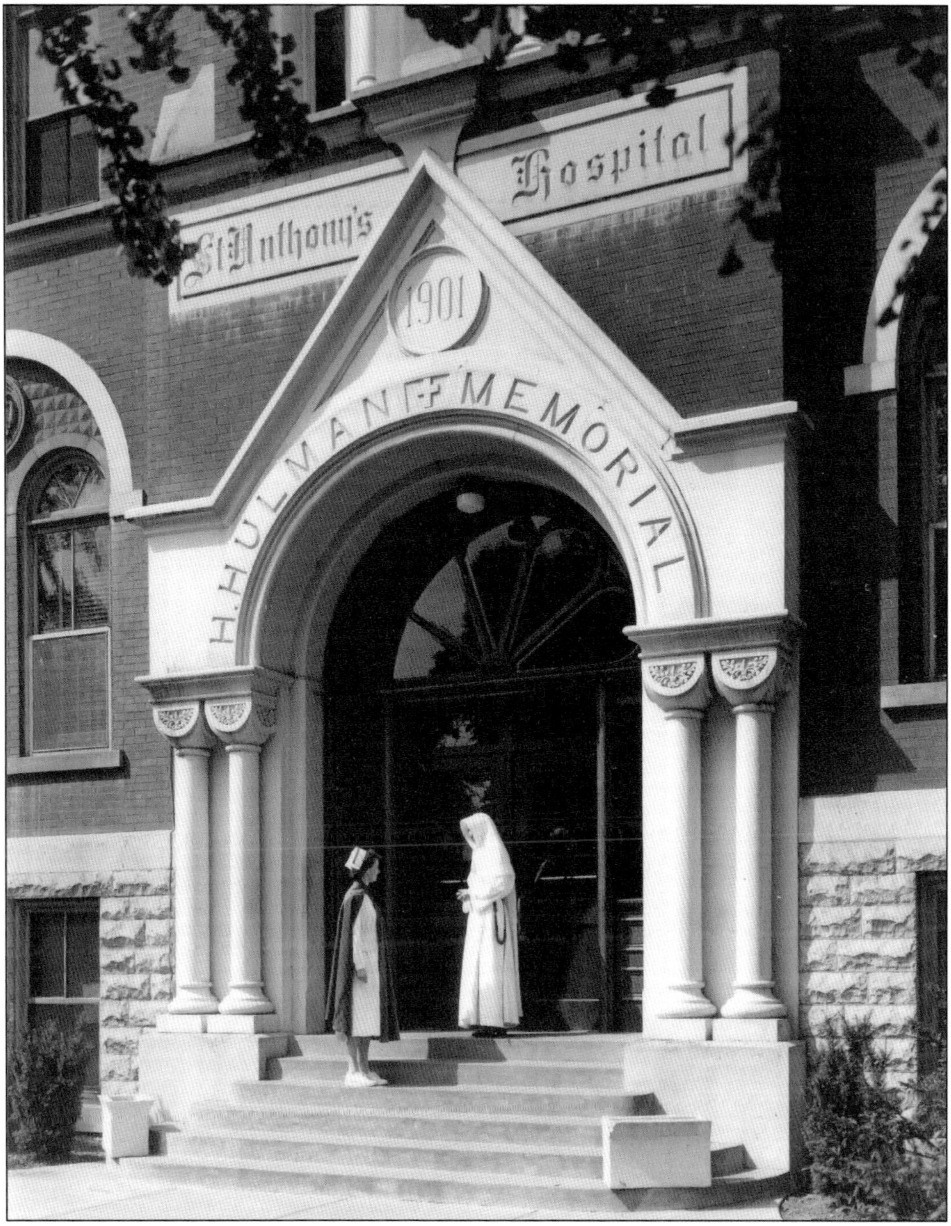

A nurse and nun converse at the entrance to St. Anthony's Hospital in the 1000 block of South Sixth Street. "H. Hulman Memorial" is visible over the entrance. On January 1, 1884, the hospital opened with an 81-bed capacity. By 1943, it could accommodate 177 patients and 30 newborns. From the original St. Agnes Academy building, several additions were made over the years. The front of the building originally faced Fifth Street and had a large lawn. In 1901, the new Hulman Memorial entrance was built to face Sixth Street, and the middle wing was added. Next came the north wing, built in 1908. A new chapel was built in 1913 and the south wing in 1922. In 1952, a new entrance was added to the 1901 entrance, and the last additions came in 1965 with a new lobby. After the nuns relinquished operation, it became the for-profit Terre Haute Regional Hospital, moving to southern Terre Haute in 1979. In 1983, the abandoned building was demolished. The land is now the site of Anthony Square senior housing. (VCHS.)

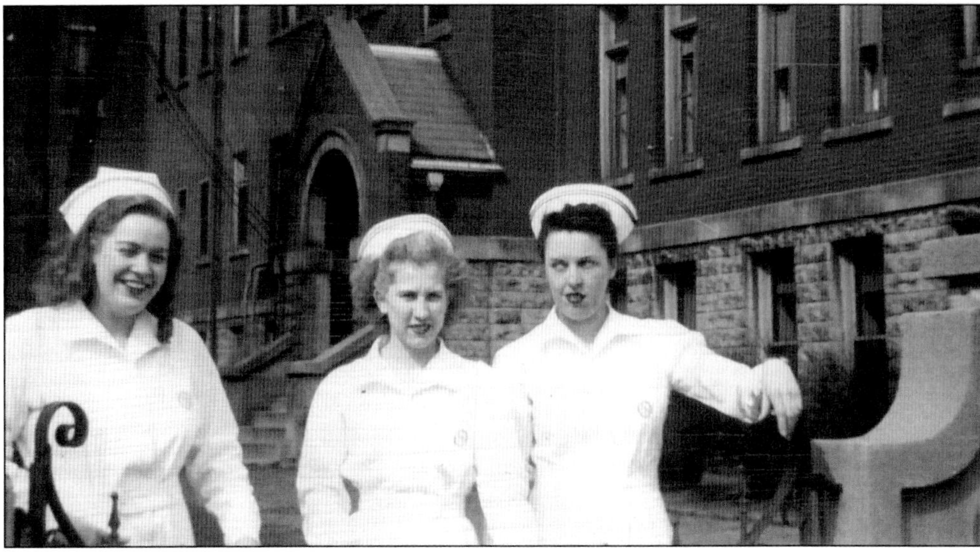

Mary Walsh (left), class of 1947 and niece of Bituminous Materials owner John Kelly, takes a break from nursing classes at St. Anthony's Hospital with friends Kathryn Ruddell (center) and Diana Sweeney (right). Student nurses received their caps at the end of the preclinical period. Colors of capes and stripes on the caps and the uniforms changed over the years. By the 1940s, the uniforms were plain white. (Anne Burkett.)

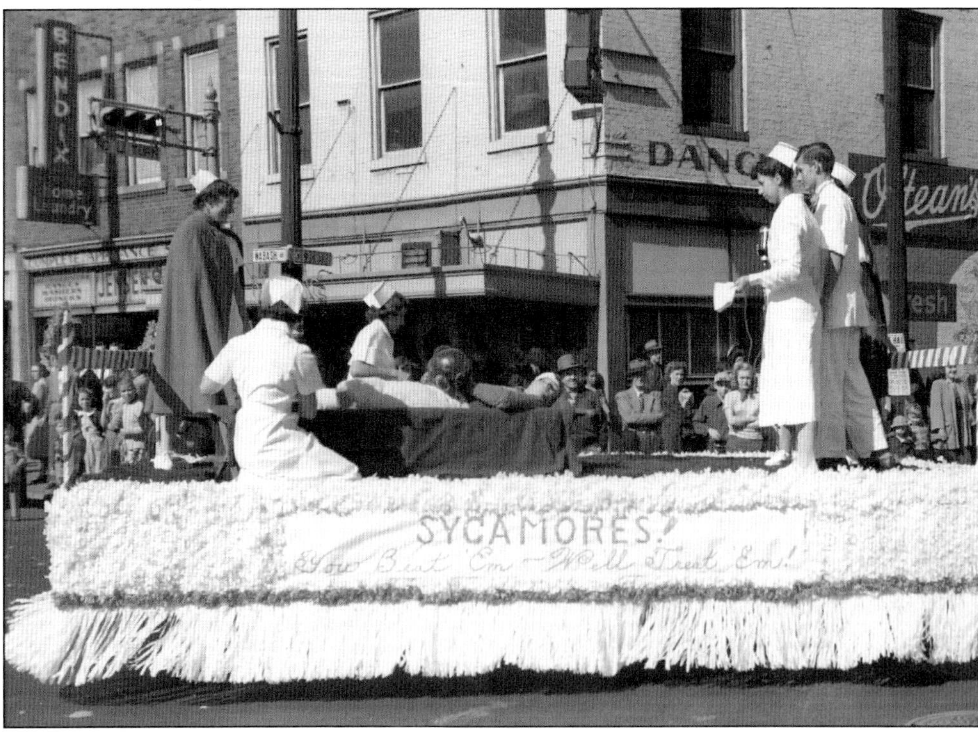

Like many other organizations in Terre Haute, student nurses at St. Anthony's Hospital joined in the festivities of the Indiana State Teachers College homecoming parade. This is one of the floats they built for the student-run parade. The slogan on the float says, "You Beat 'Em, We'll Treat 'Em." (VCHS.)

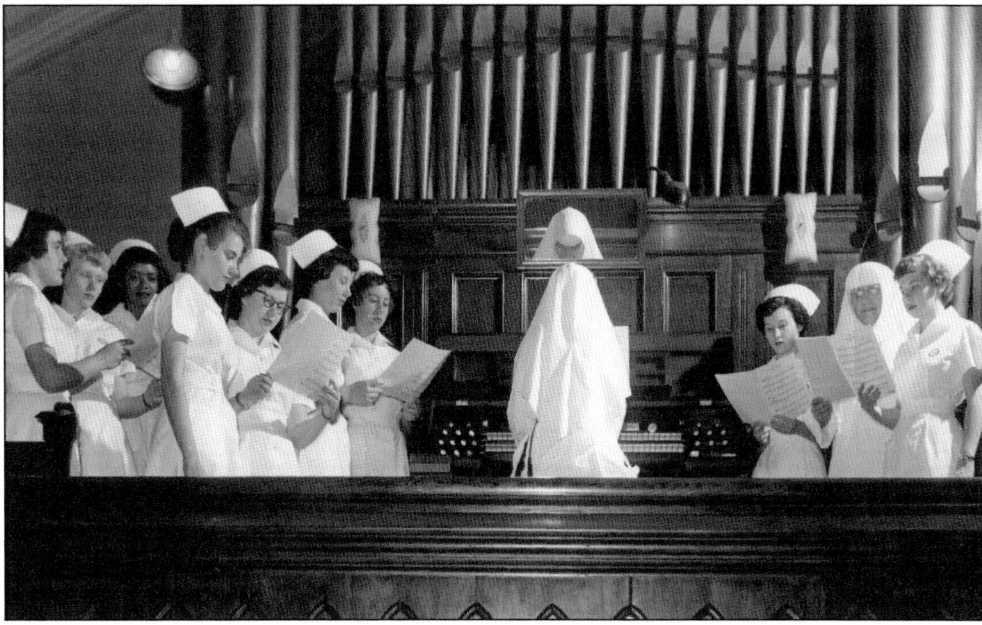

Students and Sisters of St. Francis sing during graduation for nurses from St. Anthony's Hospital School of Nursing in this June 1950 ceremony. Graduation was conducted in the hospital chapel, and High Mass was a required part of the ceremony, preceding the awarding of diplomas. It involved a religious procession, ceremony, and crowning of a statue in the chapel. (Photograph by Martin's Photo Shop; VCHS.)

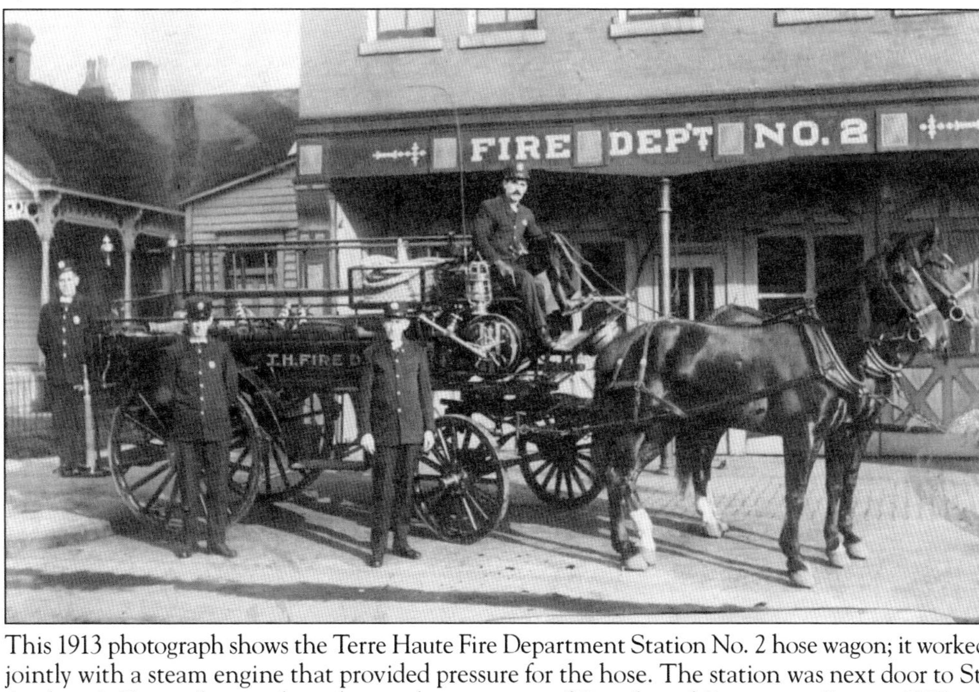

This 1913 photograph shows the Terre Haute Fire Department Station No. 2 hose wagon; it worked jointly with a steam engine that provided pressure for the hose. The station was next door to St. Anthony's Hospital grounds at the northeast corner of Fourth and Farrington Streets. William R. Root, Root Glass Company heir, dropped in frequently to listen after the station obtained its first radio. (Terre Haute Police and Fire Museum.)

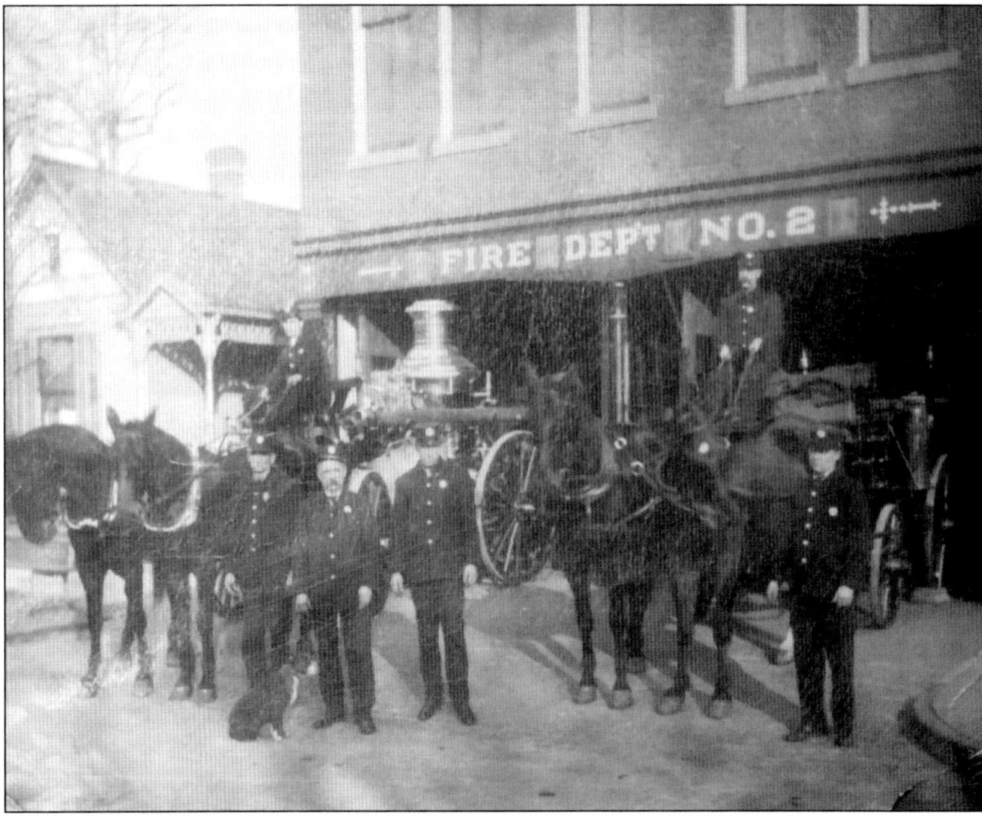

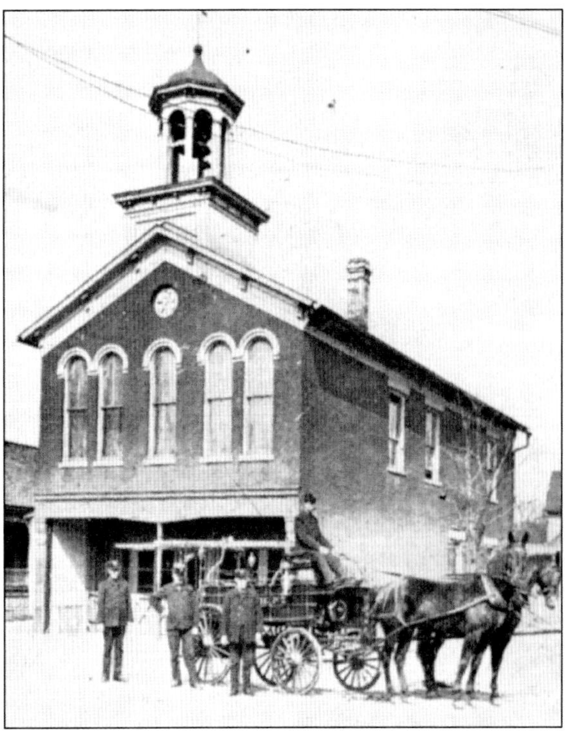

Shown here is Station No. 2's steam engine. It provided pressure to pump water through the hose on the hose wagon. When an alarm came in, the captain would ready the horses while a man in back would use kerosene on paper to start the fire, kindling to get it going, and coal to keep the fire hot. Fire plugs and cisterns provided water. (Terre Haute Police and Fire Museum.)

Any member of the public could ring the bell in the tower to alert the neighborhood; extra volunteers would rush to help. Fire Station No. 2 is shown at Fourth and Farrington Streets, where it relocated in June 1875; previously, it was at Fourth and Ohio Streets. Because of their work, firefighters lived nearby. Some went home for lunch; others stayed on duty, and their families brought them lunch. (VCHS.)

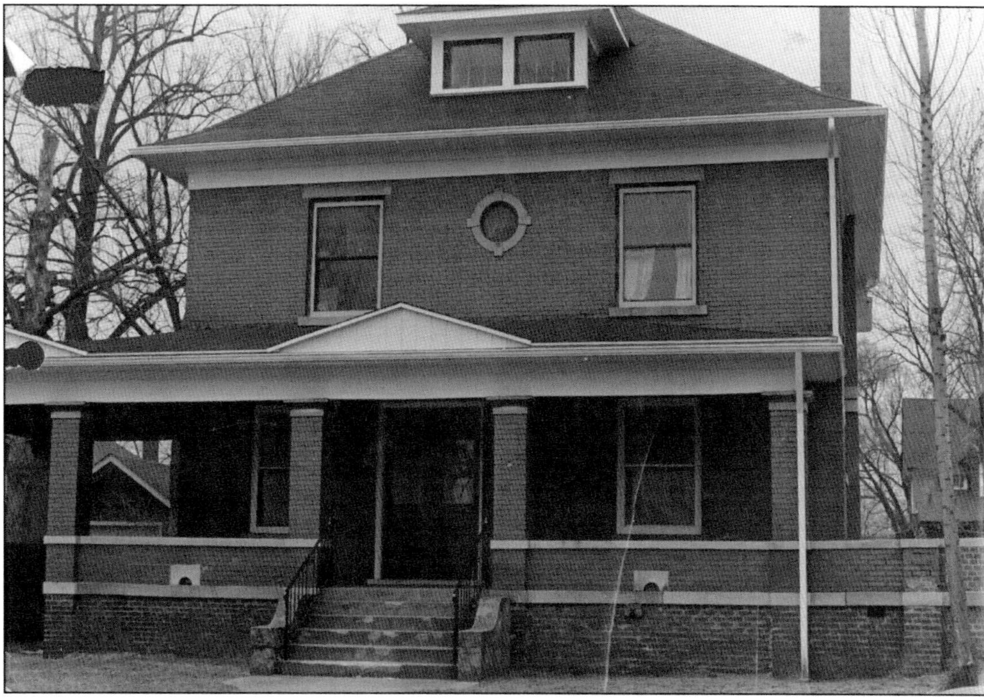

Edwin Yeakle lived at 1206 South Fifth Street, not far from Station No. 2. He was still on the job as fire inspector at age 80, making his daily rounds. He served 45 years with the Terre Haute Fire Department, rising in the ranks after his appointment in 1899. He resigned in 1944 when he felt ill and unable to do his job. He died two days later. (ISU.)

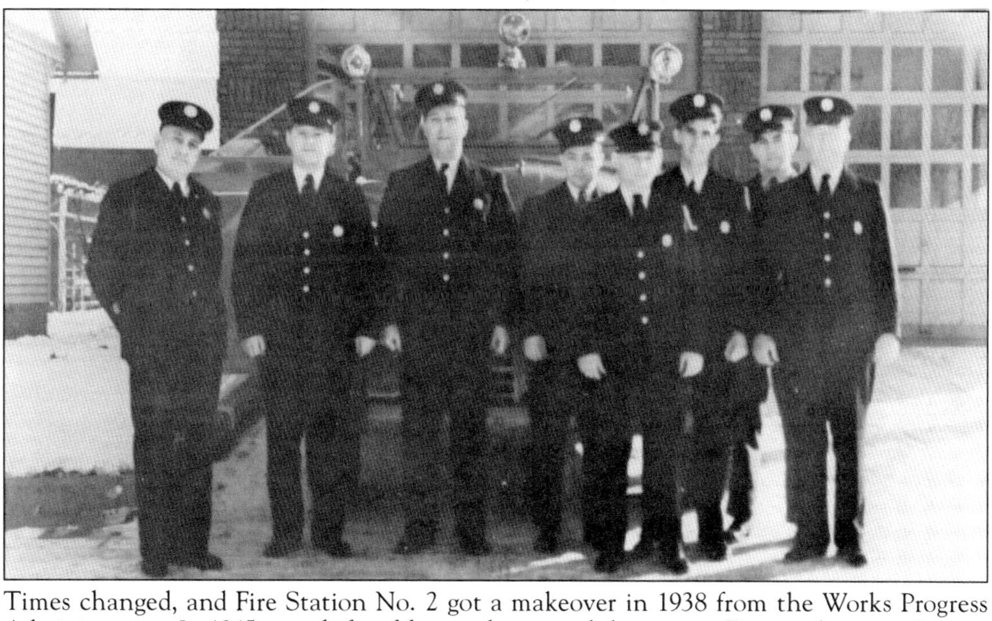

Times changed, and Fire Station No. 2 got a makeover in 1938 from the Works Progress Administration. In 1945, two shifts of four each manned the station. During that year, Station No. 2 answered 200 alarms and pumped water for a total of 18 hours and 54 minutes while fighting fires. The station also received a $9,000 American La France 750-gallon pumper. (Terre Haute Police and Fire Museum.)

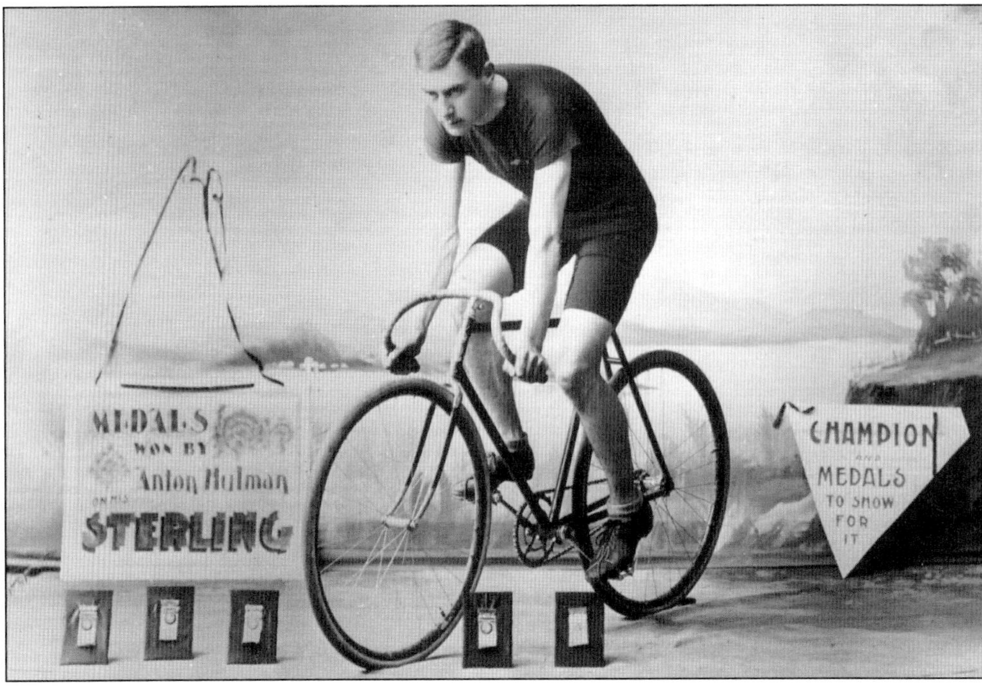

Anton Hulman Sr. raced a high wheel bicycle to 18 firsts. At age 33, he competed with a safety bicycle, shown here, winning five state championships. Gifted mechanically, at age 12 he built a house, and as an adult, he built the *Rex*, a boat complete with boiler. He worked with his father at Hulman and Company, later managing it with his brother. He was born in 1864 at Strawberry Hill. (VCHS.)

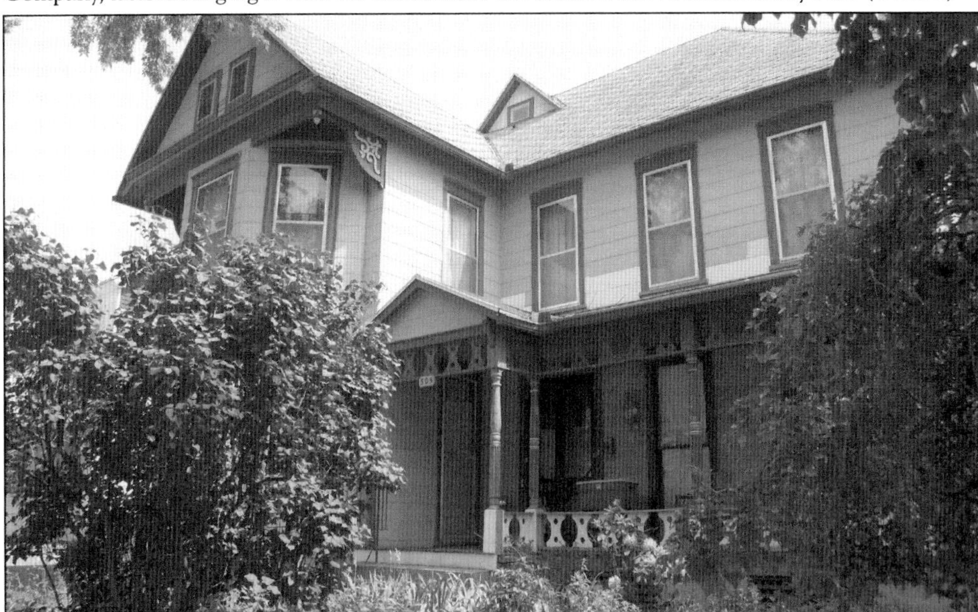

Anton Hulman Sr.'s brother Herman Hulman Jr. lived at 505 Swan Street, built around 1890. Herman headed a fund drive to improve and expand St. Anthony's Hospital. In addition, in 1917, the two brothers gave 123 acres of the Hulman farm east of town to Rose Polytechnic Institute. It allowed Rose Polytechnic to move from Thirteenth and Locust Streets and expand.

Herman Hulman Jr., also a bicycle enthusiast, is shown dressed in proper gear for 1886. He and his brother helped form the city's first bicycling club on September 12, 1884. He came close to setting a world's record on his Columbia bicycle. Herman tried his hand at other businesses, including breeding setter dogs, before joining Hulman and Company. He was born in the family's Strawberry Hill home in 1867. (VCHS.)

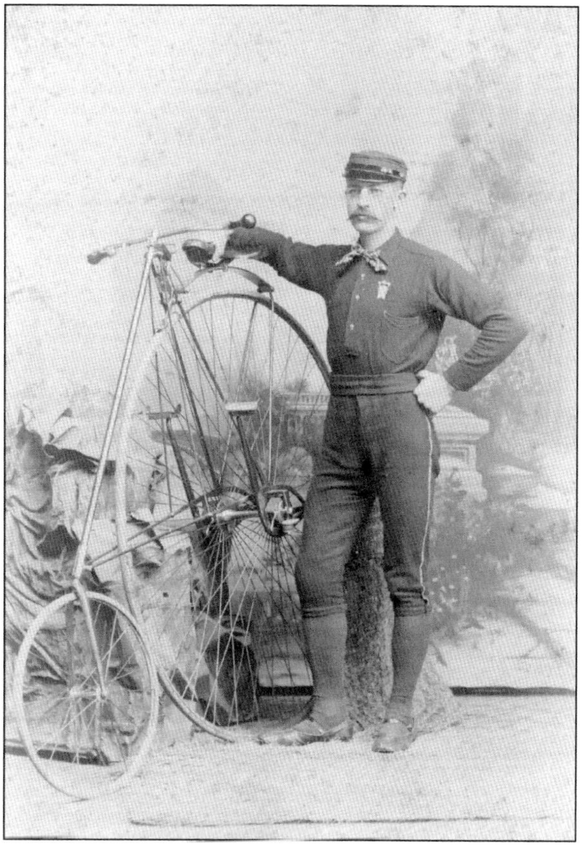

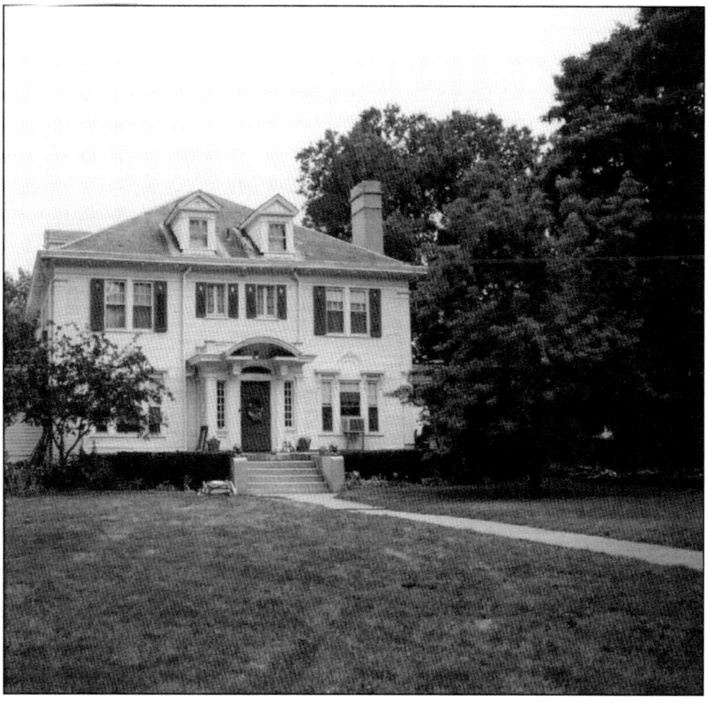

Herman Hulman Jr. lived in this house at 1320 South Sixth Street in the 1920s; after his death, his widow, Gertrude, continued here. This Colonial Revival home was built around 1905. Among other philanthropies, Herman and his brother Anton Hulman Sr. contributed $36,000 to lift the debt from Calvary Cemetery. (Photograph by J. Richard Becker Jr.)

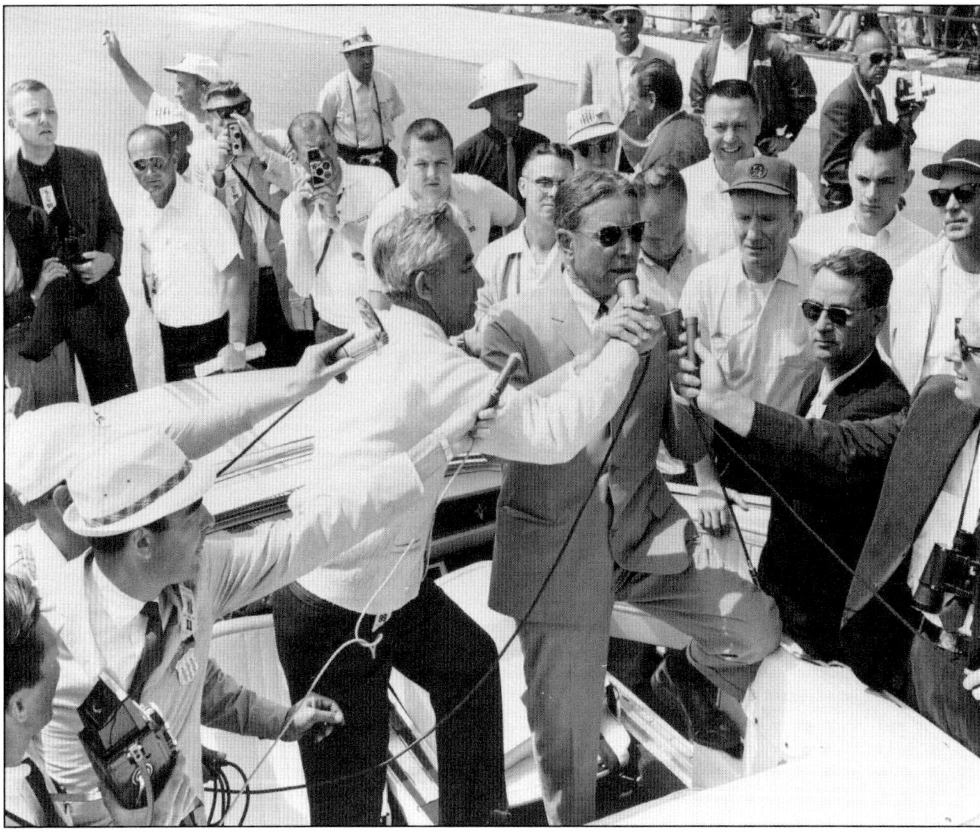

Anton "Tony" Hulman Jr. begins the 1964 Indianapolis 500 race with his trademark line, "Gentlemen, start your engines." He sometimes scribbled the line on paper as a prompt. He bought the faltering Indianapolis Motor Speedway in 1945 from a group that included World War I ace Eddie Rickenbacker, resurrecting an Indiana icon and turning the Indianapolis 500 into the "Greatest Spectacle in Racing." (Indianapolis Motor Speedway Corporation.)

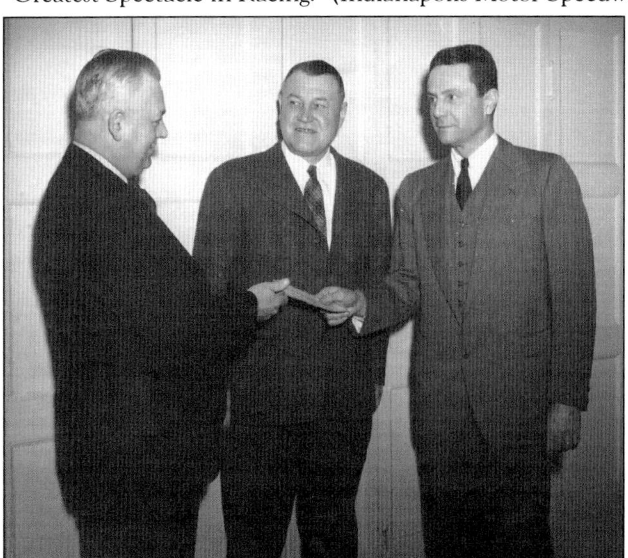

To help the community, Anton "Tony" Hulman Jr. donated a $100,000 check on April 11, 1943, to purchase 638 acres east of Terre Haute for a larger airport. Mayor Vernon McMillan had asked Hulman to chair a committee to locate land for a new municipal airport. Hulman Field eventually replaced Paul Cox Field south of town. From left to right are Harry Fitch of the aeronautics board, McMillan, and Hulman. (VCHS.)

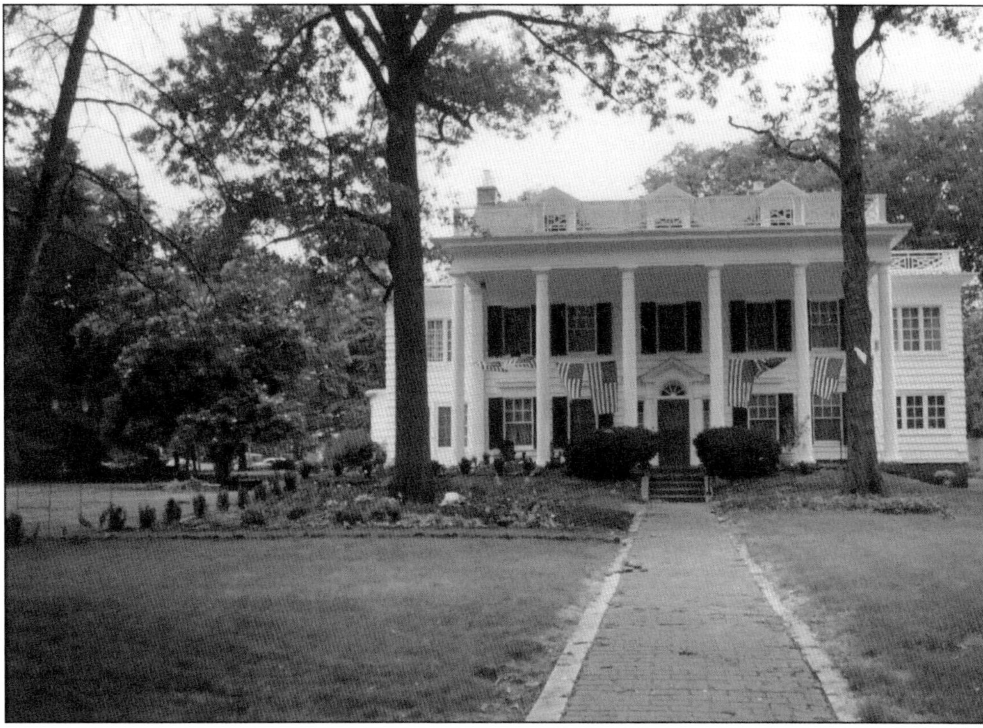

Anton "Tony" Hulman Jr. brought his bride to 1327 South Sixth Street after a European honeymoon. He and Mary Fendrich, of Evansville, bought this Southern Greek Revival home in 1927. Many celebrities stopped by during the 500-race season. The Hulman heir launched an advertising campaign that made Clabber Girl Baking Powder nationally known, and he took the helm of Hulman and Company after his father died. (Photograph by J. Richard Becker Jr.)

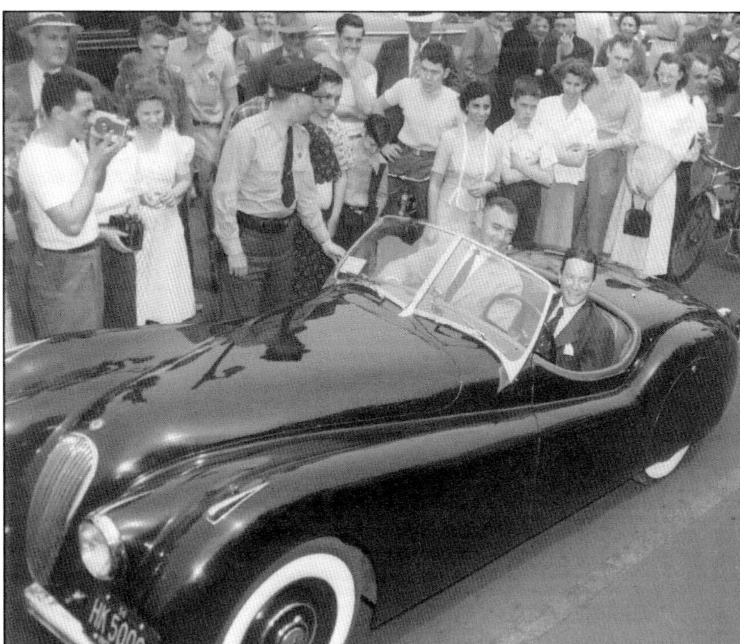

Actor Clark Gable, at left in car, was one of many celebrities who visited at 1327 South Sixth Street. Here, he rides with Anton "Tony" Hulman Jr. during a US Savings Bond drive in 1950. Though the heir of the Hulman family rubbed elbows with celebrities, people in Terre Haute knew him as just Tony, a neighbor who was hardworking, generous, and friendly. (Photograph by Martin's Photo Shop; VCPL.)

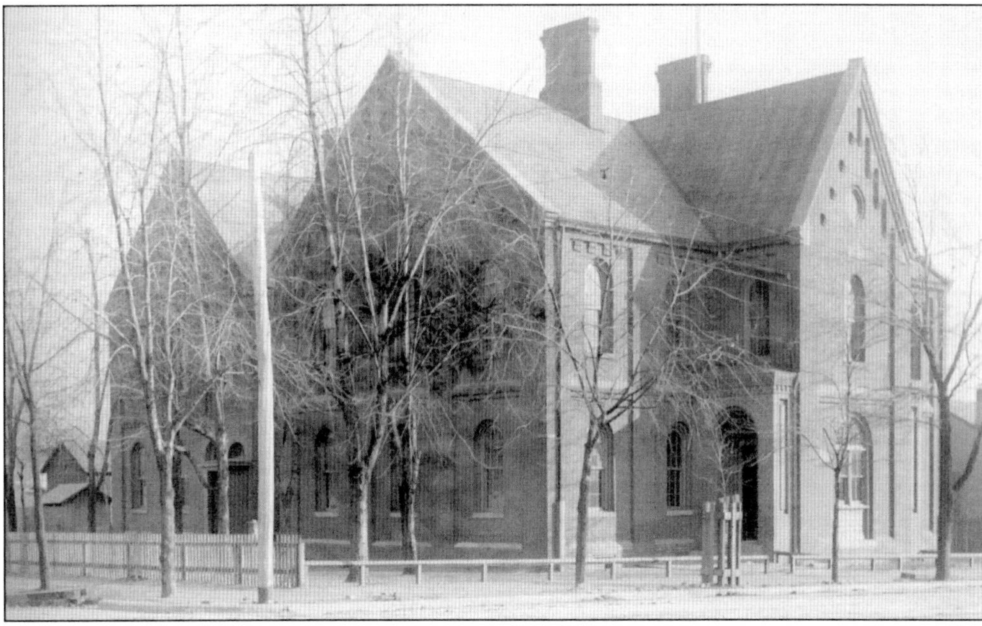

The Second District School at the southwest corner of Seventh and Swan Streets was renamed Hulman School in honor of the Hulmans when schools switched from numbers to names around 1906. The city built the school in 1867, and it was demolished in 1935. This photograph is from 1892. City school superintendent William Wiley featured several city schools in a photographic exhibition at the 1904 Chicago World's Fair. (VCHS.)

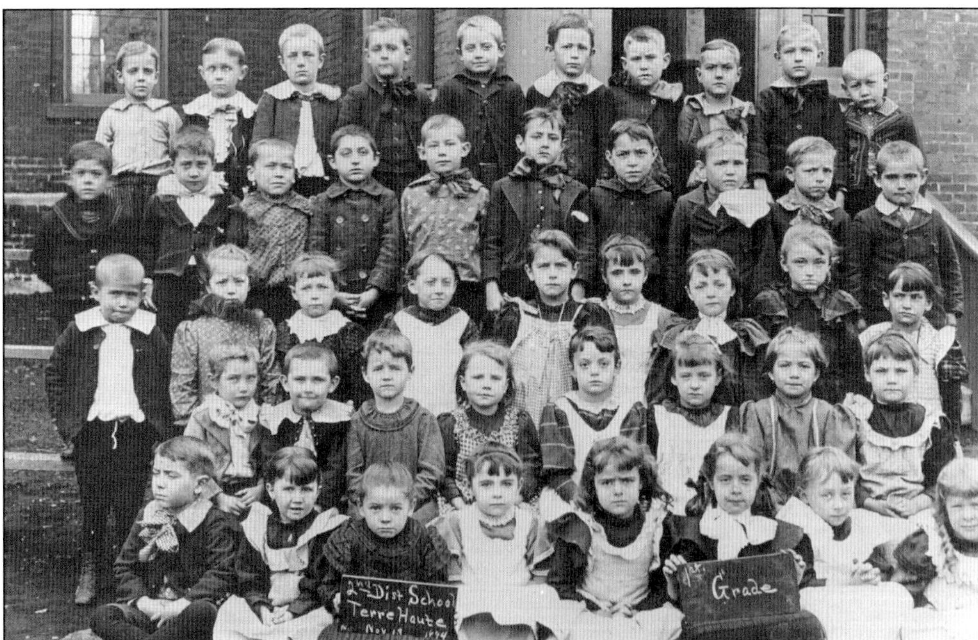

Parents dressed these first graders at Second District School in their suits and best dresses for class picture day. The teacher had a large class of eager minds to deal with; first grade contained 45 students. The day was blustery on November 13, 1894; the wind blew the neck ruffle on the girl second from left in the third row. (VCHS.)

The faculty of Second District School, later known as Hulman School, at the southwest corner of Seventh and Swan Streets, presented a stern appearance to students in this photograph from the 1880s. From left to right are (first row) Mrs. Slatz, Lulu Hale, and Jessie Cliver; (second row) May Connelly, Jennie Farnham, Alice Burnett, and Mary Lewis; (third row) Mary Reeves and Sallie Ward. (VCHS.)

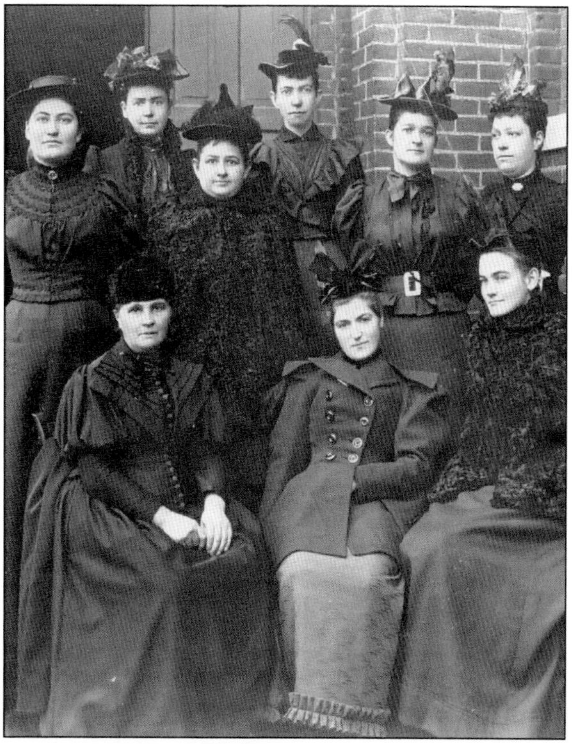

Alice Yeakle Volkers, center, was a charter member of Washington Avenue Presbyterian Church; it was three blocks south of St. Agnes Academy. As a girl in the 1870s, Alice had to stay indoors during cattle drives down Market Street (today's Third Street). Her mother, Mary Yeakle, kept her inside for fear cows might get loose and stampede toward their 917 South Fourth Street home. (Unity Presbyterian Church.)

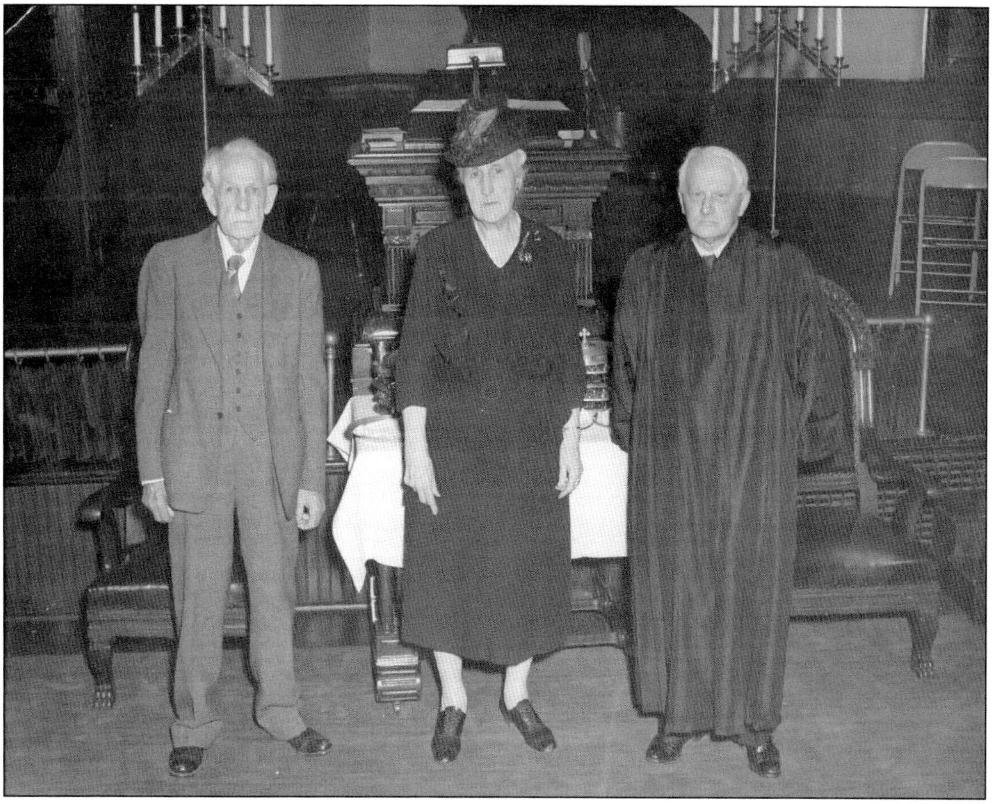

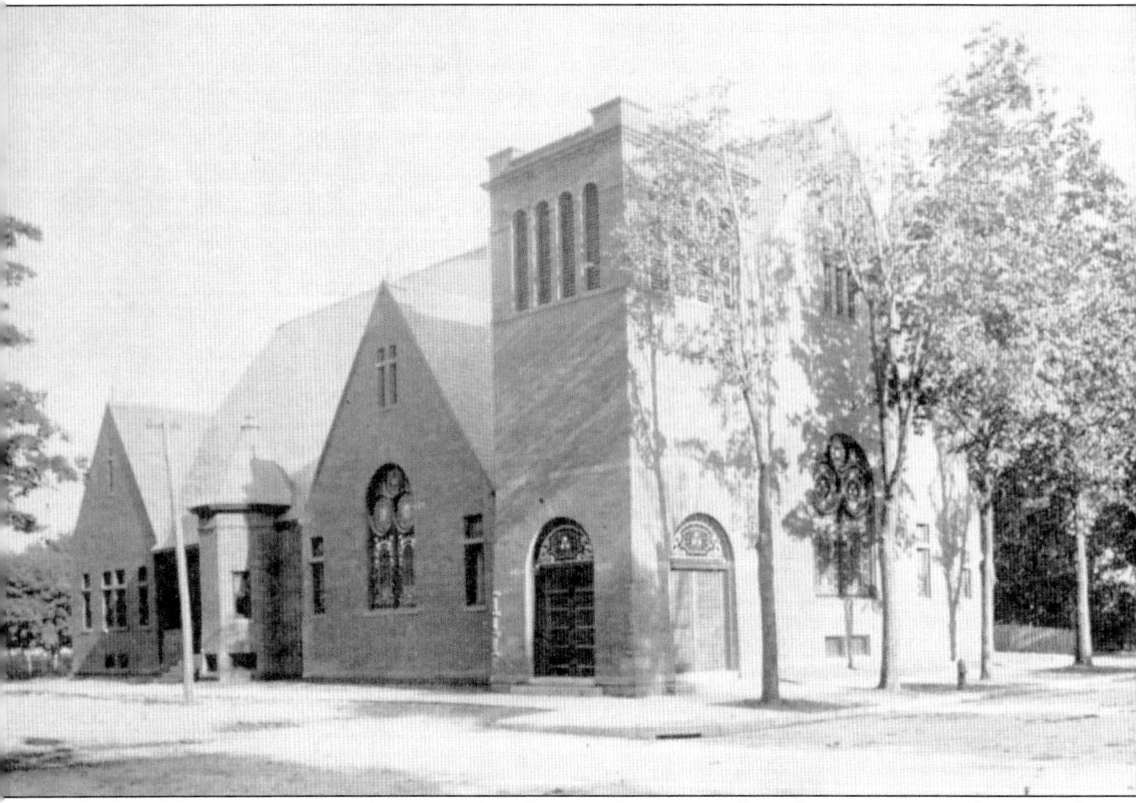

Washington Avenue Presbyterian Church at Sixth Street and Washington Avenue began with a group of Methodists meeting in St. Agnes Academy, later St. Anthony's Hospital. In 1876, the group built the Moffatt Street Church at the northeast corner of Third Street and Washington Avenue; Washington was called Moffatt Street in those days. Meanwhile, a Presbyterian group began meeting in St. Agnes Academy in 1878. Though the Methodists sold the building to the Presbyterians in 1881, some members of the congregation, like Alice Yeakle Volkers, stayed there when the Presbyterians began using the building for their Greenwood Mission. By 1884, the building was renamed Moffatt Street Presbyterian Church; the growing congregation was looking for a larger space. The cornerstone for this building at Sixth Street and Washington Avenue was laid in 1892; during construction, the congregation met in the Coates College gymnasium a couple of blocks away. The dedication of the $18,000 building was in 1894, and with it came the name change to Washington Avenue Presbyterian Church. This photograph is from 1894. (J. Richard Becker Jr.)

This interior view shows the pipe organ in Washington Avenue Presbyterian Church. The congregation purchased the organ in 1908 at a cost of $3,000, and it was renovated in 1971 for $16,000. To purchase a grand piano for the church in the early days, the women cooked and served a moose dinner to 600 people. (Photograph by J. Richard Becker Jr.)

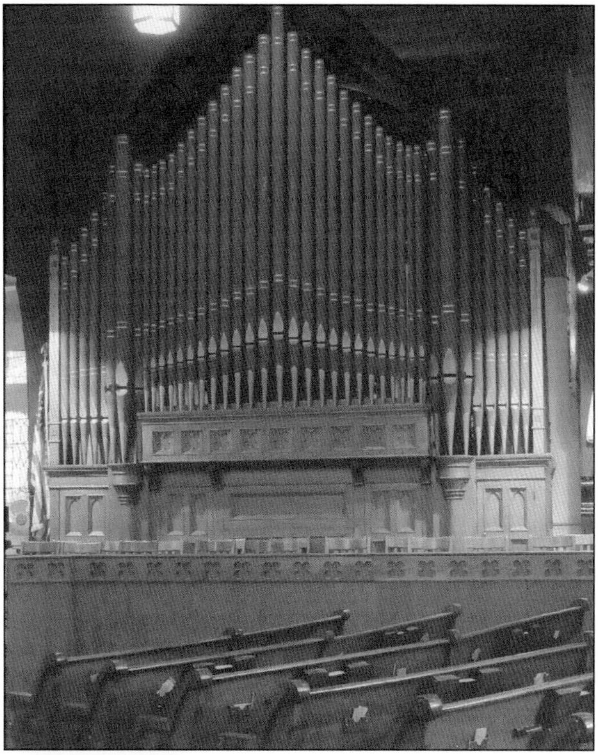

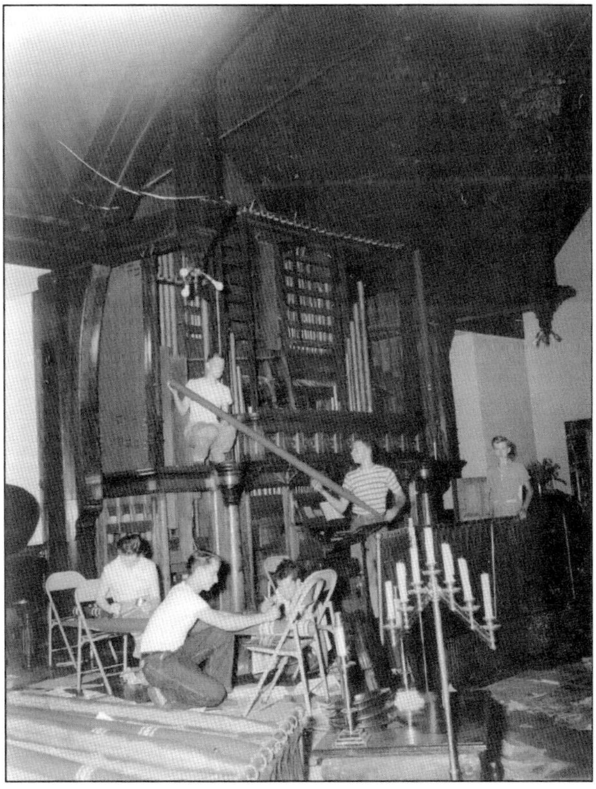

During the 1950s, the youth group at Washington Avenue Presbyterian Church decided to spruce up the pipe organ with a paint job. The young people had to number the pipes, take them apart, clean and paint them, and put them back together. Some adults viewed the proposed project with more than a touch of anxiety, but the organ worked when it was reassembled. (Unity Presbyterian Church.)

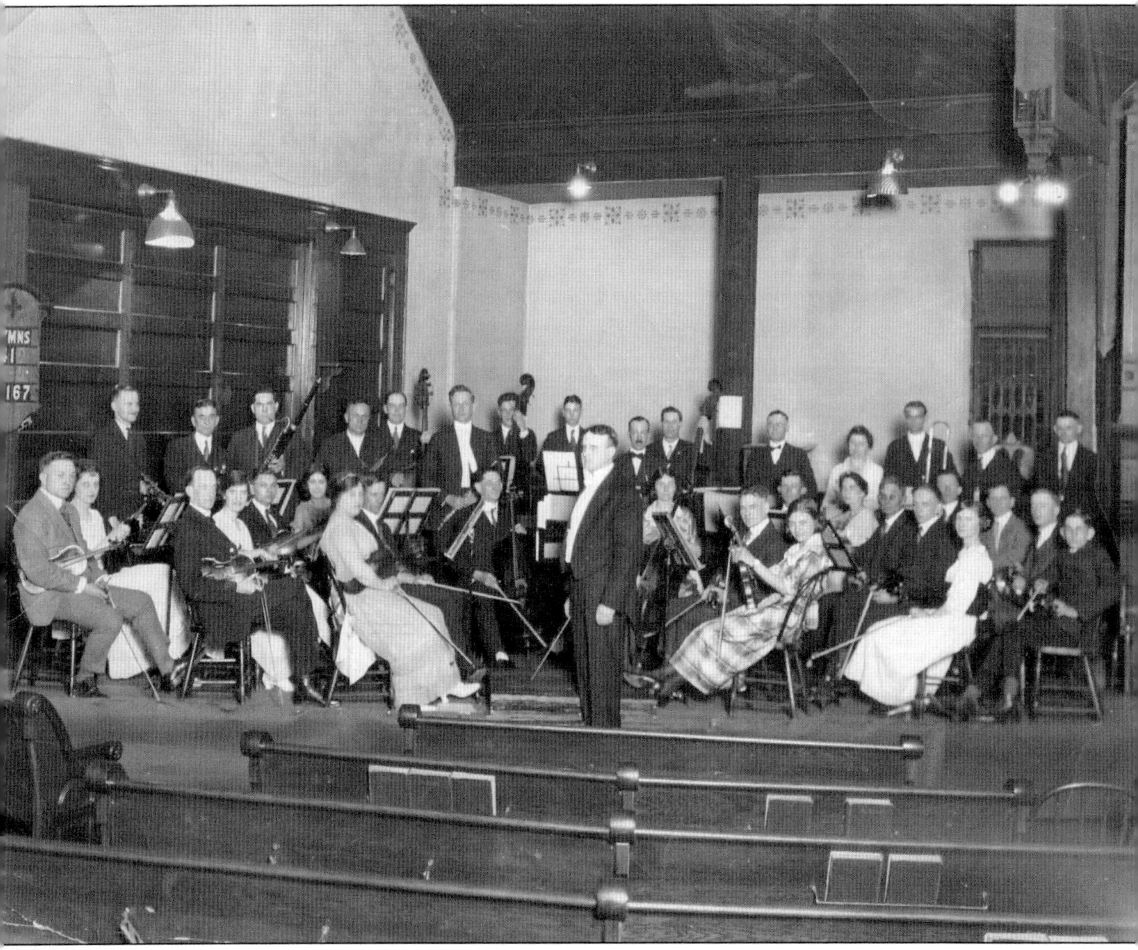

The Washington Avenue Presbyterian Church Symphony Orchestra was organized at the church in 1910, under the direction of Harry Crawford. He directed it for many years at church and community functions. This 1919 photograph shows the orchestra, a forerunner of the second incarnation of the Terre Haute Symphony Orchestra. Marguerite Kickler Miller was concertmaster of Washington Avenue Symphony. She was called to duty as concertmaster and first violinist for the new Terre Haute Symphony's first concert at 10:30 a.m. on December 4, 1926, in the Indiana Theater. Other musicians in the Terre Haute Symphony's first concert were Washington Avenue violinist Leona Fariss and flutist Victor C. Miller. Invited guests included music students from Indiana State Normal and St. Mary-of-the-Woods College. The Woman's Department Club, then on Cherry Street, hosted a private luncheon for 155 guests afterward. Among those reserving tables for private parties were Frank Hale, Bertha Pratt King, and Bess Cunningham, who entertained district Indiana Federation of Clubs officers. Musicians in the local union had pushed for the formation of the symphony. (Unity Presbyterian Church.)

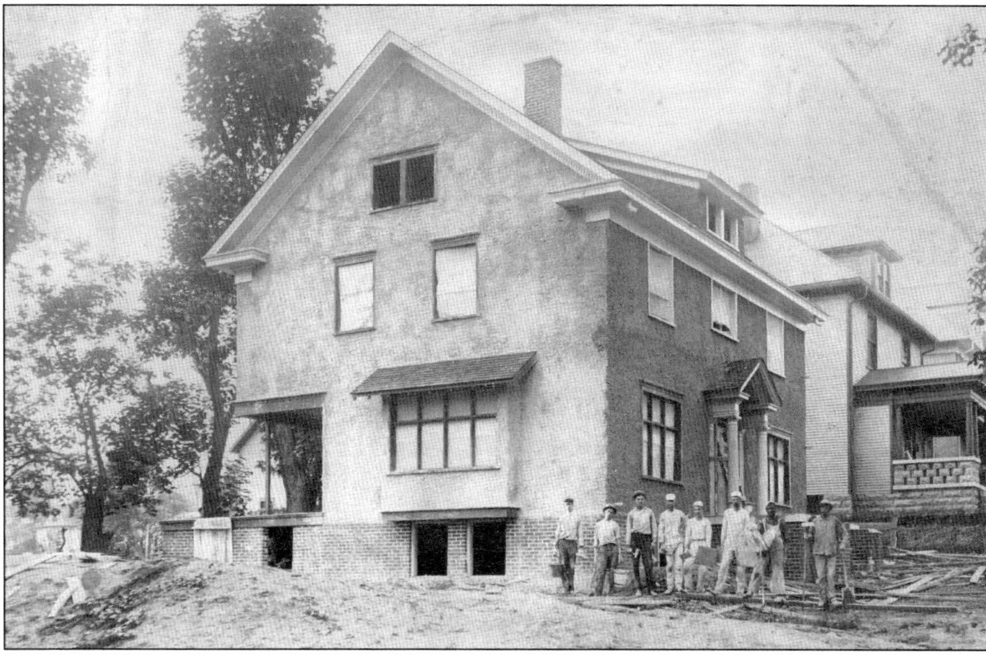

The December 4, 1926, concert of the Terre Haute Symphony Orchestra was given under the auspices of the Music Section of the Woman's Department Club and its chairman Clara H. Paige. She was an obvious choice. Her husband, Warren H. Paige, owned W.H. Paige and Company Music House downtown. The Paiges were second owners of 1645 South Fifth Street, still under construction in this 1910 photograph. (David and Sandra Roberts.)

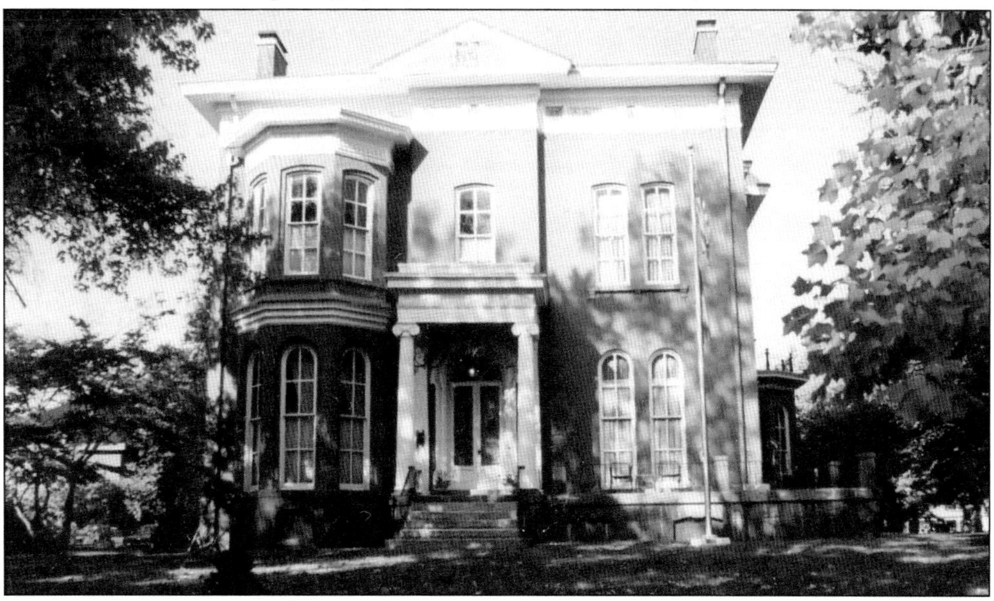

The Woman's Department Club moved to 507 South Sixth Street in 1932. The club was incorporated in 1922 when 11 women's clubs in the city united. Today, the five departments are garden and nature study, art and music, literature and drama, social service, and juniors. The Italianate-Tuscan villa house was built around 1868 for Col. Robert N. Hudson, abolitionist, state legislator, and newspaper publisher. (Photograph by J. Richard Becker Jr.)

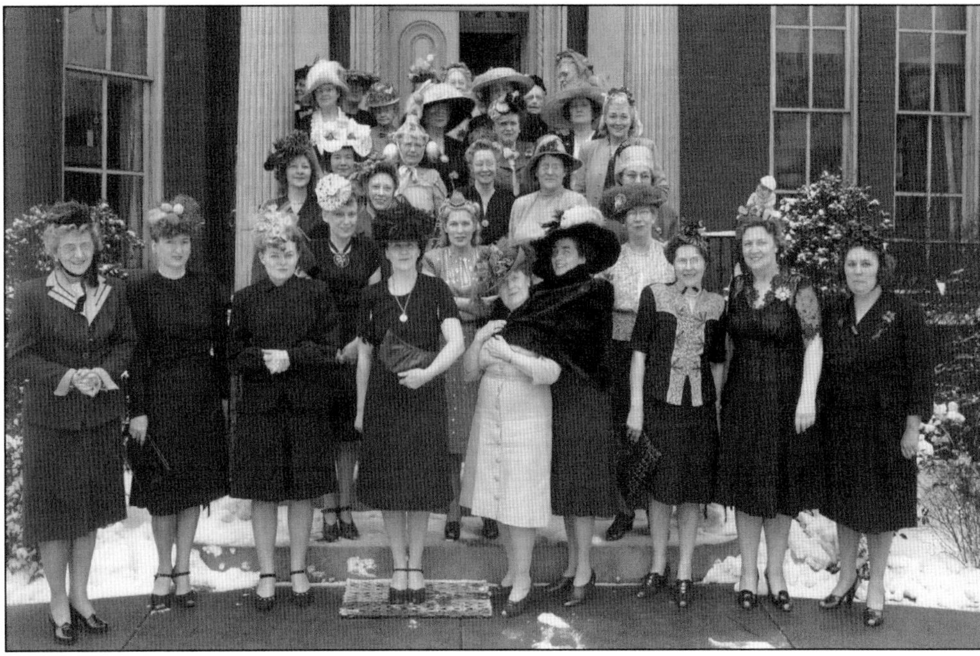

Members of the Woman's Department Club gather at the clubhouse at 507 South Sixth Street for a crazy hat contest during a meeting in 1947. Each department conducts a monthly meeting with a program of interest to members. Meetings do not take place during the summer months. (Photograph by Martin's Photo Shop; VCPL.)

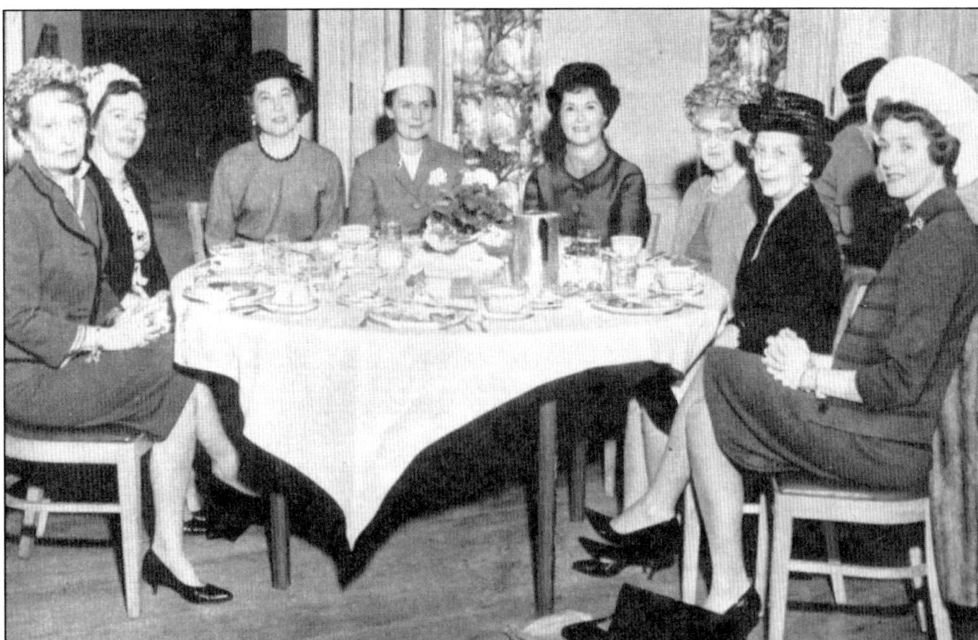

The Drama Department of the Woman's Department Club gathers for one of its monthly meetings in 1962. From left to right are Doyne Chezem, Georgia Sheldon, Luetta Lowe, Waunetta Minnis, Mrs. Lawrence Fels, Sue Tingley, Marie Drew, and Carolyn Lindley. (Photograph by Martin's Photo Shop; Tribune-Star.)

November 6, 1959, marked the first cotillion. The Woman's Department Club and the chamber of commerce joined to sponsor the first cotillion; chamber of commerce members escorted 34 young women in their debut into society. After the ceremony, fathers and daughters danced in the Mayflower Room of the Terre Haute House. The yearly tradition is now eagerly anticipated by Junior Department members of the Woman's Department Club. (Tribune-Star.)

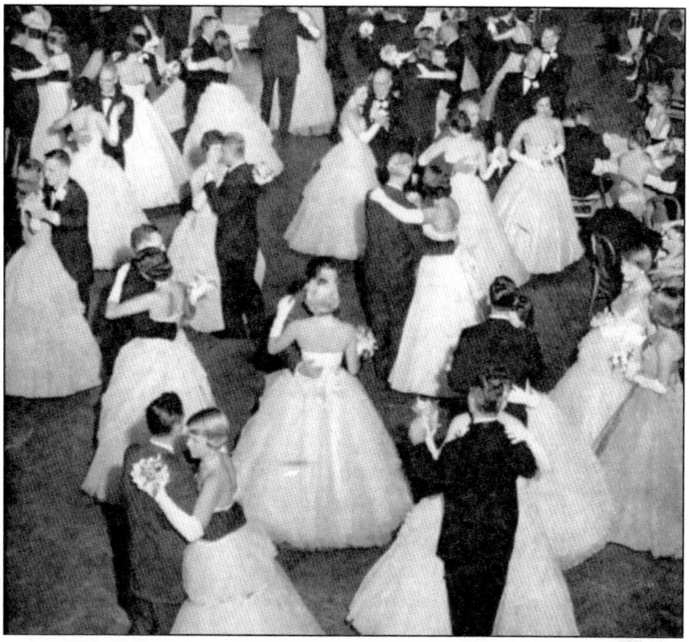

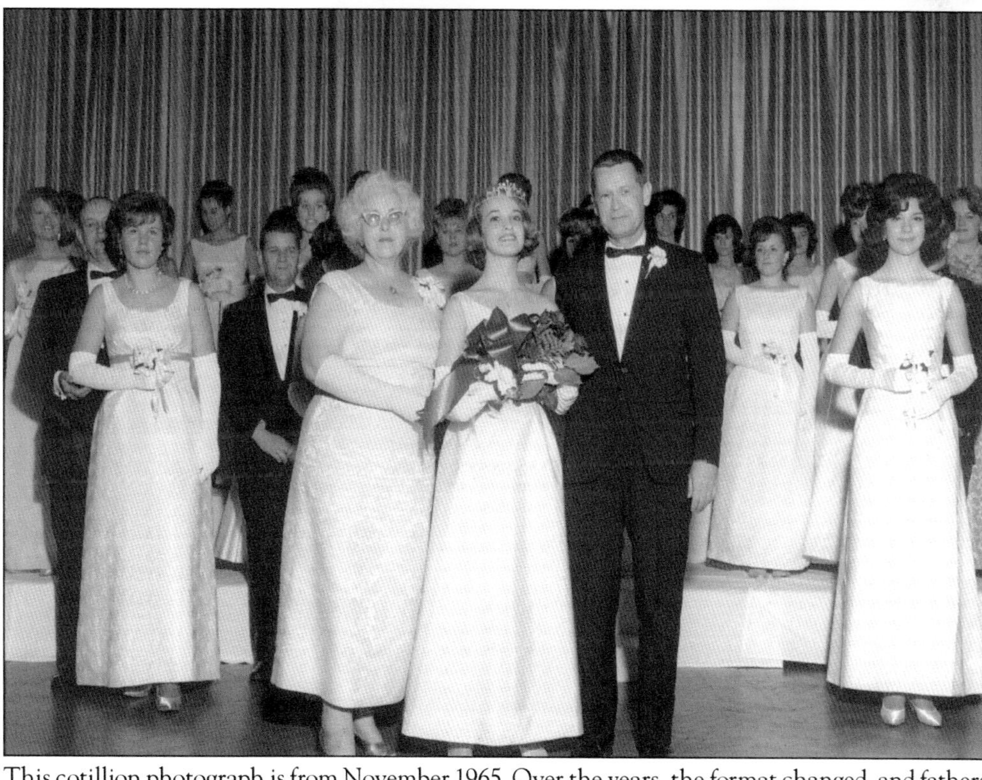

This cotillion photograph is from November 1965. Over the years, the format changed, and fathers escorted their daughters during the introduction ceremony. The cotillion also changed its focus to scholarship and honoring seniors in high school, rather than a debut into society. To join the Junior Department, girls must be 14 years old and must be sponsored by a Woman's Department Club member. (Photograph by Martin's Photo Shop; VCPL.)

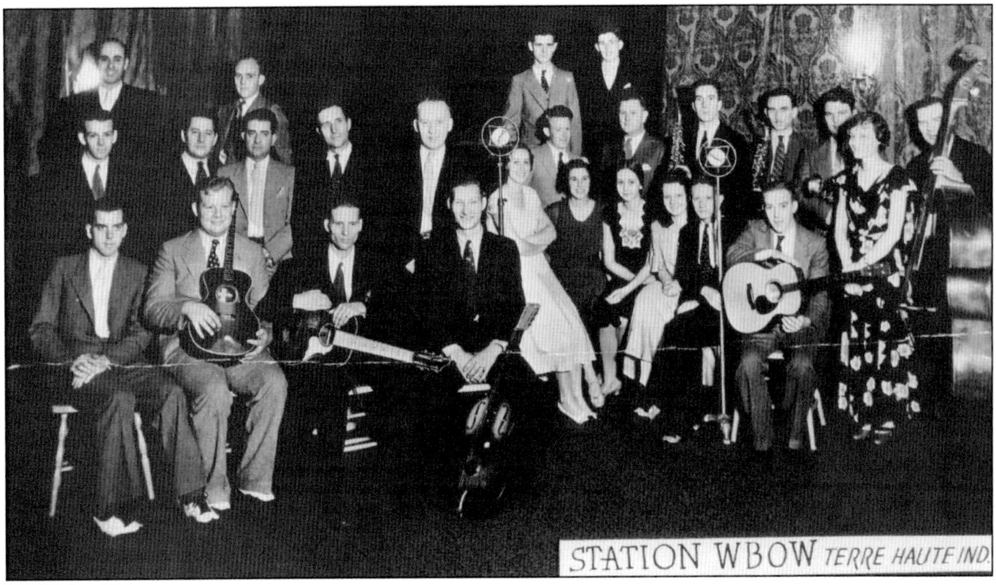

Singer Burl Ives, second from left in the first row, lent his voice to the Washington Avenue Presbyterian Church choir. The church sometimes paid college students to sing in the choir—enriching students with a little extra pocket money and enriching the choir's sound. He also earned four dollars a week in 1932 at radio station WBOW, performing folk songs on air as the Blond Tenor. (Photograph by Martin's Photo Shop; VCHS.)

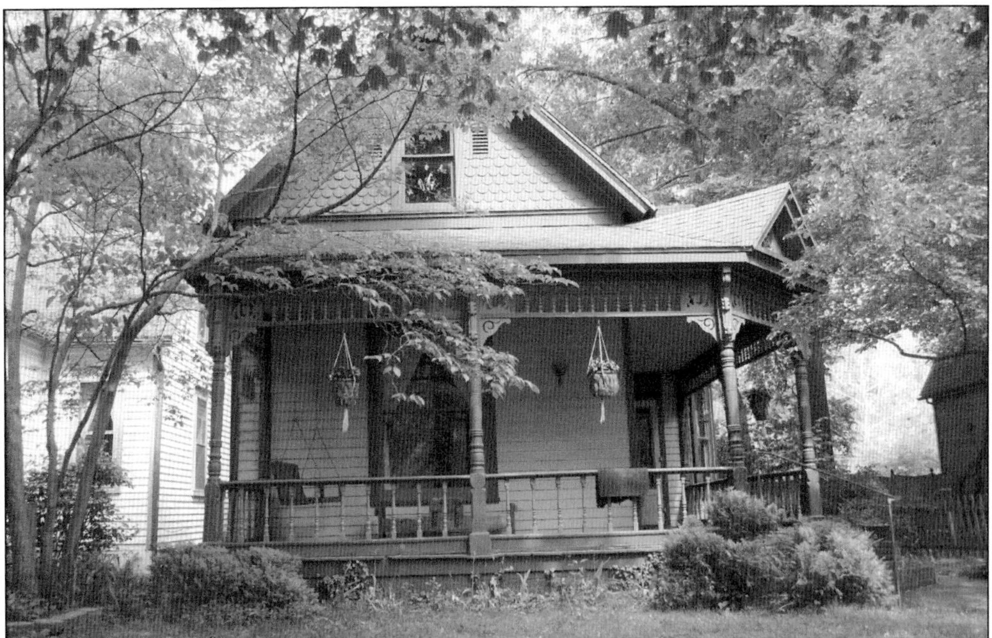

Balladeer Burl Ives took music lessons from Clara Bloomfield at 1306 South Center Street while attending Indiana State Normal. He often rode his motorcycle toting his guitar. The French-born Madame Clara encouraged him to go to New York, giving him letters of introduction. Ives said his Terre Haute experiences opened the world for him. He won an Academy Award, and his song "Poor Wayfaring Stranger" still endures.

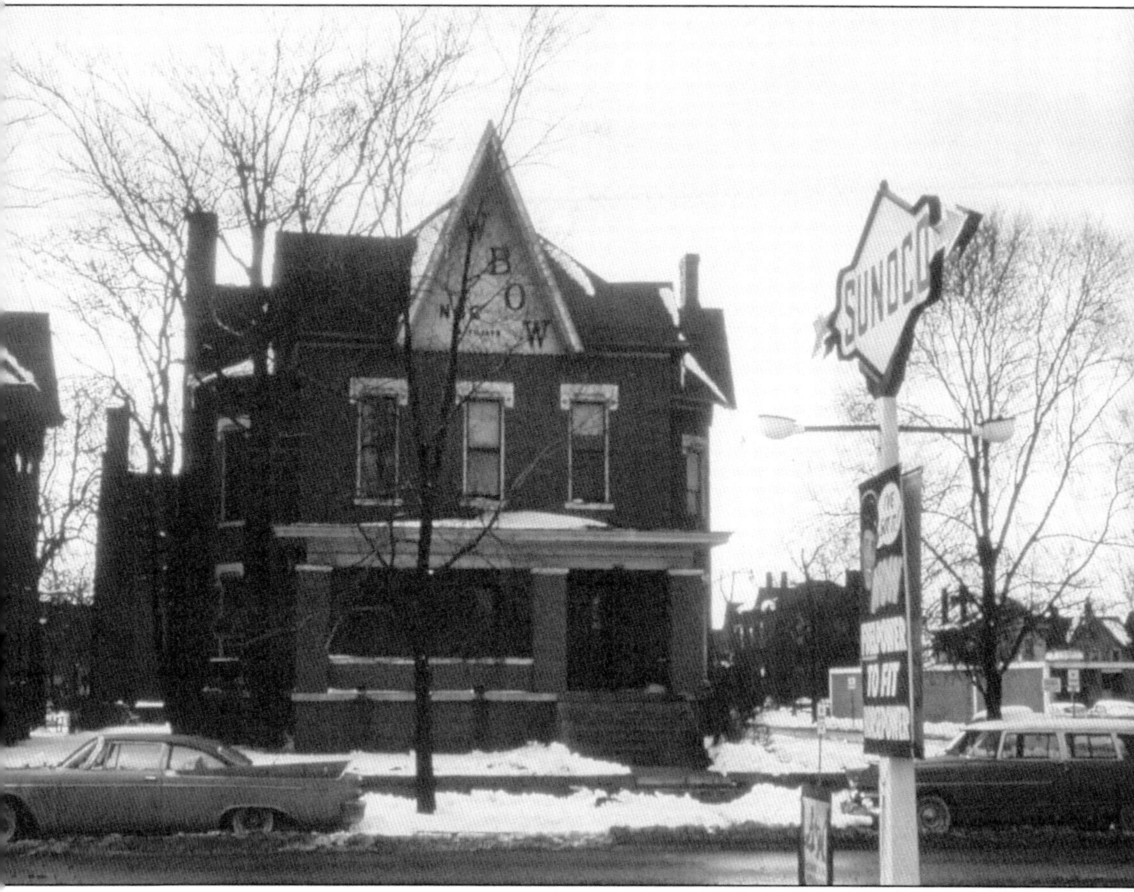

Radio station WBOW had its home for many years at 303 South Sixth Street, the southwest corner of Sixth and Poplar Streets where only a parking lot remains today. The station began in 1927 with call letters WRPI at Rose Polytechnic Institute, changing to WBOW a few years later and moving off campus. Its third location was in Farrington's Grove, beginning June 11, 1938, and staying until June 1964. On the second floor were two control rooms and two broadcasting studios for the AM and FM bands. Downstairs was the office and reception area. Many media personalities got their start at WBOW. Harry Frey, the Matinee Songster on WBOW, later became news anchor for television station WTHI and Terre Haute's answer to Walter Cronkite. Other personalities were sports reporters Cork McHargue, Darrell "Darl" Wible, and John Palmer, who later became television station WTWO news anchor. News director Martin Plascak delivered the news authoritatively. WBOW personality Ralph Tucker, remembered for his Man on the Street interviews, later served five terms as mayor of Terre Haute. (Photograph by Martin Plascak.)

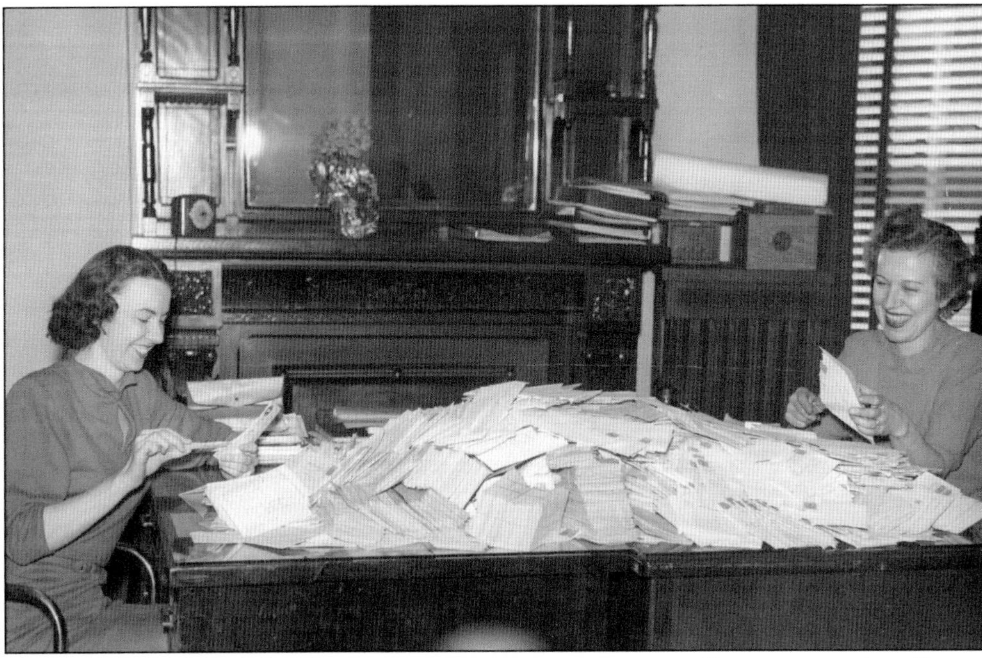

Downstairs in the office area at 303 South Sixth Street was the WBOW mailroom. Receptionist Ruth Manas (left) and promotions director Madeline Berry sort through a stack of mail in the 1940s. WBOW ran frequent promotions to catch the public's interest, and this pile of letters is likely the result of one of those. (Martin Plascak.)

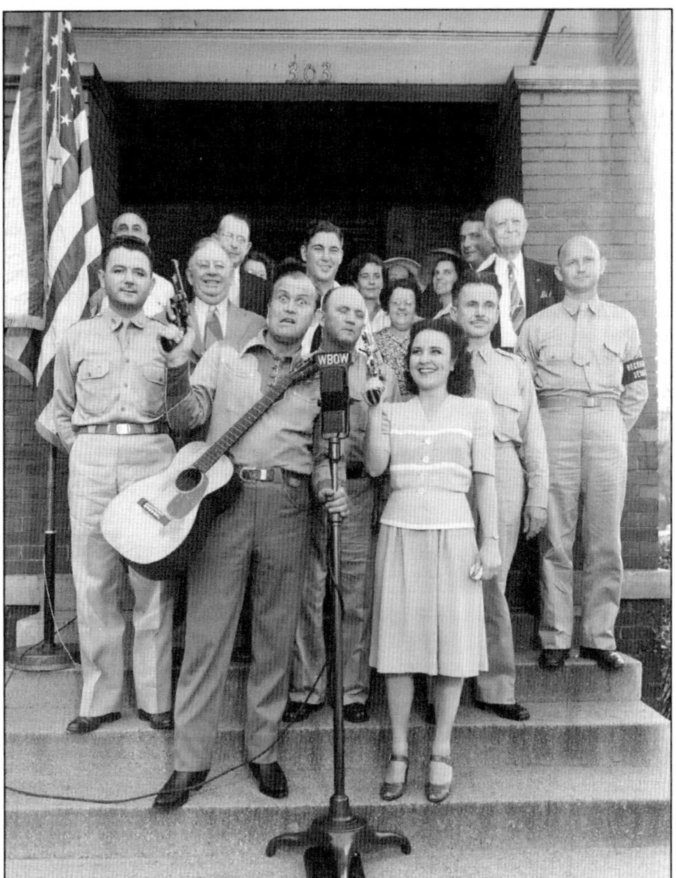

Reese Davis with his guitar and Wee Bonnie Baker (right), singer of the popular hit "Oh Johnny," mug for the camera on the steps at station WBOW. Bonnie had come to Terre Haute in the 1940s during a war bond drive. At right in the back, trying to hide, is Anton "Tony" Hulman Jr., chairman of the Vigo County war bonds staff. (Photograph by Martin's Photo Shop; Martin Plascak.)

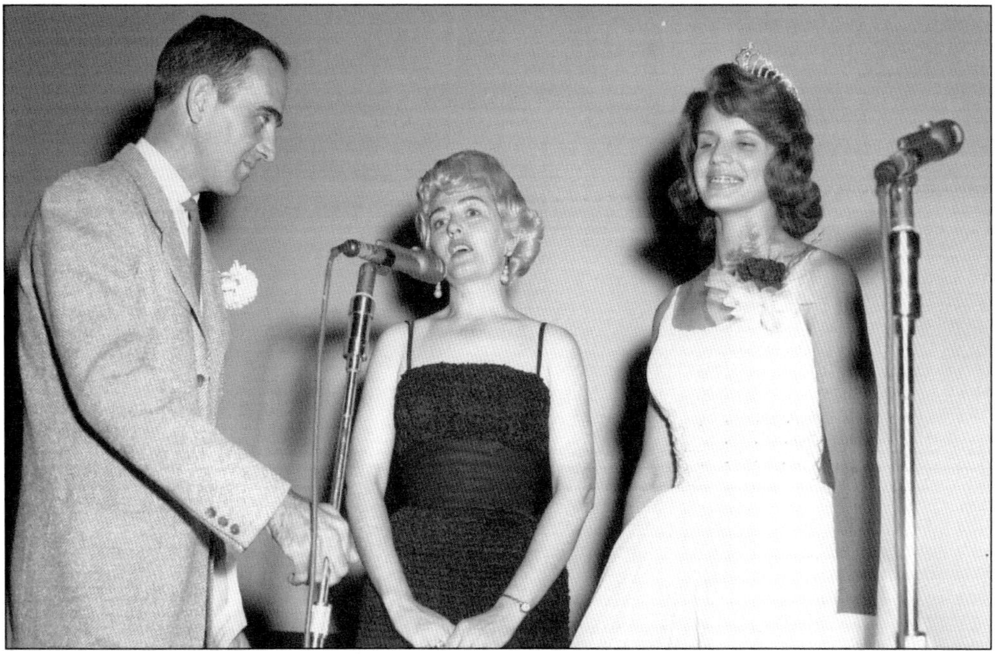

John Palmer of radio station WBOW congratulates Sue Stoehr, local winner in the Miss Teenage America pageant of 1963; her mother is in the center. Contestants arrived in a nighttime parade of open convertibles down Wabash Avenue to the Grand Theater, with crowds lining the street. Palmer served as master of ceremonies for the pageant. (Martin Plascak.)

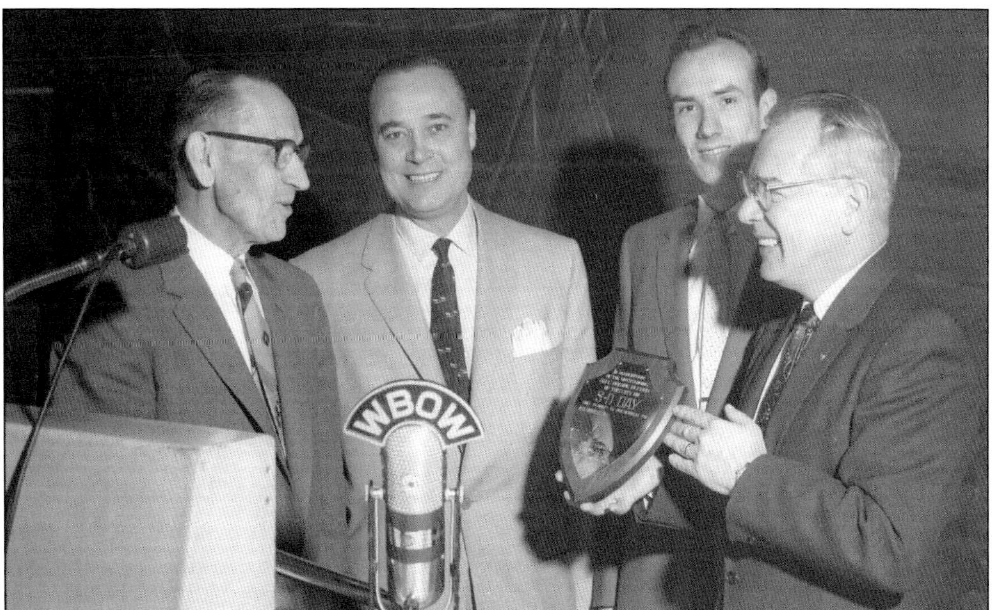

WBOW news director Martin Plascak, second from right, developed a Safe Driving Day promotion. Terre Haute challenged other communities and went 14 days without an accident. The station received the WBOW Safe Driving Day Award from the state. From left to right are an unidentified state official, Mayor Ralph Tucker, Plascak, and station manager Ferrall Rippetoe. (Photograph by Martin's Photo Shop; Martin Plascak.)

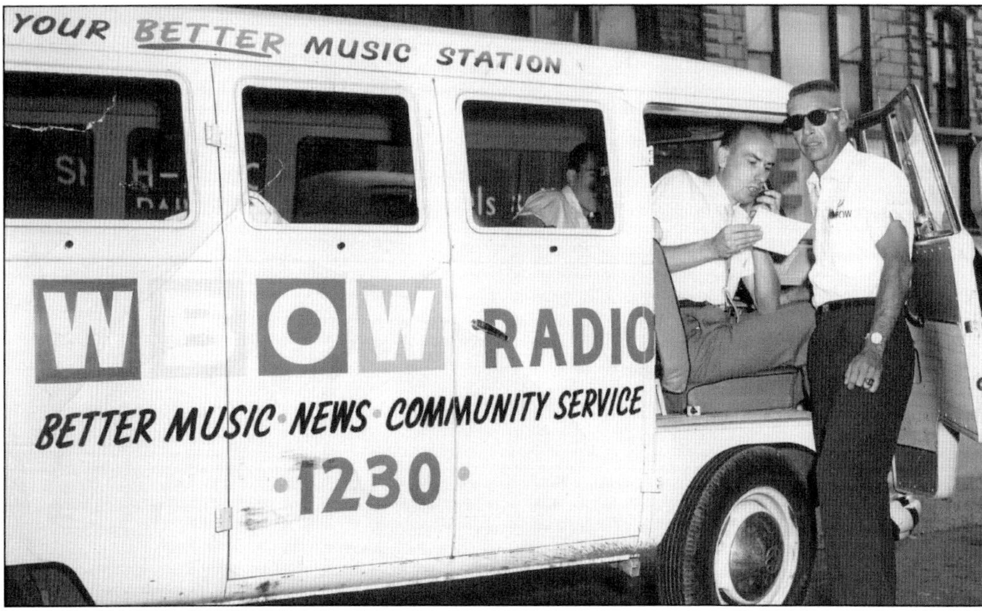

Using radio station WBOW's Red Rover news van, news director Martin Plascak interviews station disc jockey James "J.A." Austin in the photograph above. In a station promotion during the 1940s, Austin sought to beat the world's stay-awake record he had previously set. For 231 hours, Austin attempted to beat sleep in the Root Store in downtown Terre Haute. During the day, he stayed on the second floor, luring curious customers upstairs. In the photograph below, crowds watch Austin at night in Root's first-floor display window on Wabash Avenue. Spectators could win $500 for guessing the number of hours correctly. Mayor Ralph Tucker told Plascak it was the biggest crowd he had seen downtown since the end of World War II. A bleary-eyed Austin broke the record and then was taken for a medical checkup. (Both, Martin Plascak.)

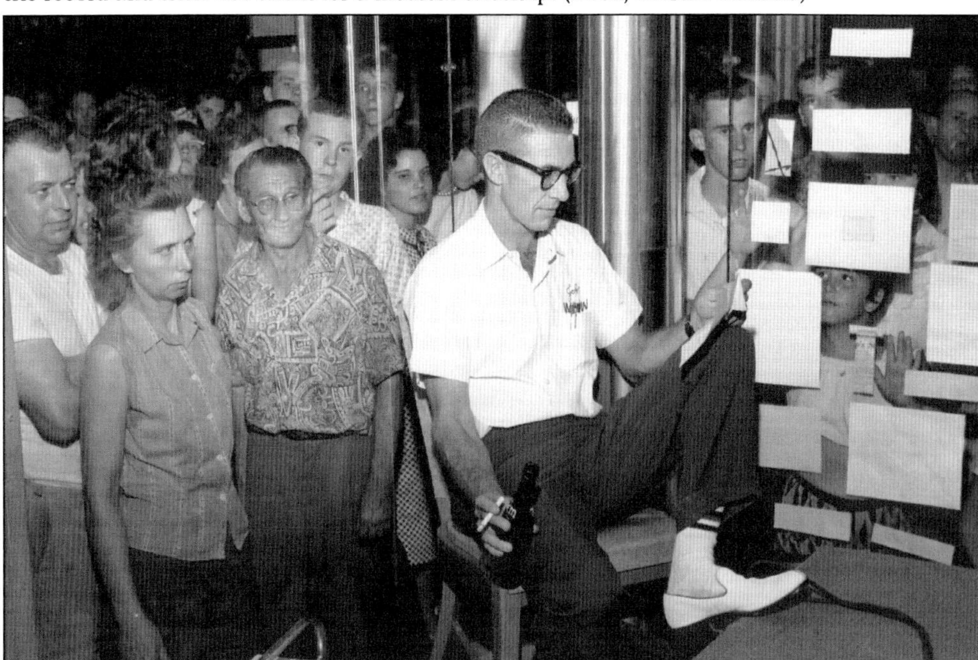

This promotional item given away in the 1950s was a radio that only received WBOW's 1230 AM frequency. The gadget resembled the ribbon microphones used in the studio. WBOW was an NBC affiliate until about 1957, carrying such shows as *Bob Hope*, *Dragnet*, and *Jack Benny*. The station then switched to the Mutual Broadcasting System for news and changed its format to Top 40 music.

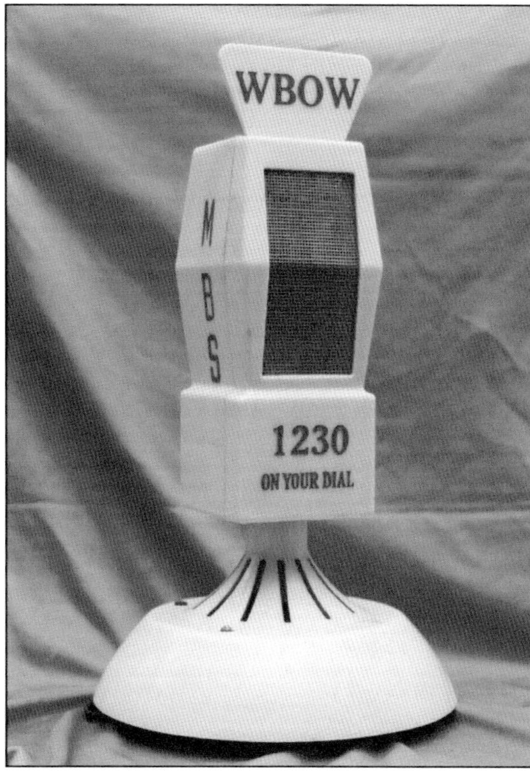

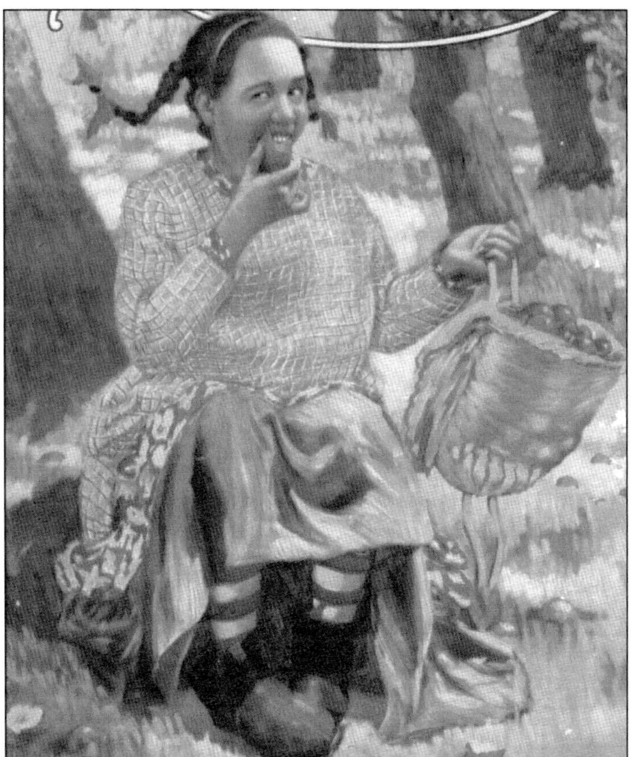

Rose Melville was a true celebrity in the early 1900s with her character Sis Hopkins. The media sensation had her own doll, two magazines, and a book. Originally, Sis was a minor character in a play about Indiana hillbillies, but it developed into a three-act musical. Melville played the pigtailed, naïve teenager on theater stages for 15 years and in several movie shorts. She grew up at 403 Willow Street, which was named Gulick Street in the 1880s and earlier. (VCHS.)

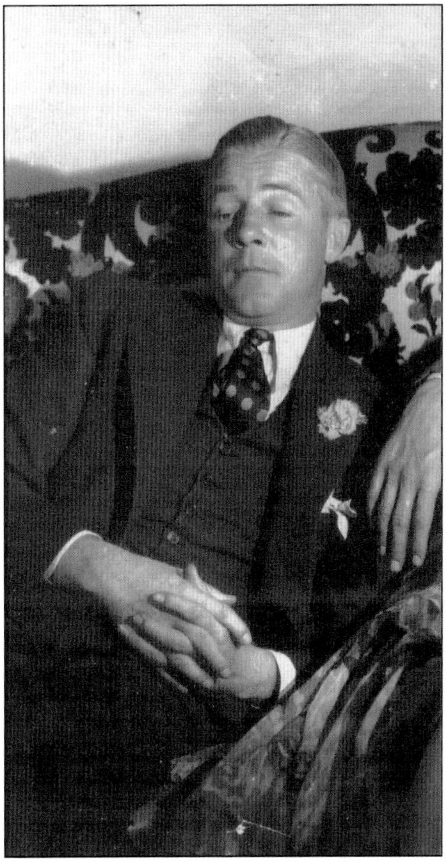

Also contributing to the entertainment industry was Farrington's Grove resident Richard "Skeets" Gallagher (pictured). The photograph below shows his boyhood home at 608 South Center Street. After trying engineering at Rose Polytechnic and law at Indiana University, he chose acting, which worked out well for him. He began in vaudeville and progressed to more traditional theater, starring in productions on Broadway as well as in Chicago and Los Angeles. He appeared in more than 50 films with actors such as Gloria Swanson and Joe E. Brown. His first "talkie" film, *The Potters* with W.C. Fields, was also the first talking film shown at the Indiana Theater in 1927. He earned great reviews as the White Rabbit in Paramount Picture's 1933 film *Alice in Wonderland*. (Left, VCHS; below, photograph by Albert Christenberry.)

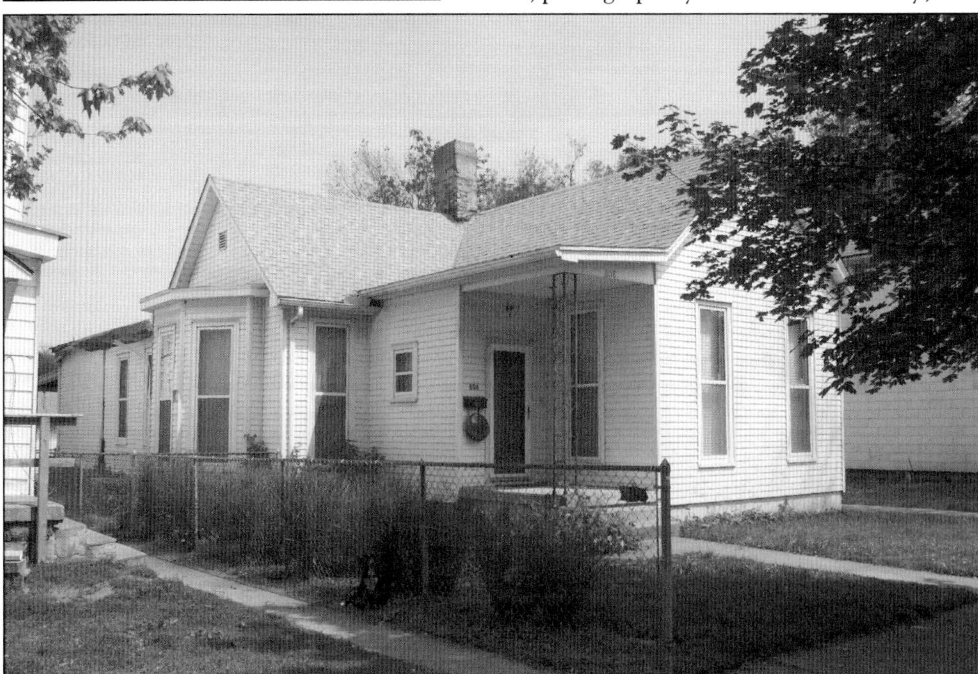

Three

Coca-Cola, a Tornado, and Strawberry Hill

The tornado of 1913 barely missed the historic homes in Farrington's Grove, but it caused loss of life, devastation in much of the city, and destroyed the Root Glass Company plant. Chapman J. Root decided to stay and rebuild—a decision that paid back in royalties. When the Coca-Cola Company announced a contest in 1915 to design a new bottle with a unique shape and feel, Root Glass Company took up the challenge and won the contest; the company received royalties from each gross produced by bottlers. Root Glass Company employee Earl R. Dean drew the design, machined the mold, and produced a prototype under incredible time pressure. Offered a choice of a $500 bonus or a lifetime job, he took the lifetime job.

In the old days, the pioneers called the area from Osborne Street south to Hulman "Strawberry Hill" because of the wild strawberries there. When Judge Samuel Gookins, a law partner of James Farrington, built a home in the area in 1848, he named it Strawberry Hill. In 1960, the Strawberry Hill Cannoneers were formed at 1504 South Sixth Street and chose their name from the area.

James Farrington Gookins, who was born at Strawberry Hill, is a man whose influence goes far beyond his birthplace, particularly in Chicago. Gookins is credited as the author of the lakefront plan for the 1893 World's Columbian Exhibition in Chicago. He proposed the idea of the Field Museum of Natural History to Marshall Field and persuaded the president of the Illinois Central Railroad to build a sea wall, making Chicago's lakefront park possible. In addition, he helped create the Chicago Academy of Design, the forerunner of the Art Institute of Chicago. In Indianapolis, he served as secretary of the Soldiers and Sailors Monument Commission; in a blind submission for the Indianapolis Circle, the obelisk design of his Munich friend Bruno Schmitz was selected. Gookins was an artist and writer for *Harper's Weekly* and other magazines. He studied art in the Royal Academy in Munich and was famous for his fanciful paintings of flowers and landscapes.

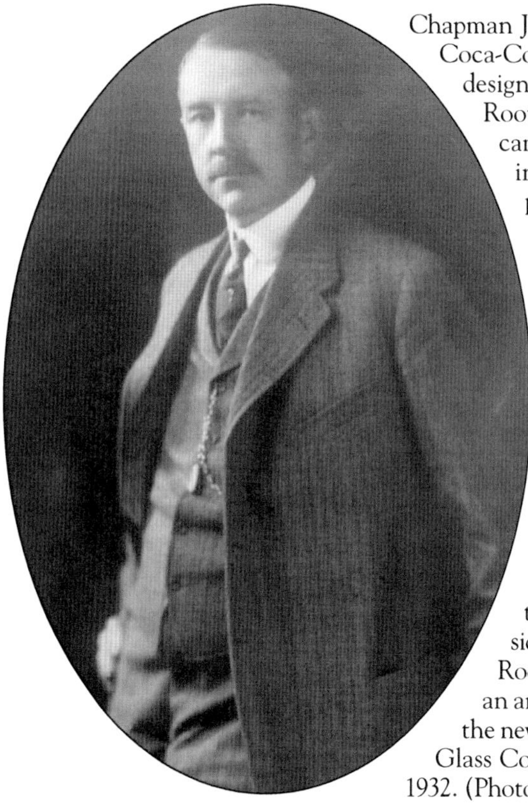

Chapman J. Root's company is linked in history to the Coca-Cola bottle; a Root Glass Company employee designed the unique shape recognized worldwide. Root, already experienced in the glass business, came to Terre Haute and established Root Glass in 1901 near Third and Voorhees Streets. It produced light green, amber, and flint bottles. Root Glass owned a 120-acre silica sand plant near Terre Haute that supplied raw materials. (VCHS.)

Chapman J. Root and his family lived at 1224 South Sixth Street for many years. Originally, this Colonial Revival home was a clapboard-sided house when it was built around 1900, but Root added brick veneer, terra-cotta details, and an arboretum. The Roots lived here in 1915 when the new Coca-Cola bottle was created. He sold Root Glass Company to Owen-Illinois Glass Company in 1932. (Photograph by J. Richard Becker Sr.)

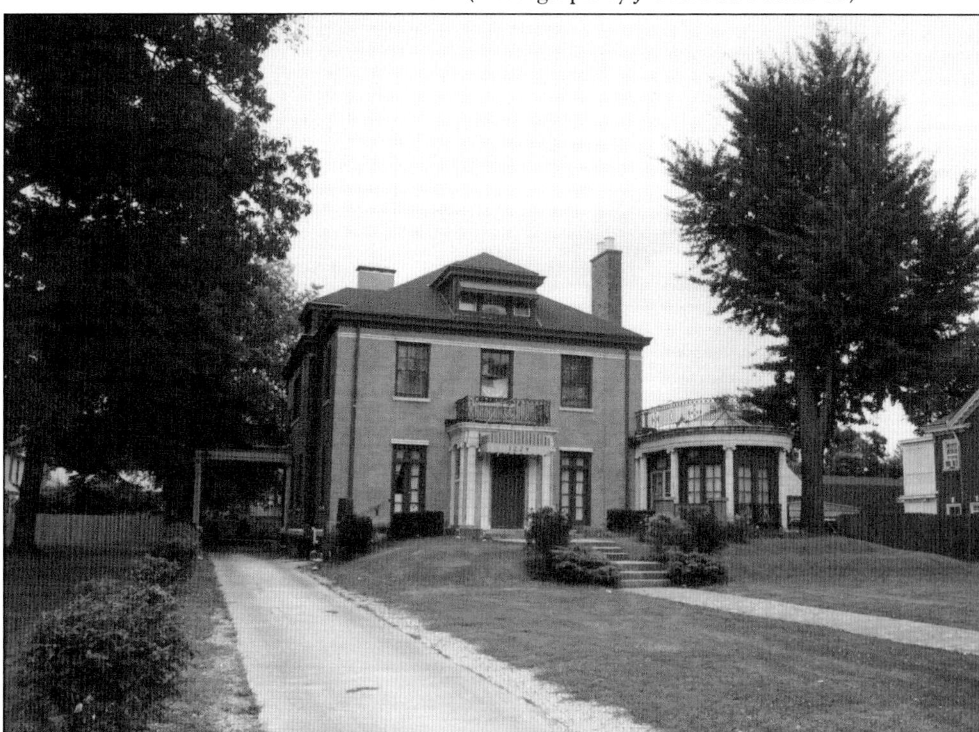

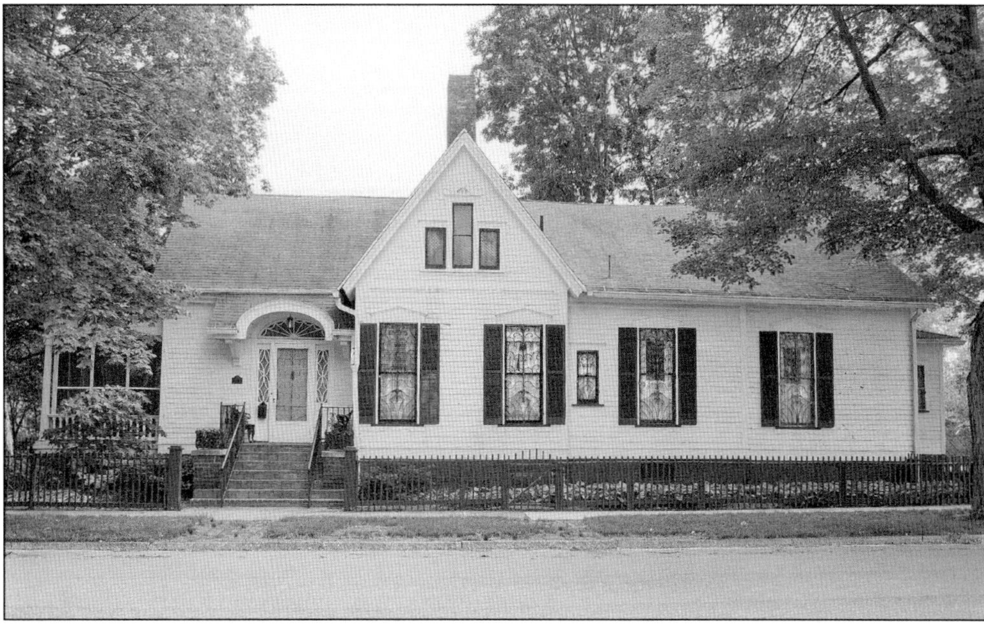

Chapman J. Root's son William R. Root lived nearby at 1503 South Sixth Street with his wife, Virginia, and son Chapman S. Root. The wrought-iron grillwork on the windows supposedly was installed after the 1932 Lindbergh baby kidnapping. Built in 1882, the house has a cupola hidden behind the trees; original owner Herbert Madison smoked in the cupola's open porch to avoid annoying his wife. (Photograph by Albert Christenberry.)

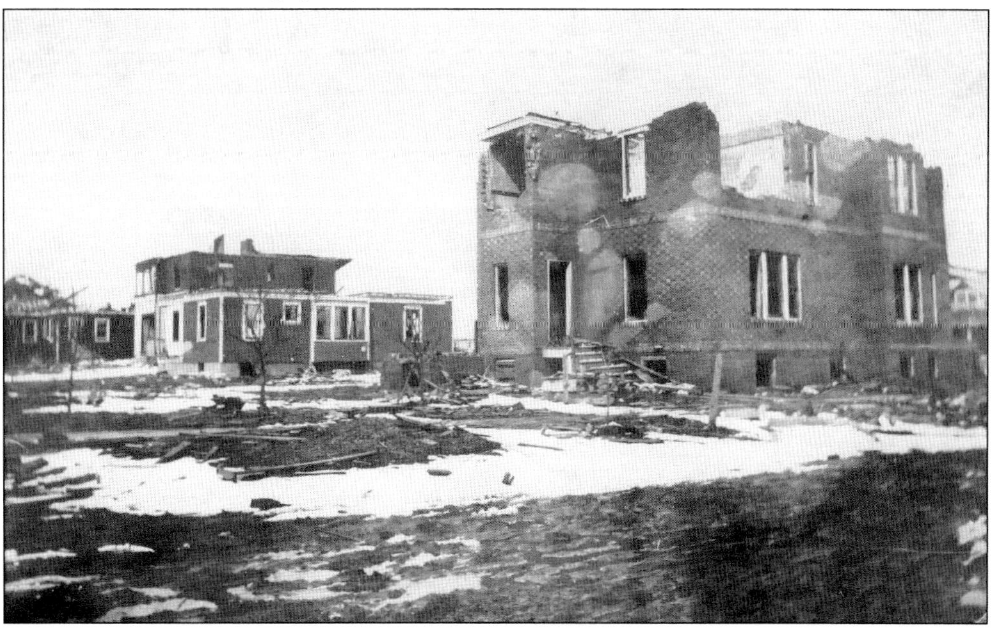

The tornado of 1913, with 100-mile-per-hour winds, cut a devastating path 500 yards wide on Sunday, March 23. This photograph of South Fifth Street shows the destruction. If the tornado's path had veered four blocks to the north, Farrington's Grove's historic houses would not exist today. Farther south, only the smokestack remained of Root Glass Company; Chapman J. Root had to rebuild. A total of 17 people died in the disaster. (VCHS.)

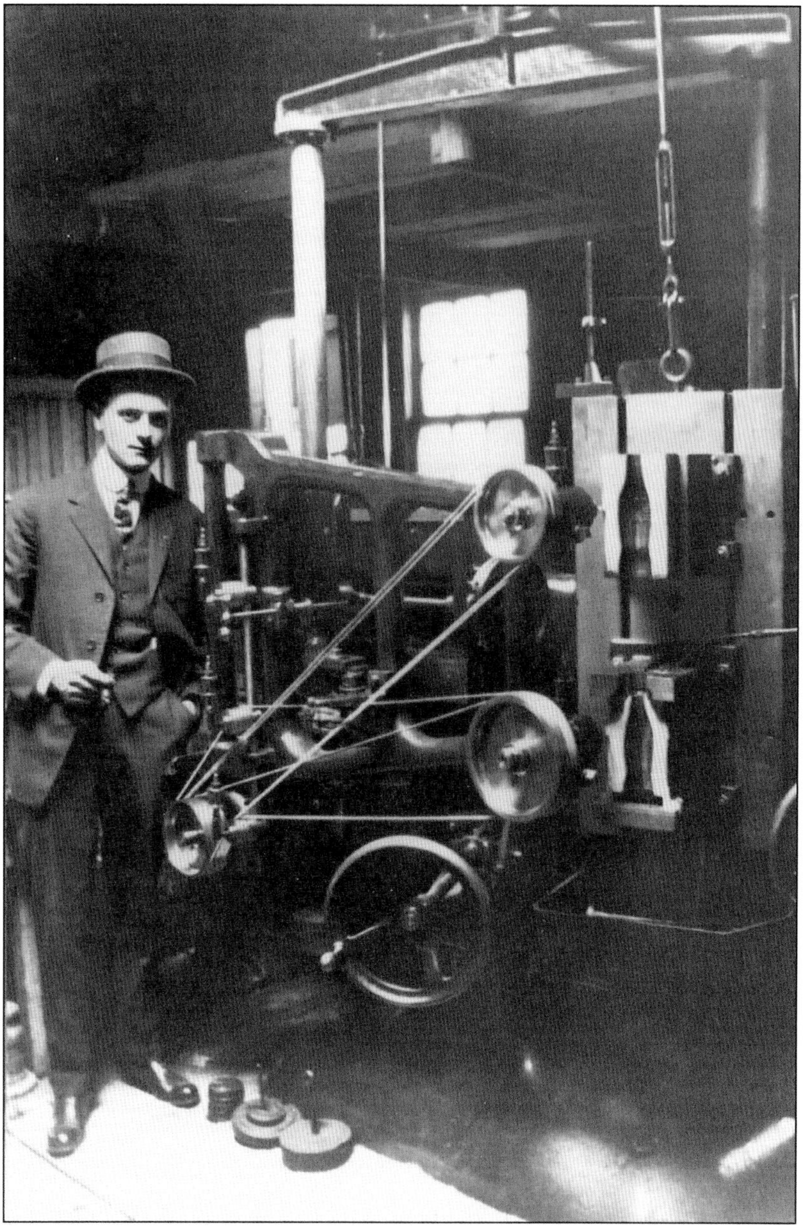

Earl R. Dean, designer of the Coca-Cola bottle, stands beside the Root Glass Company machine that produced the bottle. The mold shows the trademarked rib design that has become recognizable to 90 percent of the world. In 1915, when the Coca-Cola Company invited 30 companies to create a distinctive bottle, Root Glass Company president Chapman J. Root called three men into his office to discuss the contest. Root's chauffeur then drove Dean, who was Root's best bottle designer and machinist, and auditor Clyde T. Edwards to the Emeline Fairbanks Library for research. As a former teacher, Edwards knew his way around a library. Based on the discussion with their boss, they sought a picture of a coca plant or kola plant, representing early cola ingredients. Those encyclopedia entries contained no pictures, but Dean and Edwards did find a picture under the cocoa entry. Earl did a quick sketch from the *Encyclopaedia Britannica*. The book could not be checked out, and he had to have the design ready the next morning. (Norman L. Dean.)

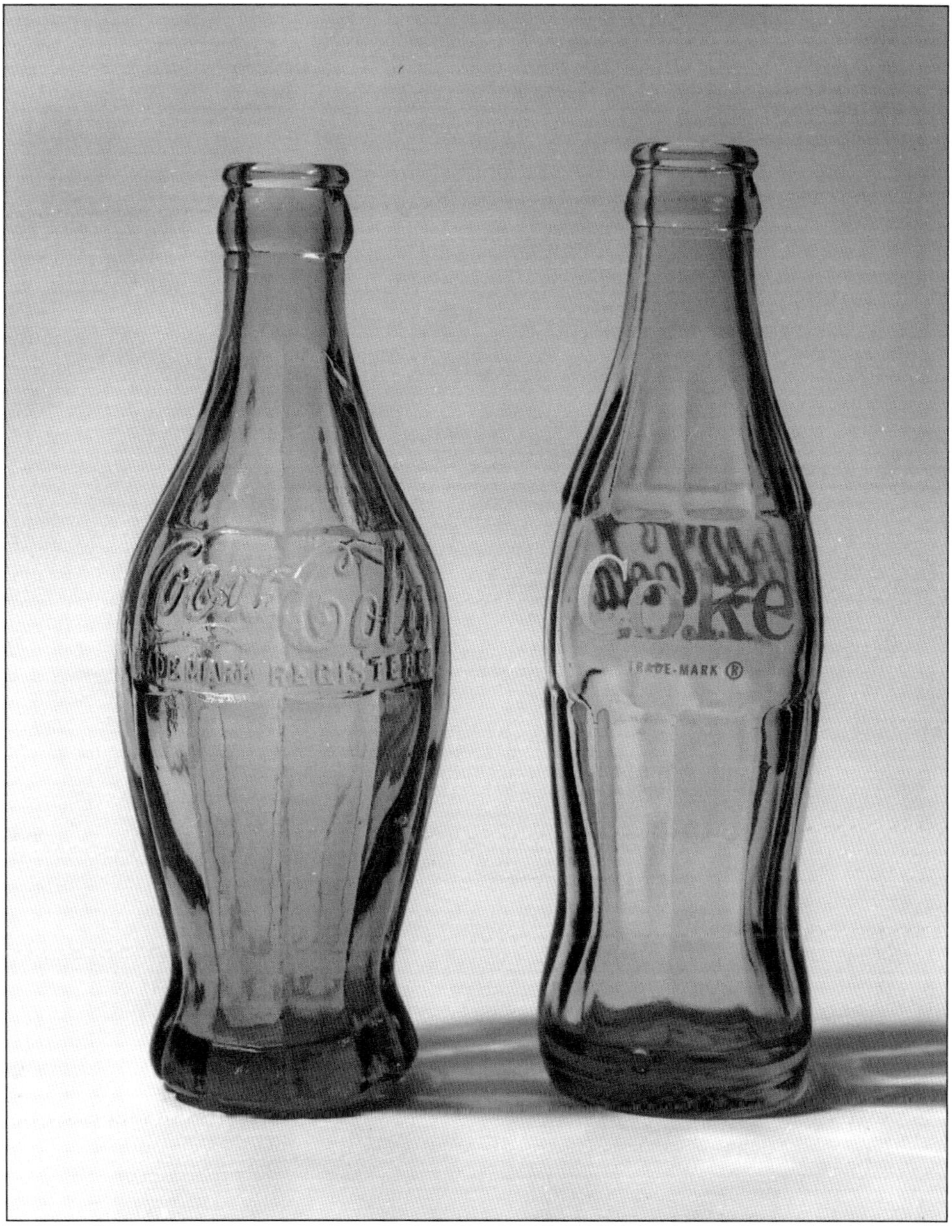

The bottle on the left is one of only two existing prototypes made by Earl R. Dean; it had the unique look and feel Coca-Cola wanted to set its product apart. On the right is a modern-day version. The ribs in the bottle are based on the cocoa pod. Actually, the pod is part of the plant from which chocolate is made. Because of the similarity in spelling, and because the encyclopedia contained no picture of a coca plant, the bottle design developed from the cocoa pod. Some have assumed the shape imitated the hobble skirt of women's clothing of the era, but that is not so. Dean said he created the design based on the cocoa pod. He consulted with his boss Chapman J. Root and slightly changed the design before it went into production, narrowing the middle to make it more stable on the conveyor line. The glass in the prototype had a greenish tinge because of the local silica sand. That color, Georgia green, became traditional for Coca-Cola bottles. (Norman L. Dean.)

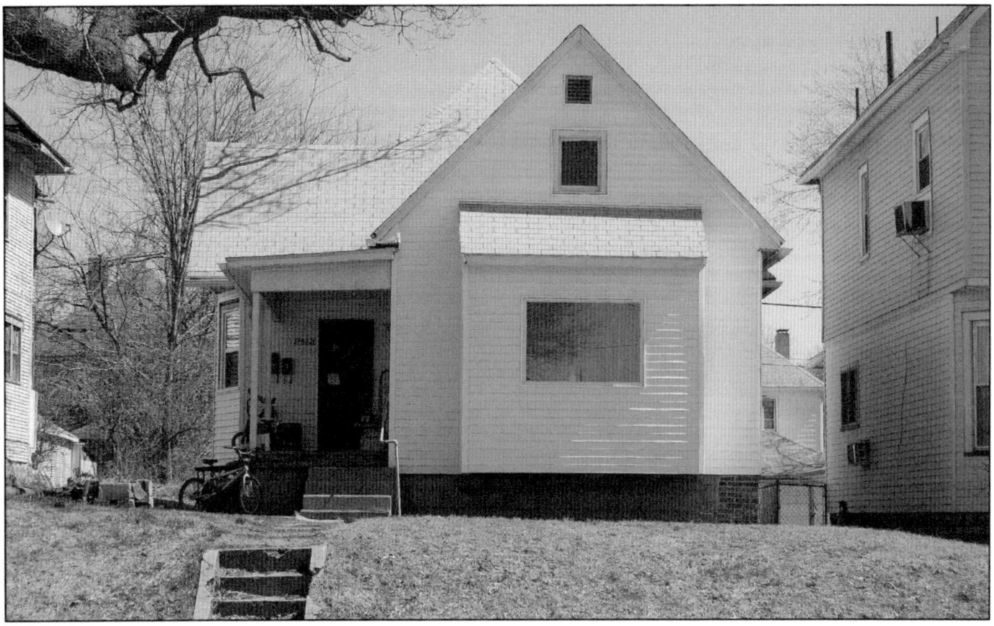

The house above, 1622 South Third Street, is where Earl R. Dean designed the Coca-Cola bottle on June 28, 1915. After the library trip, Dean checked with Chapman J. Root, took his pod sketch home, worked out logistics on the dining room table that night, and sketched a design. Root approved it in the morning. Usually, the machinist would create a wood model of a new bottle before making an iron mold, but Dean had no time. In two days, the fire under the glass tanks would shut down for inspection and cleaning. He had to go directly from his sketch to create an iron mold to pour the prototype by June 30. The photograph below shows 1616 South Third Street; Dean and his wife moved there in 1918 to live with his widowed mother and brother Cal Dean.

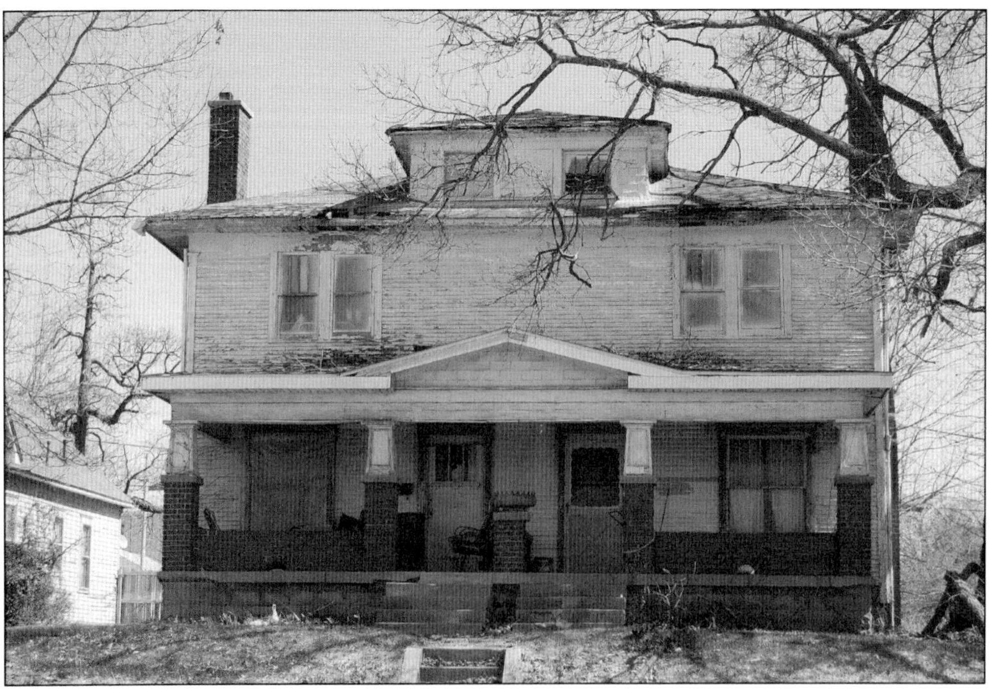

Another person who worked for Chapman J. Root was Charles A. Hay, at right in the first row. His wife, Josephine A. Hay, is in the second row, far left. The photograph shows them with neighbors in their backyard at 1719 South Sixth Street. Charles was a professional glassblower who came from Patterson, New Jersey, to work for Root Glass Company. (C. David Hay.)

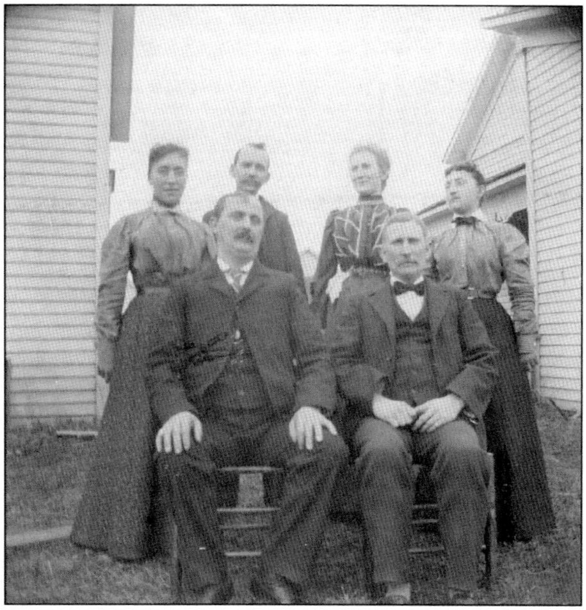

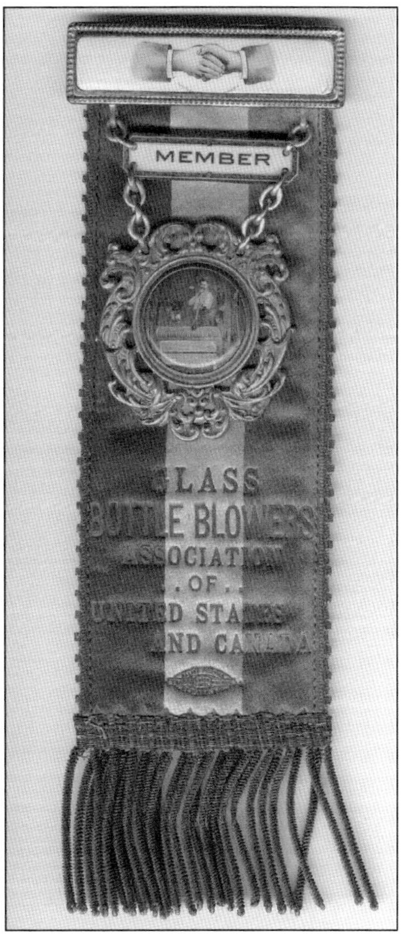

Unions have an important history in Terre Haute. Like many other workers at Root Glass Company and other glassworks in the city, Charles A. Hay was a member of the Glass Bottle Blowers Association union. The ribbon is red, white, and blue on the front. The reverse of the ribbon is black and has the words, "In Memoriam: Glass Bottle Blowers Association of United States and Canada." (C. David Hay.)

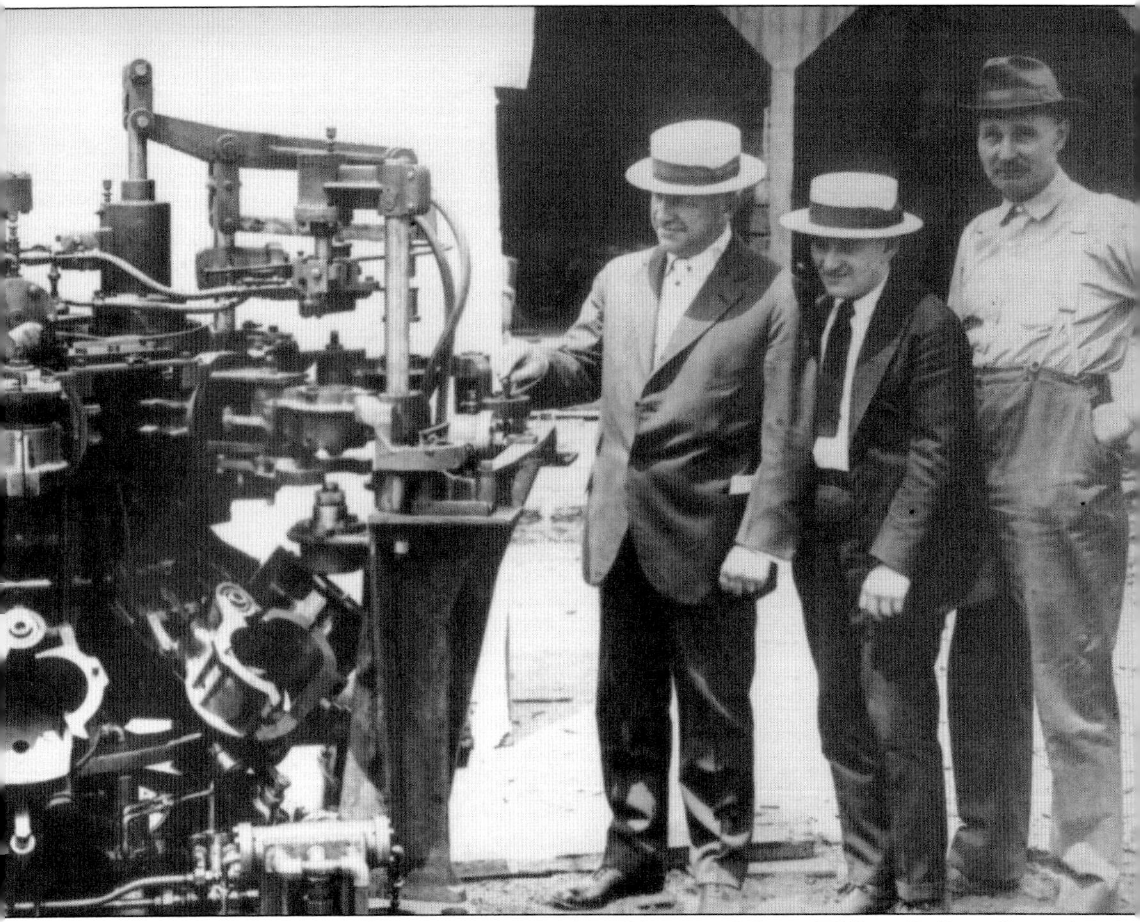

From left to right, Root Glass Company president Chapman J. Root, William R. Root (his only child), and plant superintendent Alexander Samuelson look over some bottling machinery. The younger Root died June 23, 1932, in a plane crash near Farmersburg along with his friend Paul Cox, who piloted the plane. Witnesses told investigators the plane sounded like it was having engine trouble. Both men were charter members of the Terre Haute Aero Club and boosters of aviation. Cox had returned to Terre Haute after World War I as a war hero and a first lieutenant in the air service. He spent 15 months on the Western Front, instructed other aviators, and downed one German plane. Dresser Field, the municipal airport south of town, was renamed Paul Cox Field in his memory in 1933. Today, the area is the site of Terre Haute South Vigo High School. (VCHS.)

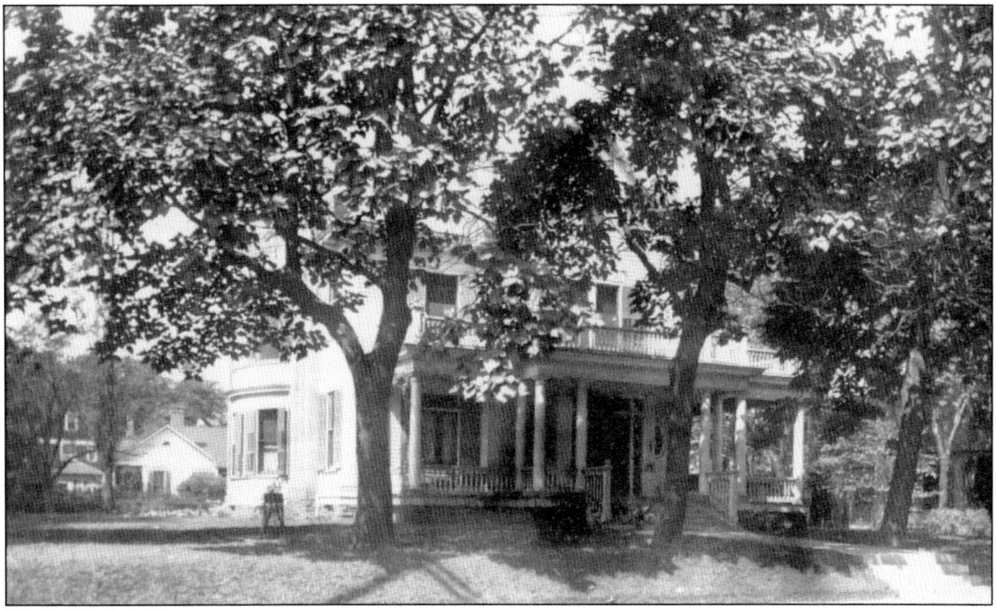

Paul Cox grew up at 931 South Seventh Street, shown here in 1907. After returning from World War I, he joined his father in John S. Cox and Son automotive equipment dealers. John owned one of the first cars in town. When this house was built around 1900, the Coxes installed a "magnificent pipe organ" with keyboard in the west parlor and pipes in the dining room. (J. Richard Becker Jr.)

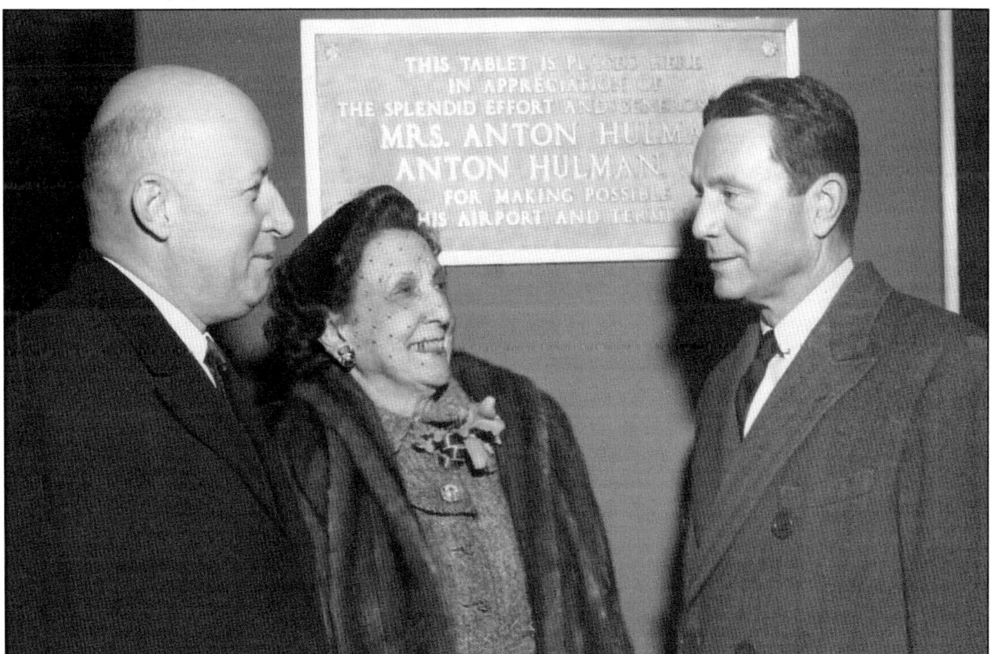

A later occupant of 931 South Seventh Street was Grace Hulman, widow of Anton Hulman Sr. She is shown at the dedication of the Hulman Field terminal in this photograph from November 29, 1953. Hulman Field eventually replaced Paul Cox Field as Terre Haute's municipal airport. From left to right are Ed Whalen, Grace Hulman, and her son Anton Hulman Jr. (VCHS.)

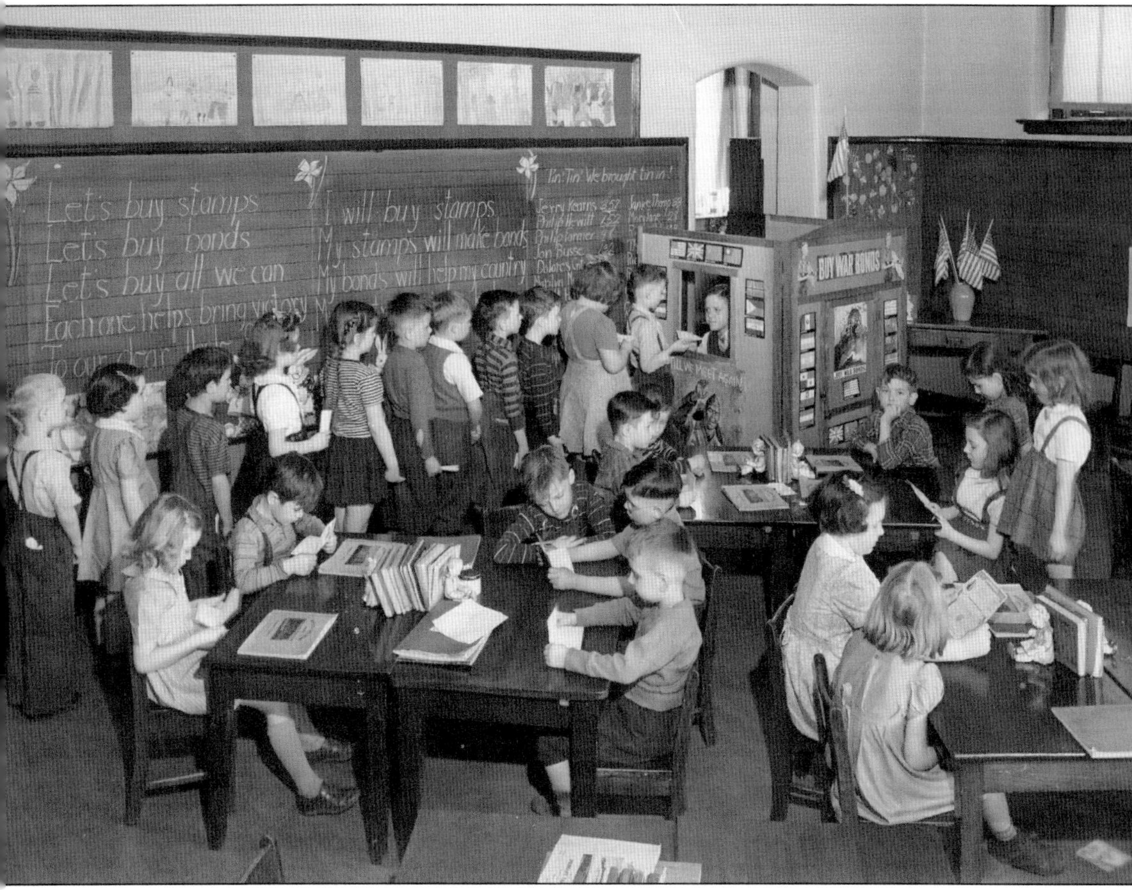

Charles A. Hay's grandson C. David Hay is the boy in the booth during a war bond drive at Fairbanks School, which formerly stood at the southeast corner of Sixth and Hulman Streets. He is selling stamps to other students in Miss Kelly's first-grade class of 1942–1943. Students would buy stamps to fill a book and exchange books for war bonds. David won the coveted title of Lieutenant Tin for bringing in the most scrap metal for the war effort. Of course, he did have an edge. Because of his diligent work on the safety patrol, the principal told him to take his red wagon to the local groceries. She also told the grocers he was dependable and would pick up their scrap metals regularly. Third in line to buy war stamps in this photograph is Jerome Kearns, who grew up to become a judge in Vigo County. (Photograph by Martin's Photo Shop; C. David Hay.)

This was the front entrance to Fairbanks School on Sixth Street near Hulman Street, which opened in 1906. The school's architecture was Neo-Jacobethan, derived from early-17th-century England. School lore says the old desk in the office of Farrington Grove School, which replaced Fairbanks, belonged to Orville Connor, the first principal of Fairbanks. He taught 8A and 8B and lived nearby at 1318 South Fourth Street. (VCHS.)

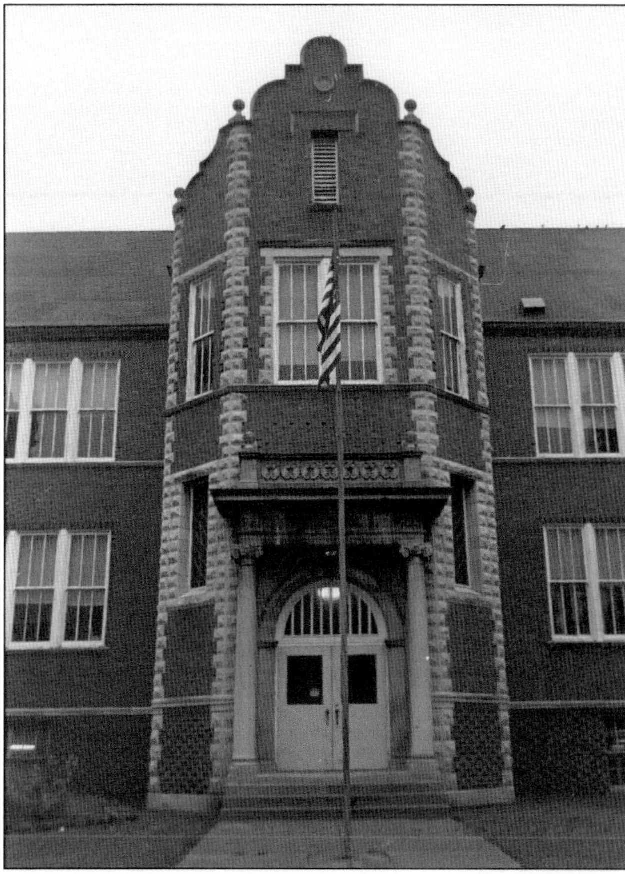

This photograph of a Fairbanks School class is from 1938; as usual, it is hard to get everyone to look at the camera at the same time. Thomas Tanoos is second from right in the first row. He grew up to join the Terre Haute Police Department, working his way through the ranks to become chief of detectives. (Mary Ann Tanoos.)

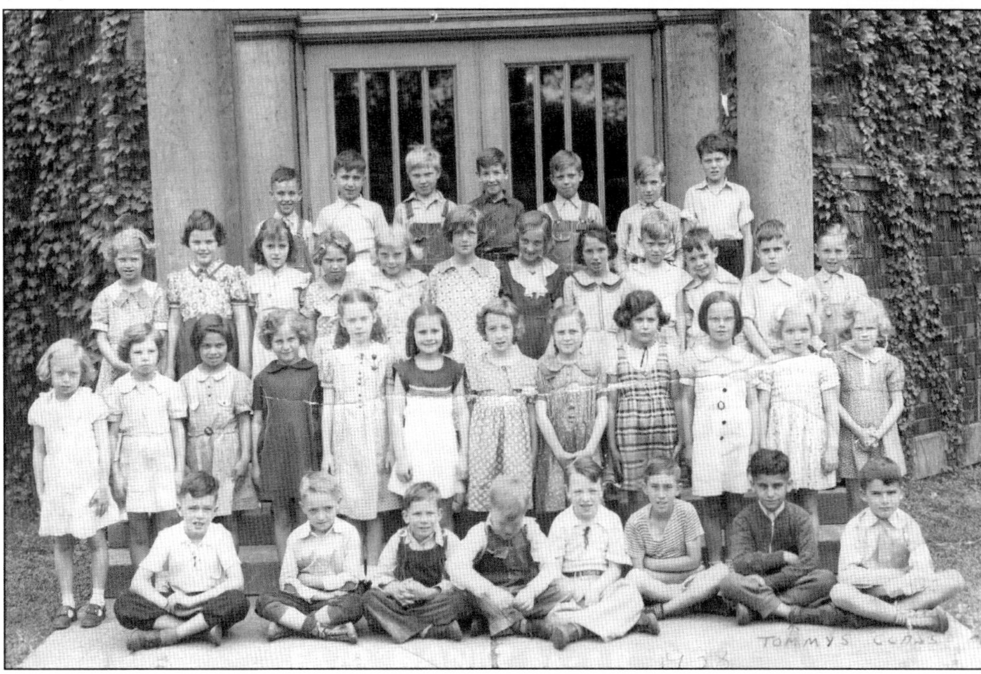

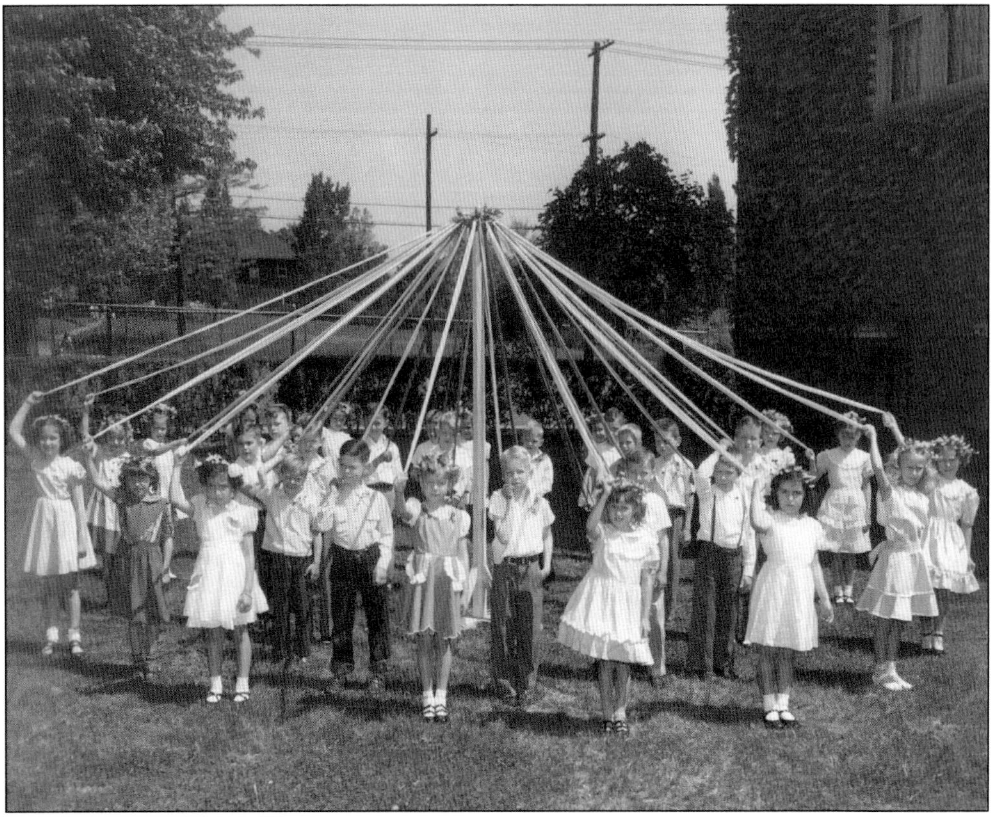

Students at Fairbanks School dance the Maypole dance on May 1, 1950. In the 1950s, the tradition of celebrating May Day was popular in elementary schools, with outdoor events and games to welcome the arrival of spring. Some trace such celebrations back to the feast of Flora, the Roman goddess of flowers. (Photograph by Martin's Photo Shop; VCPL.)

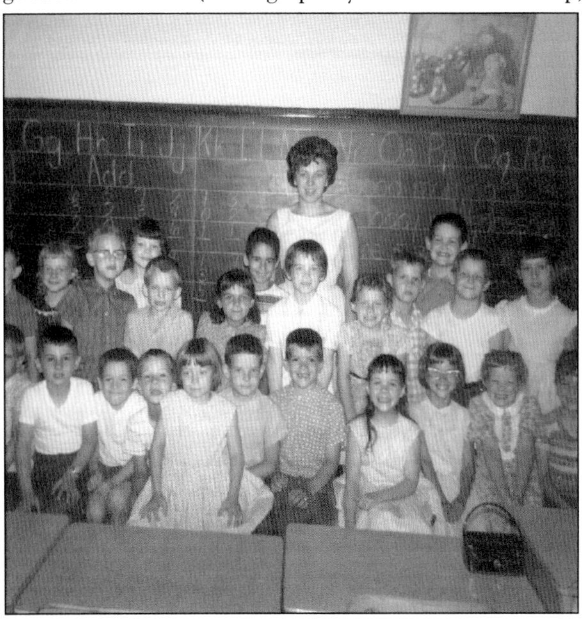

Here, one of the primary-grade classes at Fairbanks School mugs for the camera with their teacher in this photograph from the 1960s. Standing to the left of the teacher, Mrs. White, is Anthony Tanoos. He grew up to become an attorney with the firm of Fleschner, Stark, Tanoos, and Newlin. (Mary Ann Tanoos.)

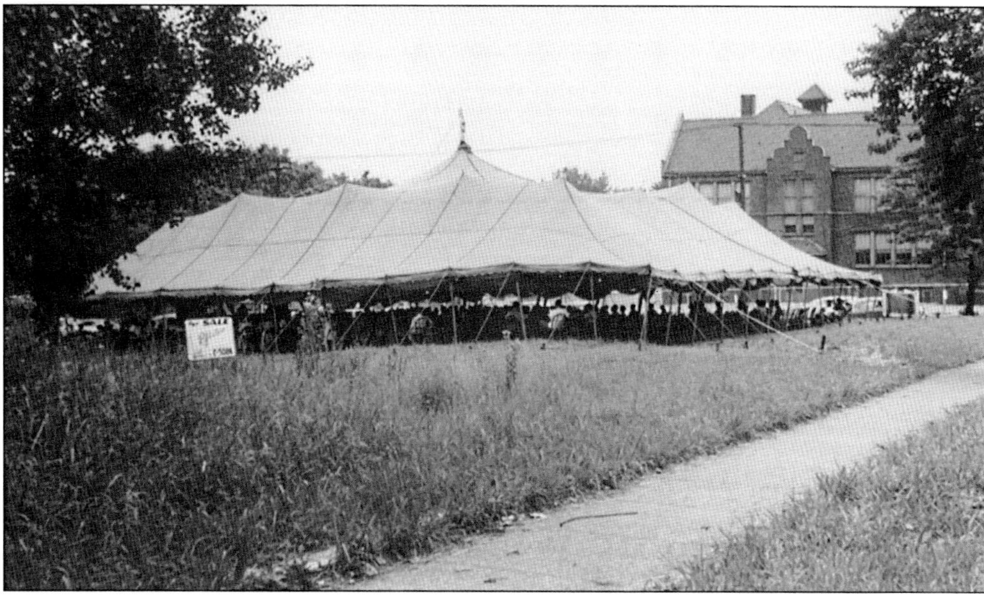

Fairbanks School is visible in the distance; this vantage point looks south on Sixth Street past Hulman Street. J.G. Vrydagh, a Terre Haute architect who designed several public buildings, designed Fairbanks School. In the foreground is a summer tent meeting of the Vigo County Holiness Association in July 1951. During the rest of the year, neighborhood children used the vacant lot for baseball. (VCPL.)

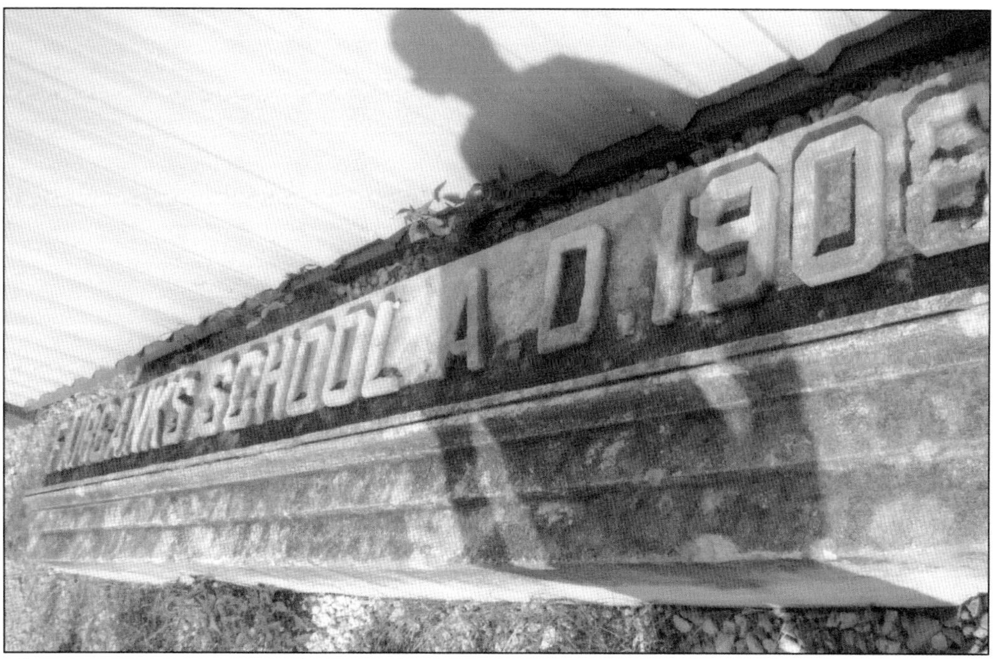

This stone piece once stood above the entrance to Fairbanks School. Demolition occurred during June 20–24, 1988. While Fairbanks demolition was under way at the north end of the block, construction for the new Farrington Grove School was beginning at the south end. Just as Fairbanks School had honored early pioneers, the name change honored James Farrington, another early resident of the area. (Daniel Tanoos.)

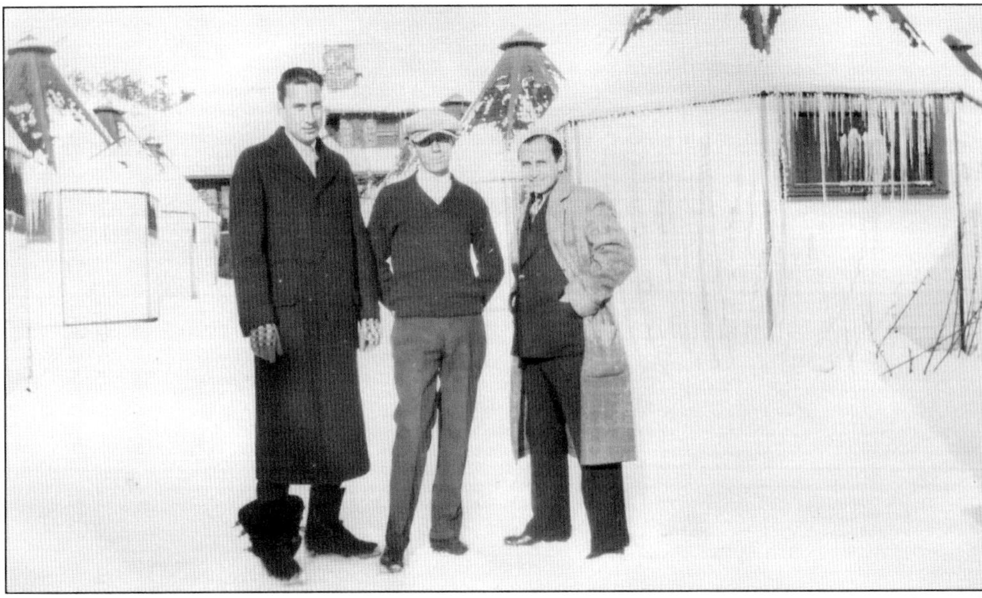

Glassblower Charles A. Hay's son Charles A. Hay Jr., at left, also lived at 1719 South Sixth Street. He nearly died from tuberculosis but recovered after treatment at the Modern Woodmen Tuberculosis Sanatorium in Colorado Springs, shown here. He operated a mercantile store, using his garage and attic for storage. At first, he sold door-to-door, but then people came to him to order housewares, rugs, and linoleum. (C. David Hay.)

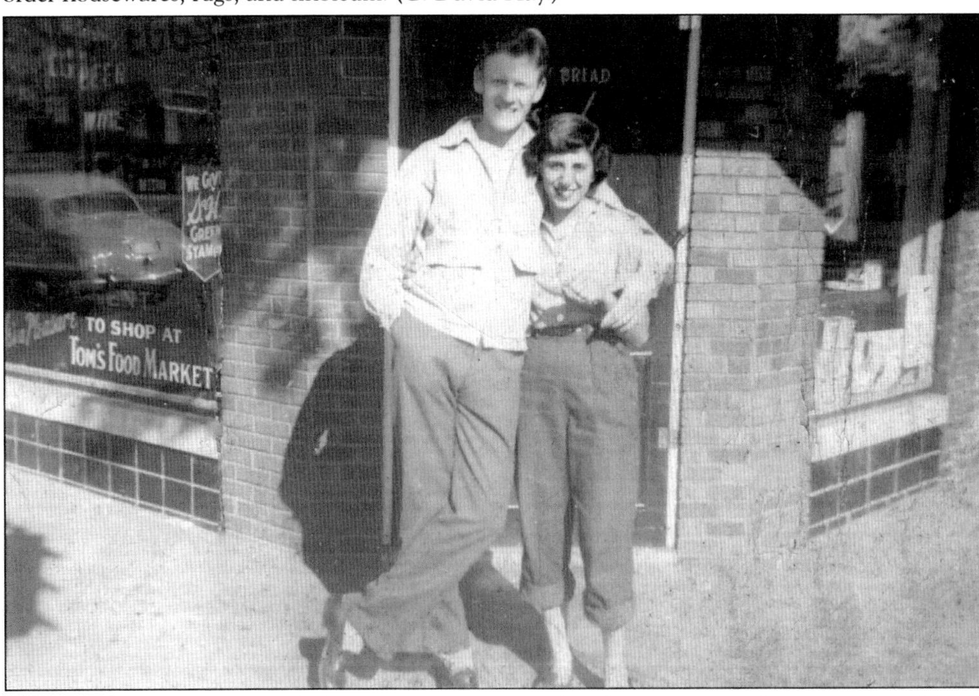

Also operating in Farrington's Grove was Tom's Food Market on the northeast corner of South Seventh Street and Washington Avenue. Thomas J. Nasser operated the market. In front of the store is his daughter Mary Ann Nasser with neighbor Robert Heidenreich. Also in Farrington's Grove were Albert Nasser's Market and Kay Nasser's Market. (Mary Ann Tanoos.)

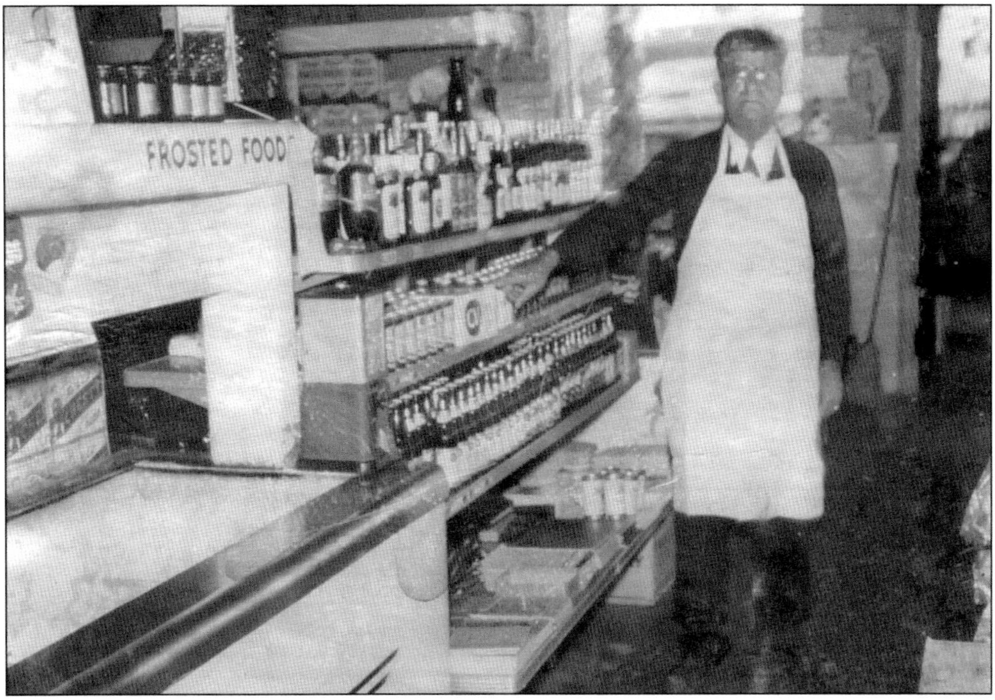

Thomas J. Nasser stands in his market on the northeast corner of South Seventh Street and Washington Avenue. From 1900 to the 1920s, several Syrian families came to Terre Haute from the town of Ein-el-Shara. They immigrated seeking a better life and freedom to practice their Christian Orthodox faith. (Mary Ann Tanoos.)

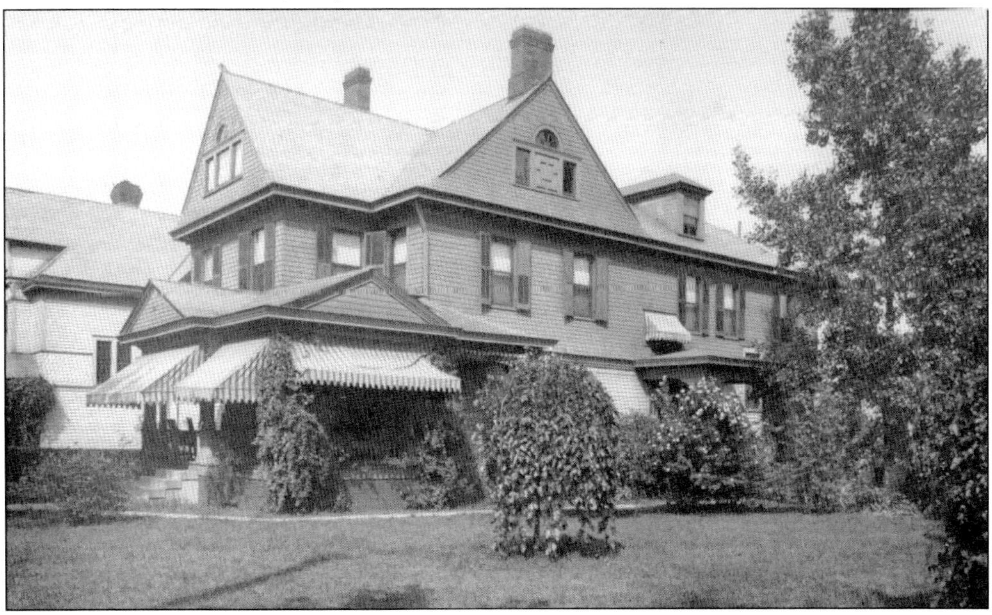

Fred B. Smith, who owned 1504 South Sixth Street in the early 1900s, founded Merchants Distilling Company around 1898. He also invited Bertha Pratt King to town to tutor his son. The house was built in 1894 and has had several changes to the exterior since this 1907 picture. In 1960, its backyard was the founding place of the Strawberry Hill Cannoneers. (J. Richard Becker Jr.)

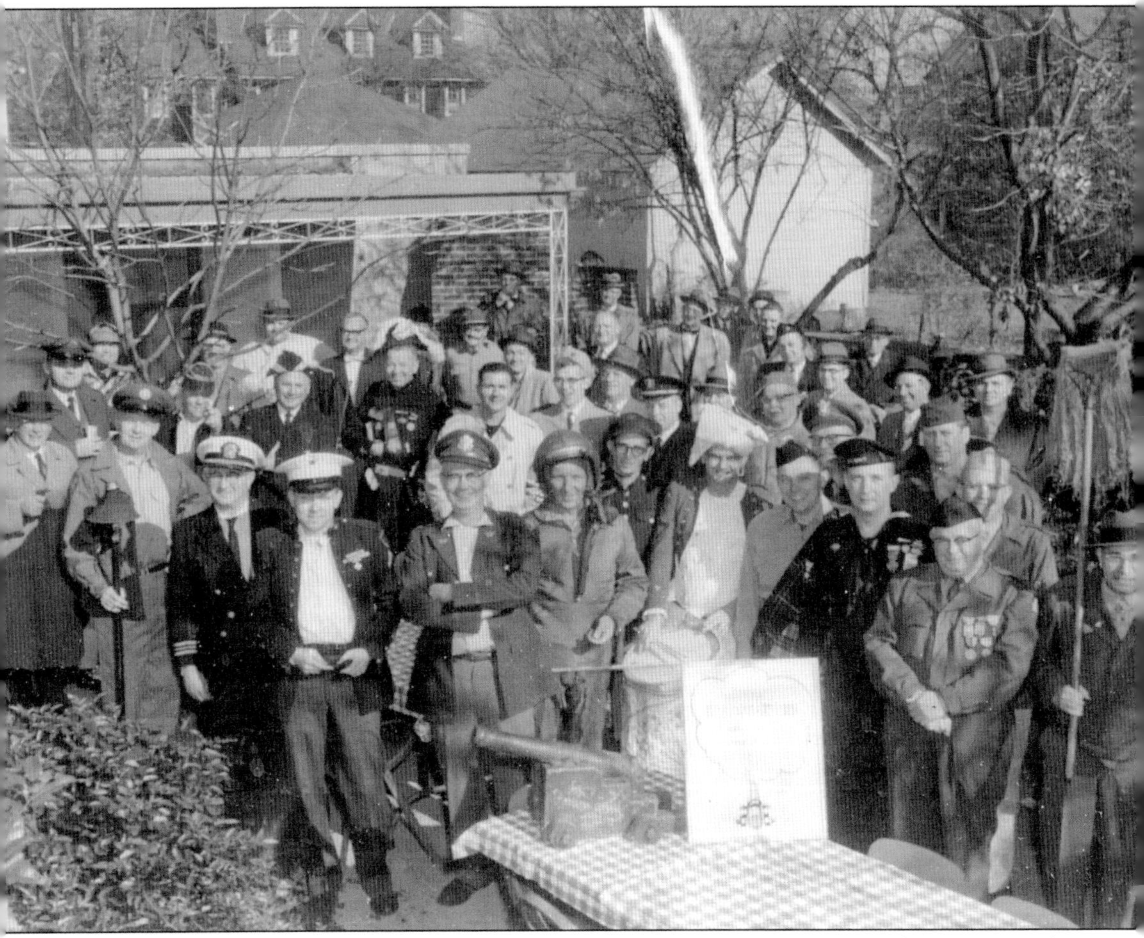

This photograph shows the birth of the Strawberry Hill Cannoneers on November 11, 1960, when attorney Lenhardt Bauer invited 57 friends to a cookout. In military fashion, the invitation told the 57 they were ordered to report for duty. To surprise Bauer, his friends dressed in World War II and alternative military regalia, marched down Sixth Street, and presented themselves for inspection at 1504 South Sixth Street. At the cookout, they formed the Strawberry Hill Cannoneers with Generalissimo Lenhardt Bauer as commander. They chose the name from the southern section of Farrington's Grove. The cannon on the table is an 1834 French salute cannon Bauer bought at an antique shop in Philadelphia. The size of the group was originally 150—limited by the size of their stew pot. Tongue in cheek, their standing orders noted the battery was "selfishly dedicated to the mutual entertainment of all members." Activities in later years included a Cannon Ball so the wives could participate. Bauer is in the first row, third from left. (Photograph by Martin's Photo Shop; Frederick T. Bauer.)

This official cap of the Strawberry Hill Cannoneers, called a kepi, belonged to P. Pete Chalos, a four-term mayor of Terre Haute. The kepi is red; the patch contains a red strawberry and golden cannons. According to the group's standing orders, "it ain't a golf or fishing cap" and could be worn only for official functions. The quasi-military battery billed itself as Terre Haute's "last line of defense." (John R. Becker III.)

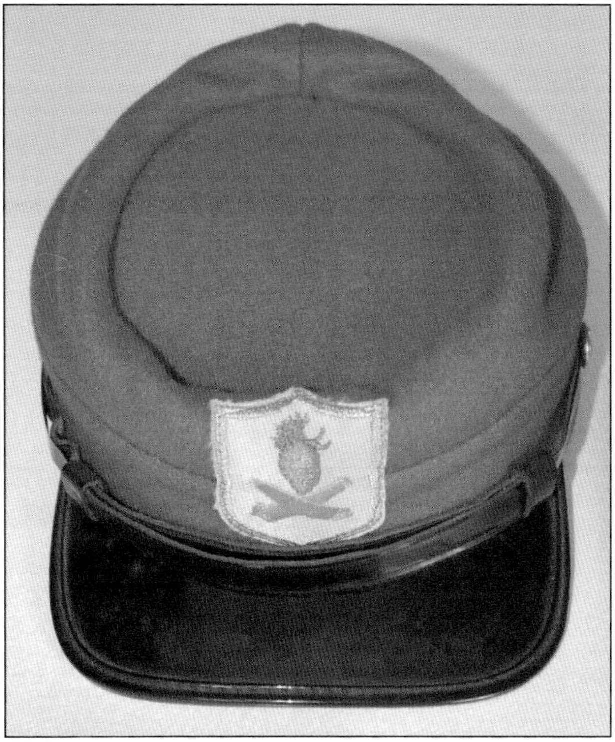

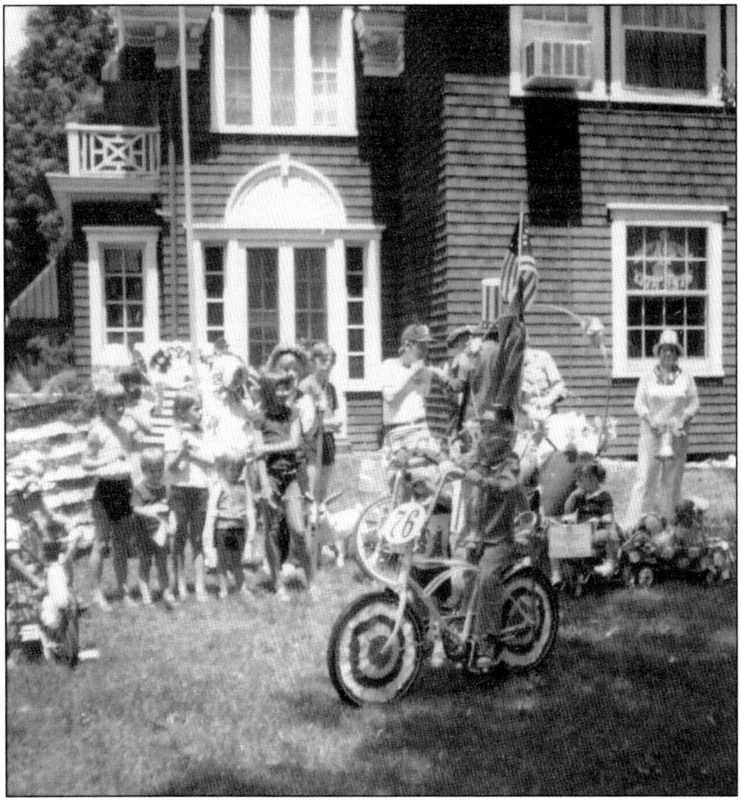

This gathering of children at the home of Gene Vaughn at 608 Putnam Street preceded a parade. It began with bell-ringing. All the kids decorated bicycles, tricycles, and baby carriages and then assembled to parade down the street, accompanied by watchful parents and relatives on the sidelines. After the parade, judges determined the winners in the costume and decorating divisions. The neighborhood then shared a pitch-in picnic. (L. Edward Harbour.)

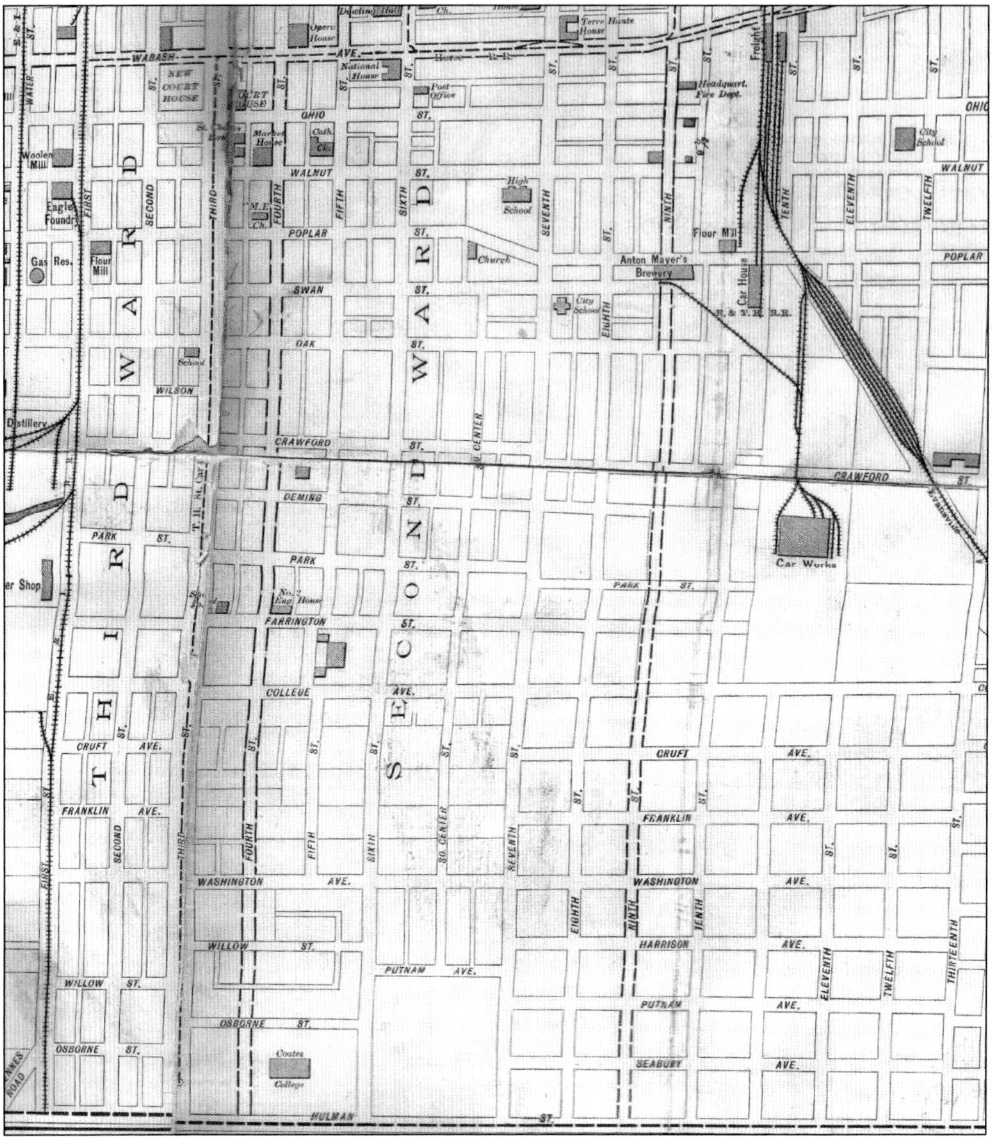

This 1887 map shows the area of Farrington's Grove Historic District. The area south of Osborne Street—spelled Osborn before 1886—was known as Strawberry Hill because of the wild strawberries the pioneers picked there. When Judge Samuel Gookins built his mansion south of Osborne between Fourth and Fifth Streets, Strawberry Hill was the logical choice for its name. The mansion later was the home of Coates College. The exact location of the long-gone building has been debated, but the bottom of this map shows its outline south of Osborne. Visible on the map is the outline of Terre Haute Female College on Fifth Street, between Farrington Street and College Avenue; it later became St. Agnes Academy and then St. Anthony's Hospital. Northwest of the hospital is the outline of Fire Station No. 2. West of the firehouse is the outline of Third District School. By this year, Market Street was renamed Third Street, and Moffatt Street was renamed Washington Avenue. (VHCS.)

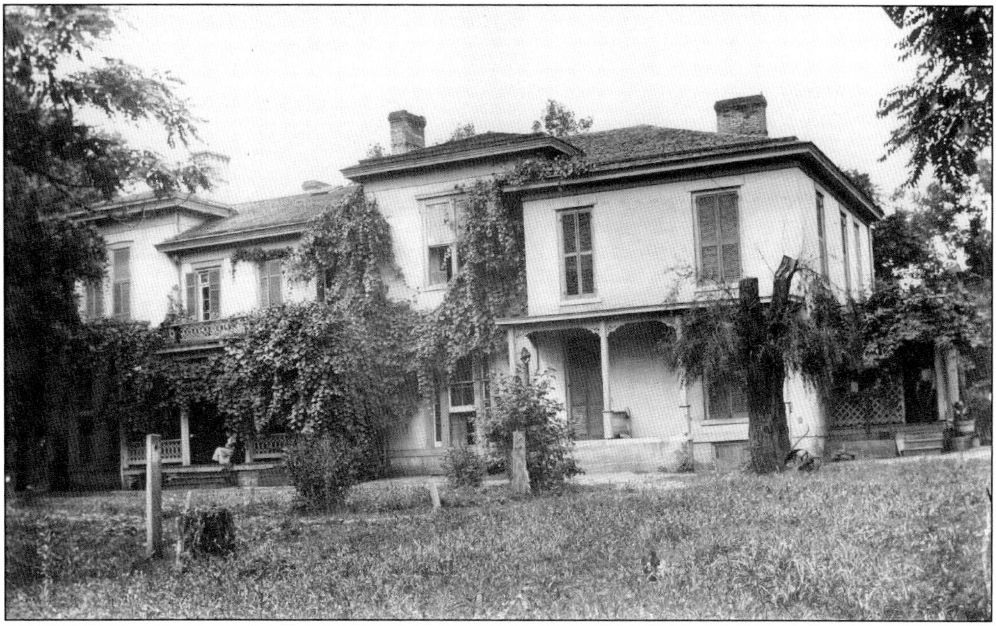

In 1848, Samuel Gookins, who had been a law partner of James Farrington and later served on the Indiana Supreme Court, built this enormous mansion, Strawberry Hill. It stood in the center of a 20-acre tract and had 24 rooms. This north view would have been visible from Osborne Street. He sold it to Herman Hulman Sr. in 1863, but returned in the 1870s. He died there in 1880. (VCHS.)

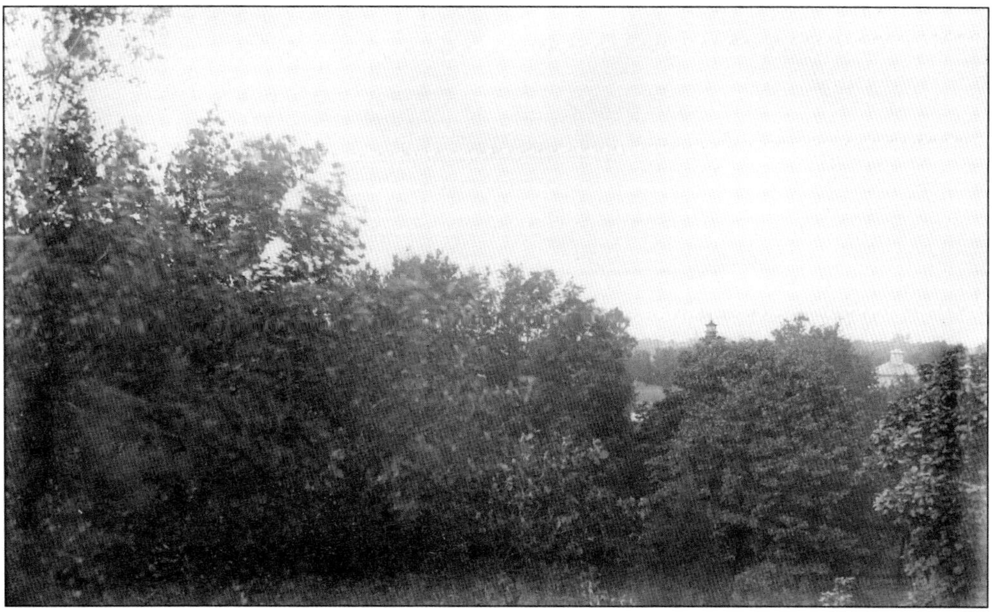

This 1862 photograph from the northeast rooftop of the Strawberry Hill mansion at Fifth and Osborne Streets shows the view to the north. In the distance is the distinctive octagonal cupola of Terre Haute Female College, later St. Agnes Academy. Strawberries were so plentiful here that when Samuel Gookins hosted a strawberry feast in 1851, the guests—including 200 youth from a local school—could not eat them all. (VCHS.)

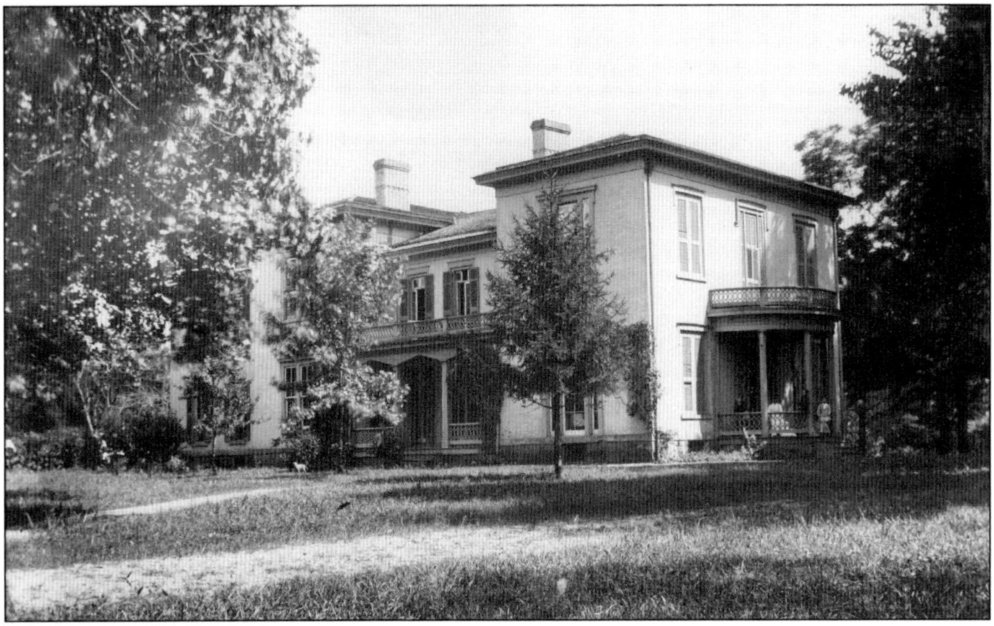

This is the south view of Strawberry Hill. Anton Hulman Sr. and Herman Hulman Jr. were born here in the 1860s while Herman Hulman Sr. owned it. Samuel Gookins repurchased it. Later owners sold it to Jane Coates, of Greencastle, who opened Coates College in 1885. The school closed after the 1896–1897 school year because of a lack of funding after her death. It was demolished around 1905. (VCHS.)

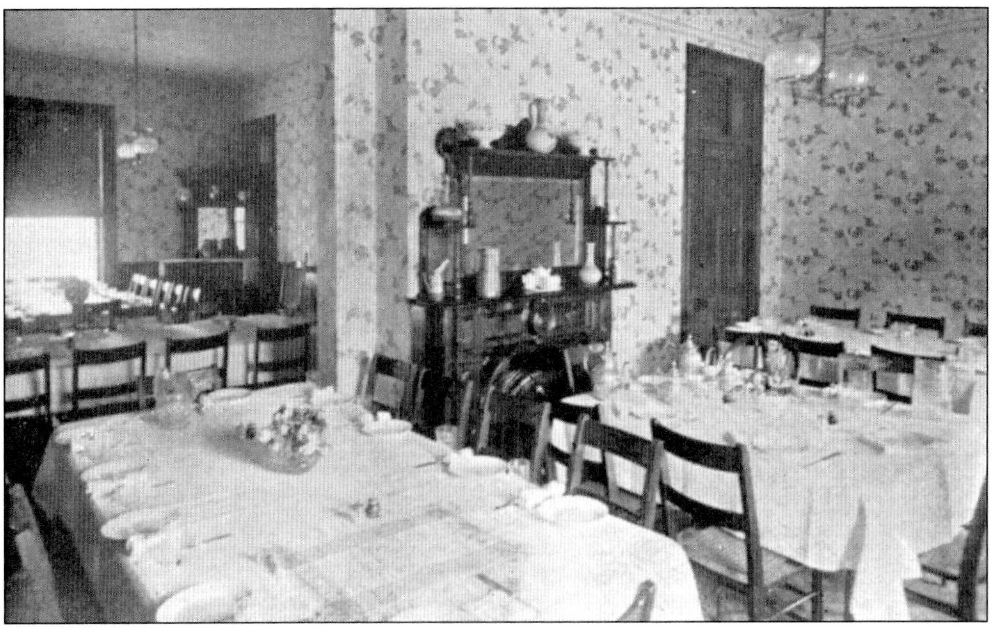

This photograph shows two of the dining rooms of Coates College with tables properly set for dinner. Jane Coates bought 13 acres of the former Samuel Gookins property, including the Strawberry Hill mansion. She added a separate school building and gymnasium. The estimated value of all property was $100,000, and she endowed the college with $20,000. The Coates College curriculum was modeled after Vassar and Wellesley Colleges. (J. Richard Becker Jr.)

James Farrington Gookins, named after his father Samuel Gookins's friend, spent his youth at Strawberry Hill. Painter, writer, and planner, Gookins's influence was felt beyond Terre Haute. He was involved with the Soldiers and Sailors Monument Commission of Indianapolis and pushed for Chicago's lakefront park and the Field Museum. He also helped formulate the Chicago Academy of Design, the forerunner of the Art Institute of Chicago. (VCHS.)

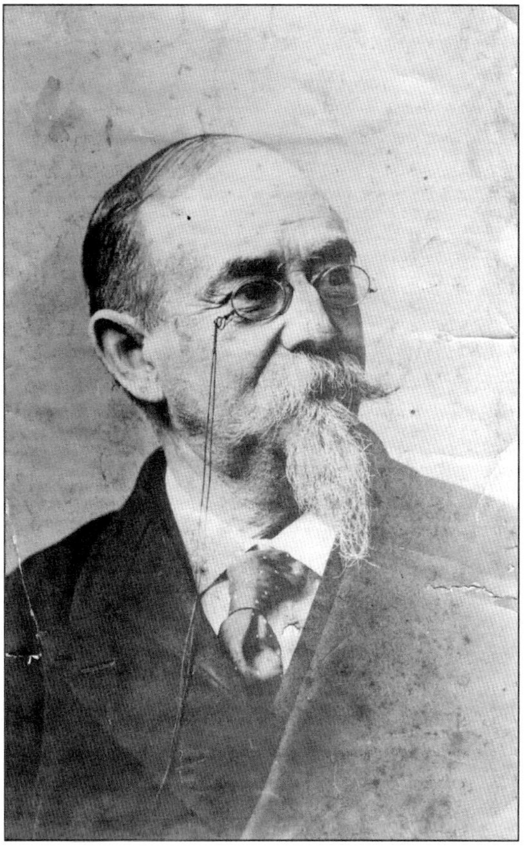

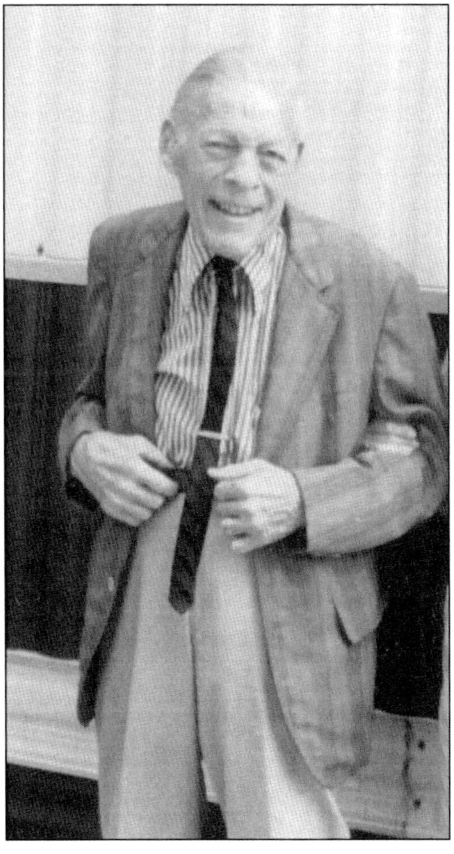

John Rogers Cox, shown in his later years, worked at the Art Institute of Chicago from 1948 to 1965, teaching primarily figure drawings. He was the first director of the Swope Art Museum in Terre Haute when it opened on March 21, 1942. William Turman, chairman of the art department at Indiana State Teachers College, offered him the post. (Eleanor Cox Riggs.)

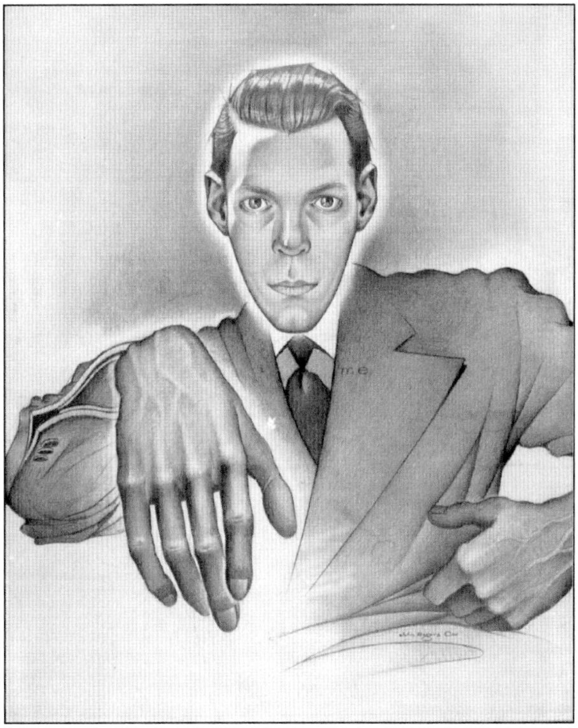

This self-portrait of the young John Rogers Cox is from about 1938. When William Turman offered Cox the director's job at the Swope Art Museum, the irony was that Cox had had trouble getting a job in art. Suddenly, at age 26, he found himself one of the youngest museum directors in the country. (John Rogers Cox 1915–1990, *Me*, pencil on paper, 1938, Swope Art Museum, Terre Haute, Indiana.)

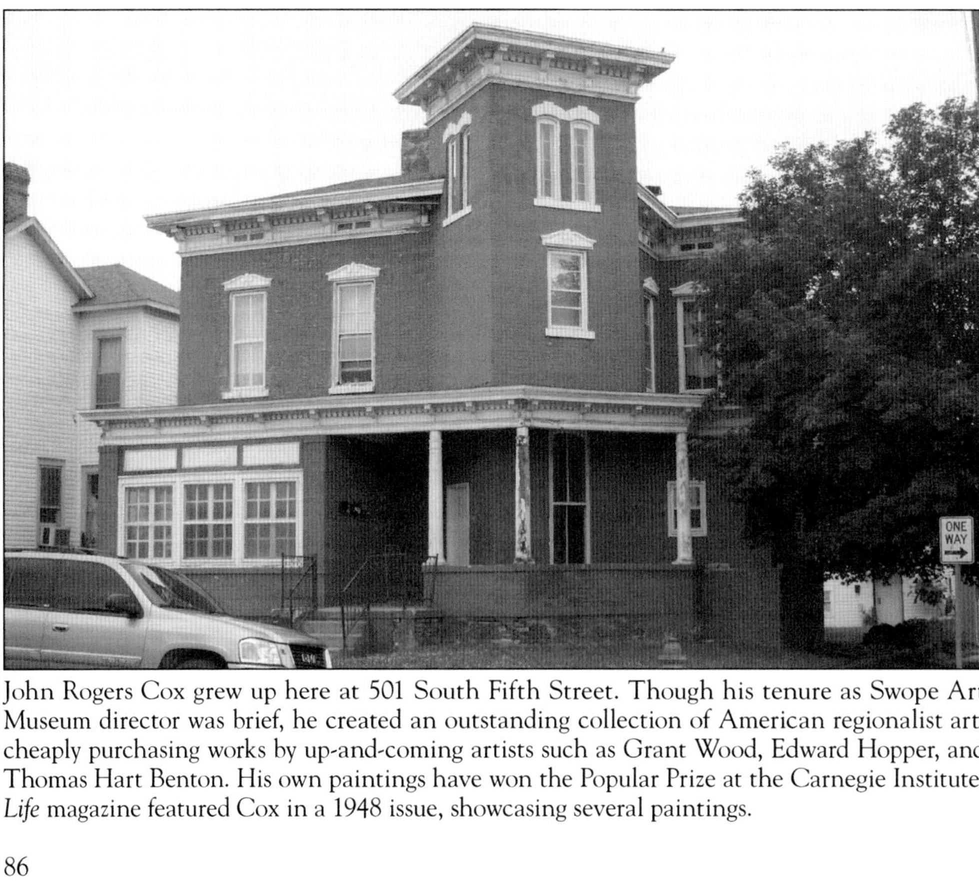

John Rogers Cox grew up here at 501 South Fifth Street. Though his tenure as Swope Art Museum director was brief, he created an outstanding collection of American regionalist art, cheaply purchasing works by up-and-coming artists such as Grant Wood, Edward Hopper, and Thomas Hart Benton. His own paintings have won the Popular Prize at the Carnegie Institute. *Life* magazine featured Cox in a 1948 issue, showcasing several paintings.

Another educator in the area was Walter Piety Morgan. These wedding portraits of Walter and his bride, Effie Jane Elliott, were taken March 11, 1893. Walter served as superintendent of Terre Haute city schools from 1906 to 1908 and lived in the Farrington's Grove area while attending high school and later Indiana State Normal. From 1912 to 1942, he served as president of Western Illinois University (WIU) in Macomb, Illinois, the longest tenure of any WIU president; his name is still honored in the community. Walter grew up in a log cabin in Prairie Creek. He detested his middle name *Percy*, so when he discovered in church birth records that his middle name was written only with a *P*, he adopted his mother's maiden name *Piety* for his middle name. (Photographs by Walter Piety Morgan.)

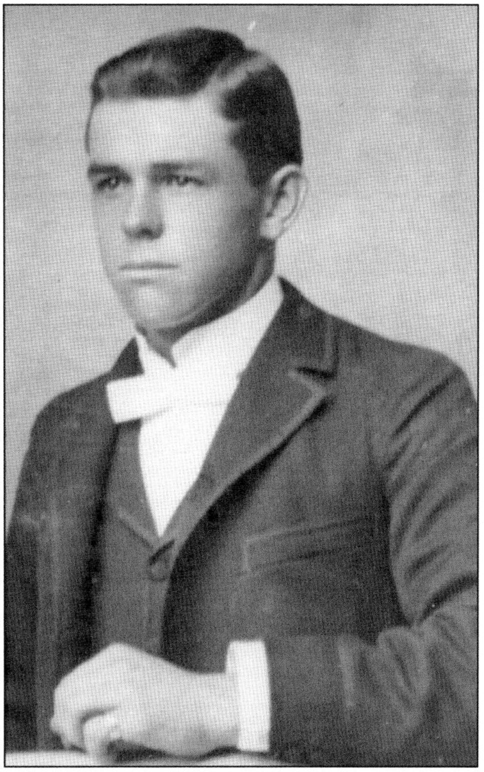

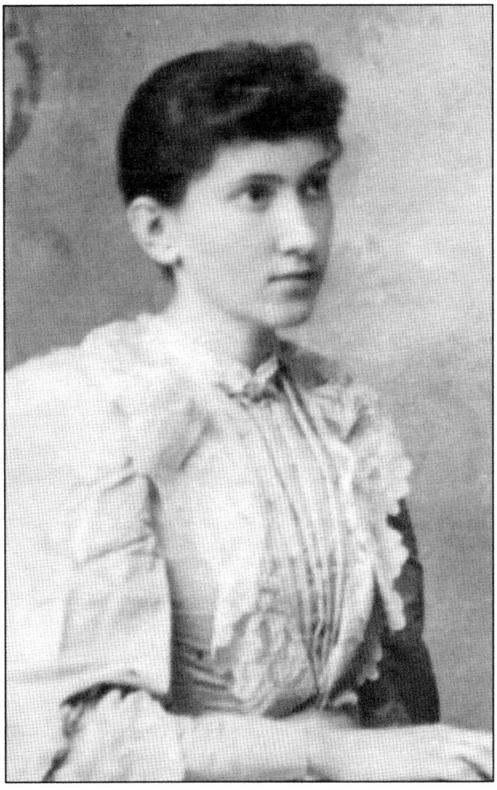

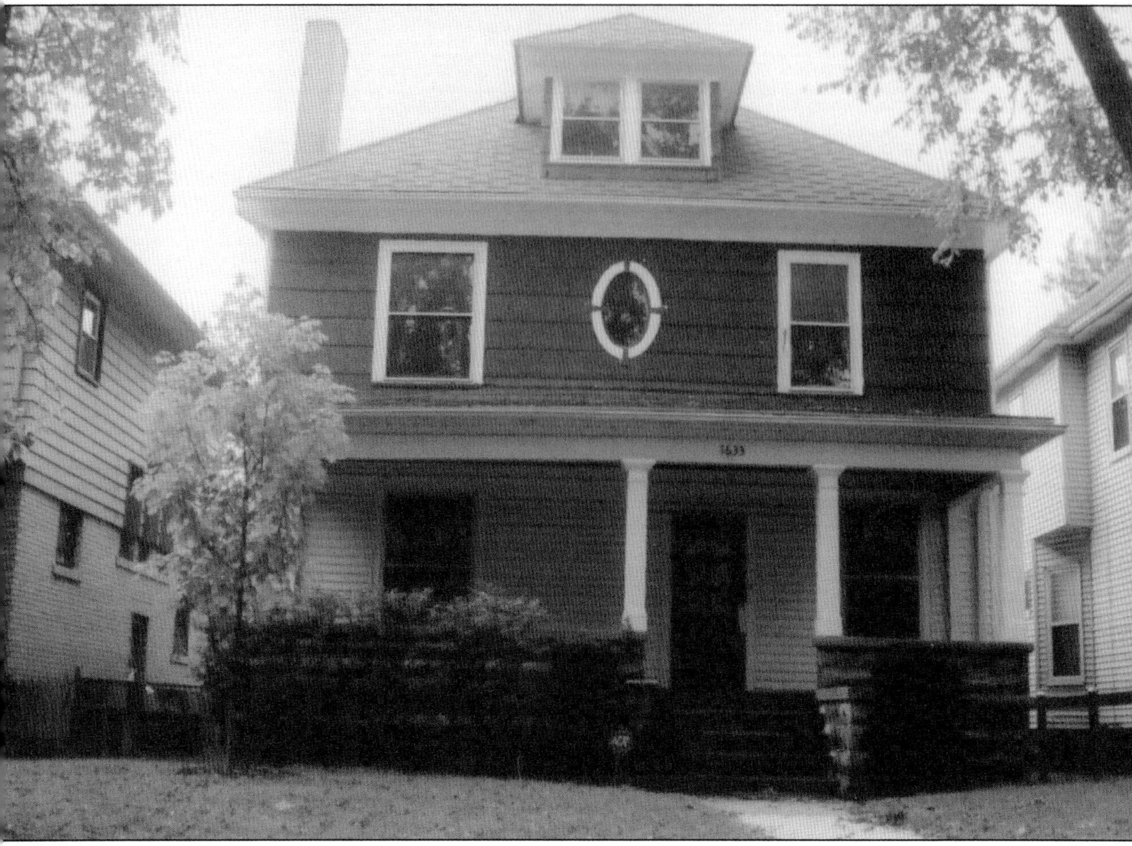

Walter Piety Morgan and his family moved around the corner from their house on Willow Street to 1633 South Fifth Street, which he built in 1905. The style is American Foursquare. The Morgans did not live in the house long; after he served as superintendent of Terre Haute city schools, the family left for Chicago in 1908 so he could pursue further administrative opportunities. While this house was under construction, Morgan carefully oversaw the details and kept an account sheet of money invested. Among items listed were $450 for the lot, $225 for plumbing, $35 for wiring, $100 for a furnace, and $1,200 for carpentry work. He also spent $3 on trees, although the lot already contained some old trees. In addition, he had a darkroom installed so that he could pursue his interest in photography. (Photograph by Barbara Morgan.)

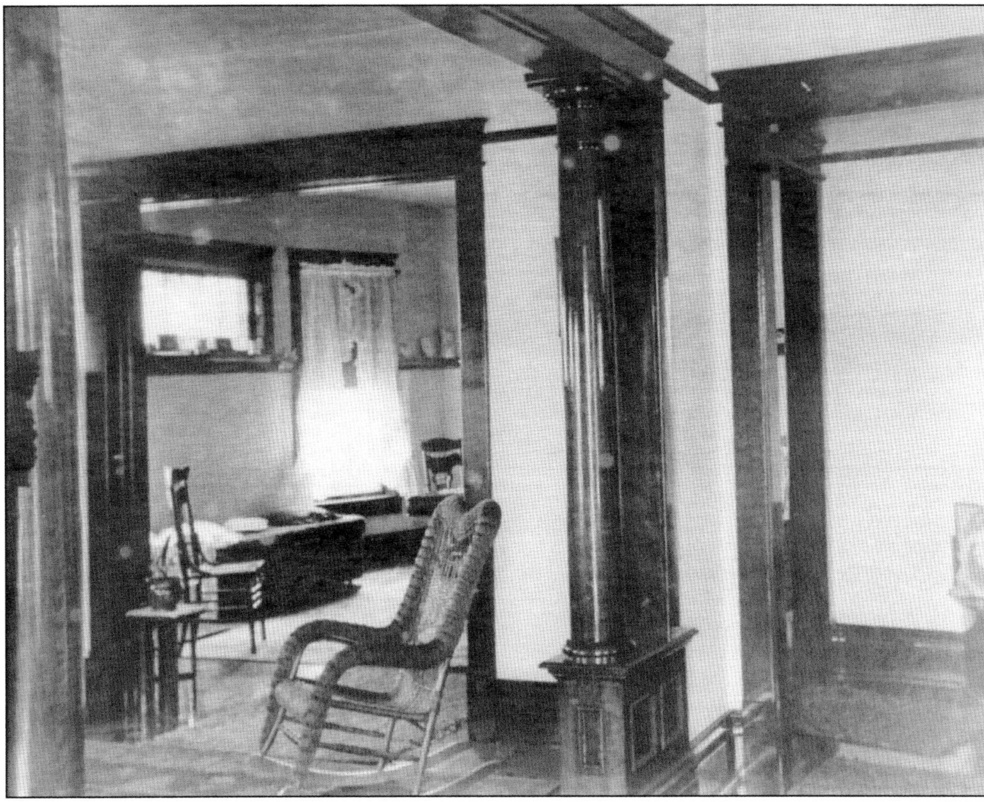

In many respects, the Walter Piety Morgan house at 1633 South Fifth Street has remained the same over the years. He took the above photograph looking from the entry into the parlor and dining room around 1906. The photograph below shows a similar view of the house decades later, taken by his granddaughter. Varnishing the floors in 1905 cost $10. Morgan paid $5 for the darkroom on March 10, 1906. He installed an expensive $45 mantel in the parlor, but a later owner removed it because she thought it looked too old-fashioned. (Above, photograph by Walter Piety Morgan; below, photograph by Barbara Morgan.)

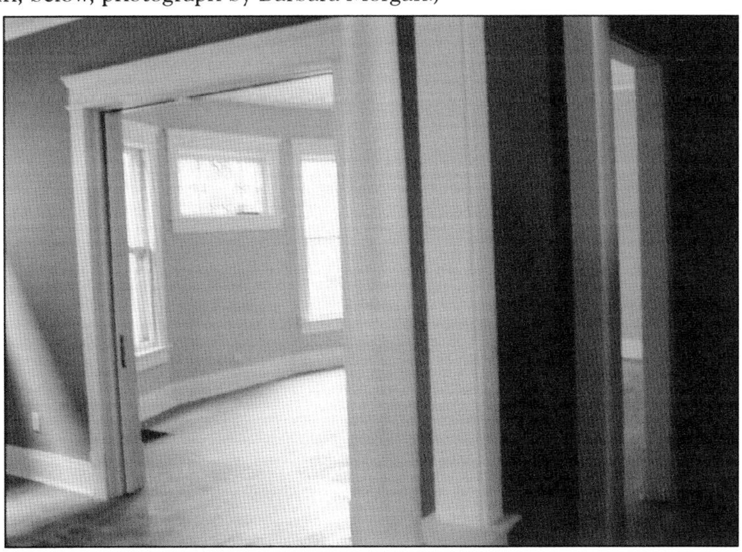

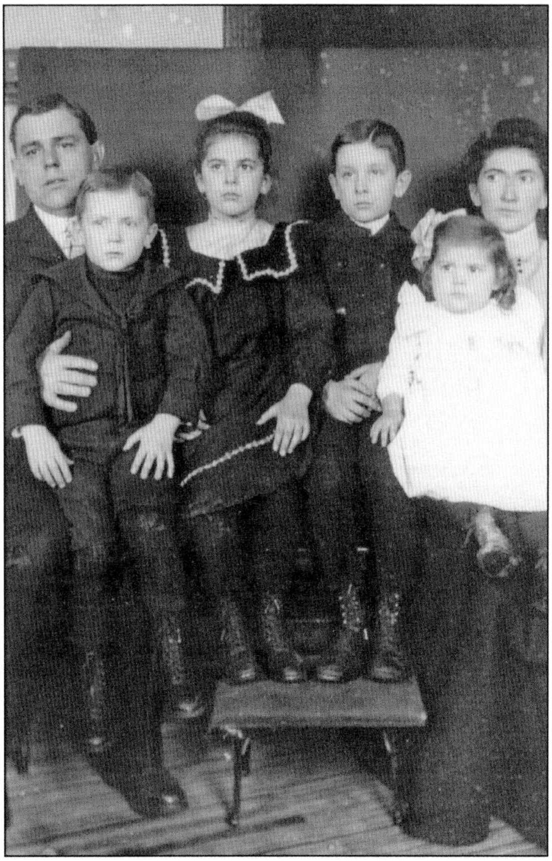

Effie Jane Elliott Morgan was so slender her husband could fit both hands around her waist. Here, they pose for a portrait with their children in 1903. From left to right are Walter Piety Morgan, William (born in 1898), Mildred (born in 1895), Ralph (born in 1893), Lucile (born in 1901), and Effie. They were living at 433 Willow Street; the house no longer exists. (Photograph by Walter Piety Morgan.)

This house at 415 Willow Street belonged to Benoni and Sarah DeBaun, uncle and aunt of Walter Piety Morgan. Benoni was a teacher and mentor to Morgan. Before Morgan married in 1893, he lived with the DeBauns on South Third Street while attending Indiana State Normal. He attended college during the springs and summers from 1888 to 1895 and taught at rural schools during the winters to earn money. (Photograph by Barbara Morgan.)

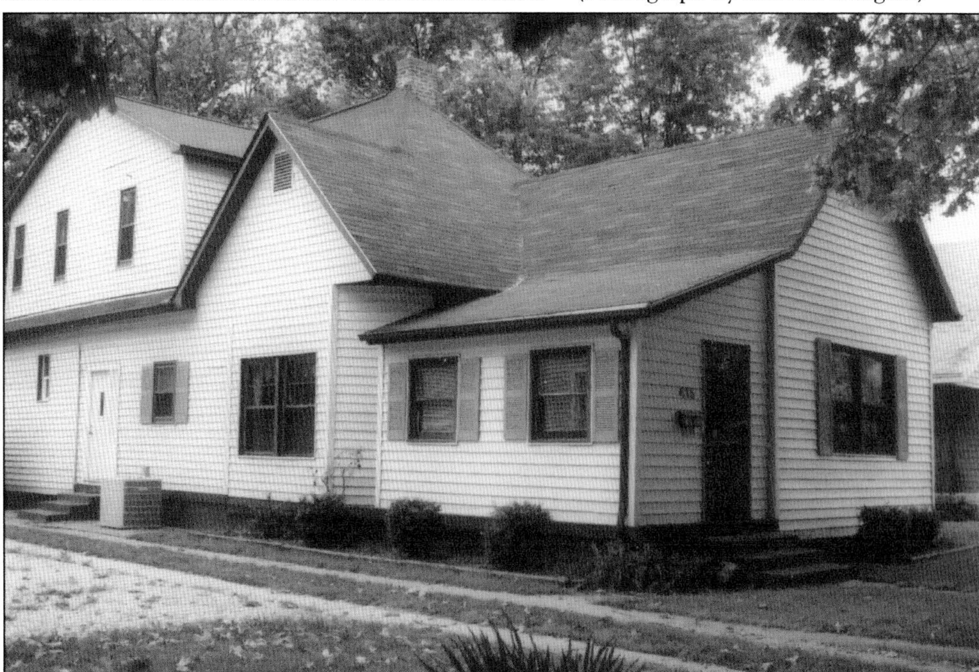

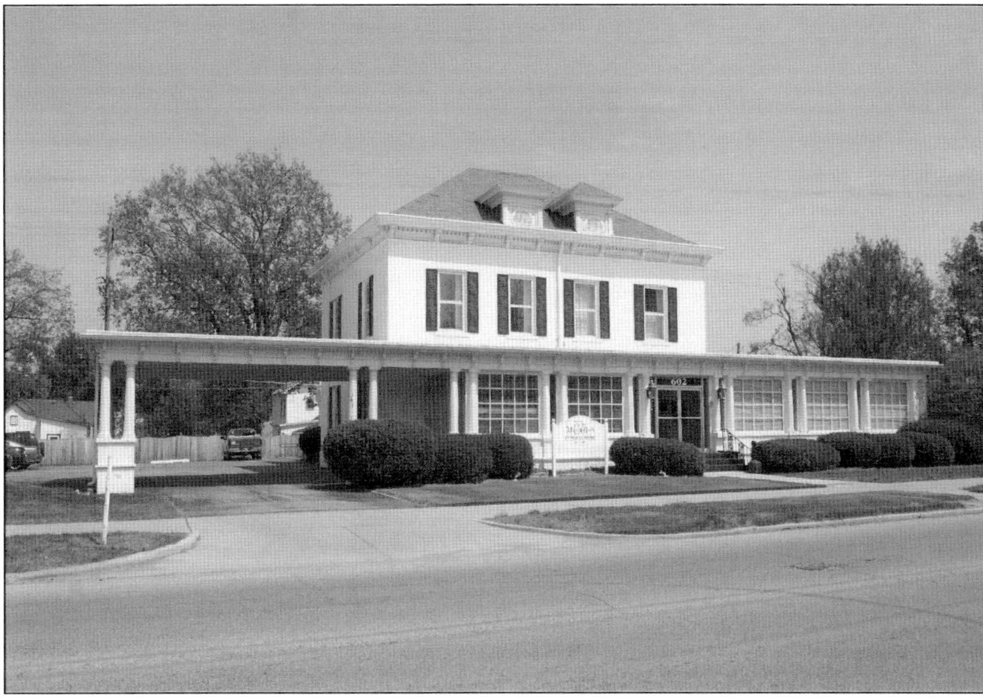

Benoni and Sarah DeBaun were related to the DeBaun family that began a funeral home business in Terre Haute. Another family connected with the funeral industry was the Ryan family, which began operating Patrick J. Ryan Funeral Home from 602 South Seventh Street in 1957; the business began in 1875 at another location. Today, it is Mattox-Ryan Funeral Home.

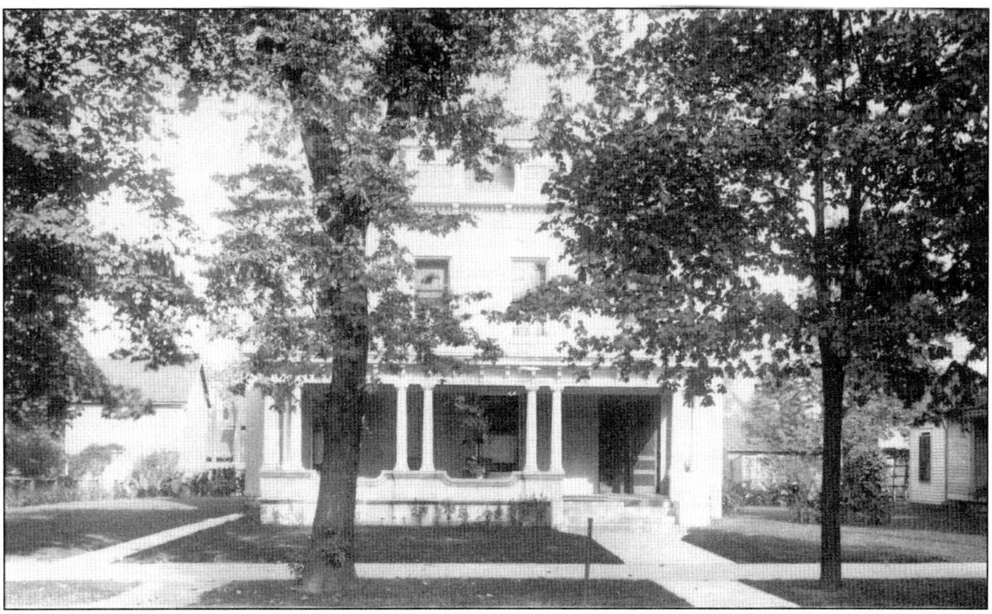

In 1907, the building at 602 South Seventh Street looked like this. The owner, F.C. Goldsmith, was president of Vigo Commission Company, a wholesale company that sold fresh fruits and vegetables to many of the small neighborhood groceries. He was also president of Goldsmith Ice Cream Company. The house was built in 1876 in the Italianate style. (J. Richard Becker Jr.)

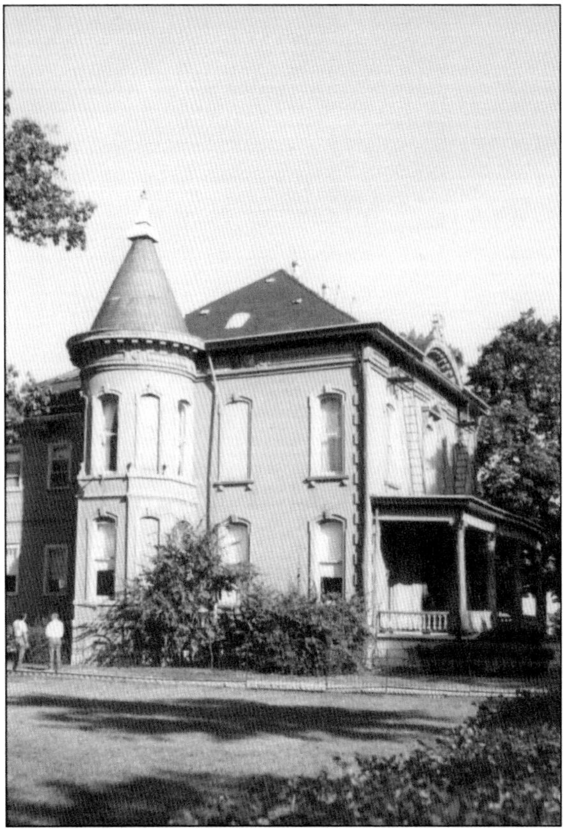

In the 1950s, the building at 405 South Sixth Street was the Martin-Tearman Funeral Home. The Italianate-style home was built in 1871 for Demas Deming Jr., son of early settlers. He was president of Deming Land Company and president of First National Bank, among other business interests. In 1967, Dr. Daniel Cheek bought it for a residence and dental office. Patients received treatment in the round tower. (J. Richard Becker Jr.)

This home at 1617 South Fifth Street has been home to two generations of dentists and an osteopath. The Queen Anne–style house was built around 1913, and members of the Minnis family have lived there ever since. The first was Dr. Joseph C. Minnis Sr., an osteopath in Terre Haute for many years. Next was Dr. Joseph C. Minnis Jr., who went into dentistry. (Judy Minnis Lowe.)

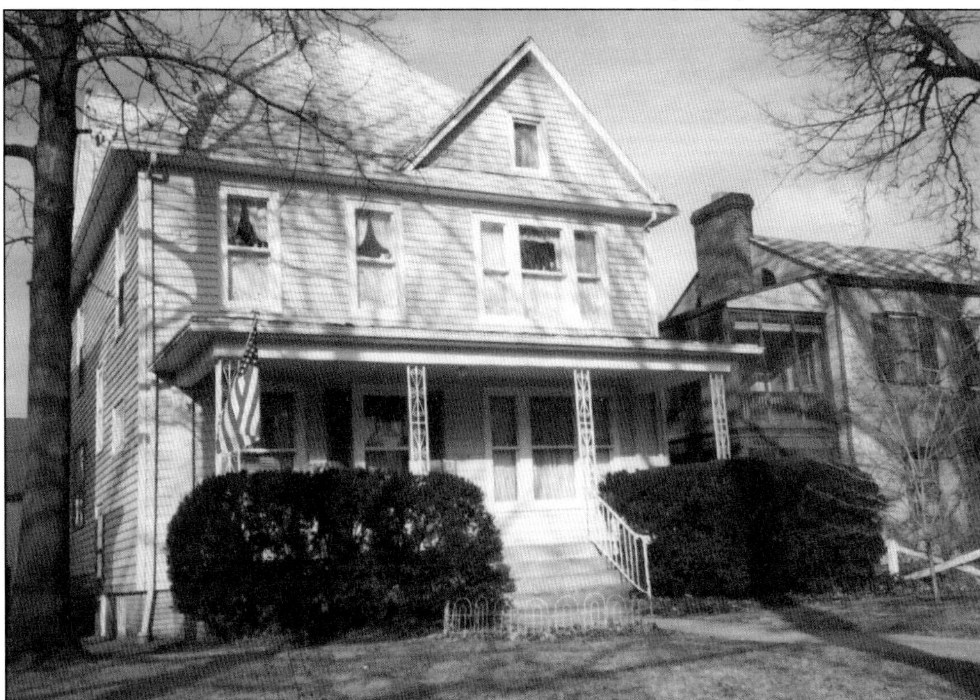

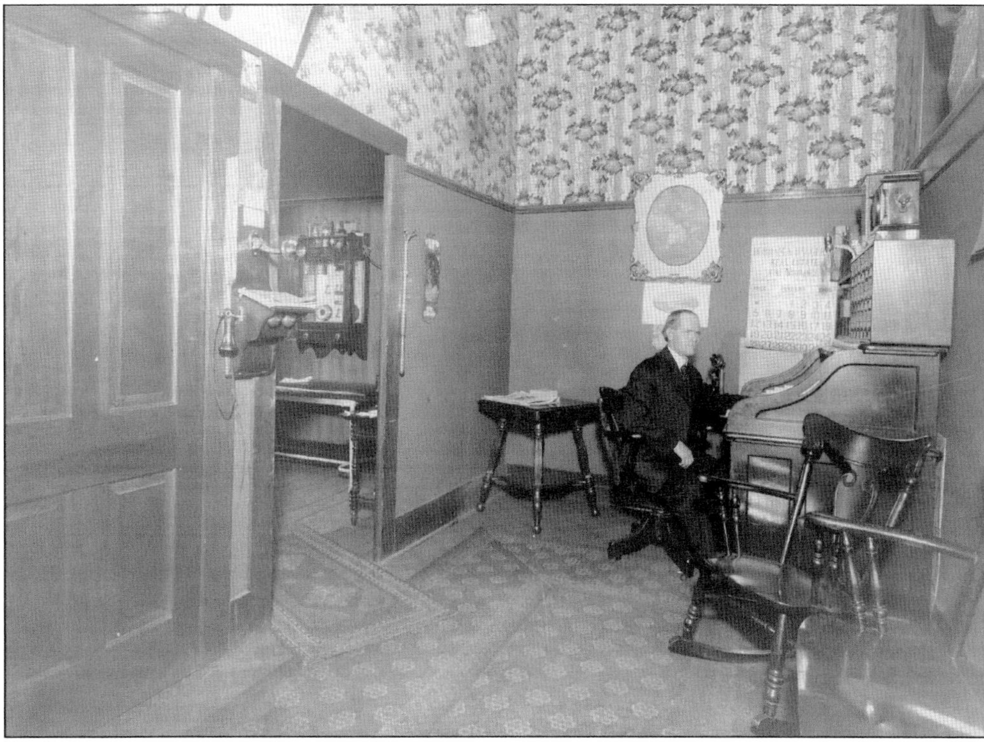

This photograph shows Dr. Joseph C. Minnis Sr. in his office in downtown Terre Haute in 1908. An old-fashioned telephone is visible on the wall. As an osteopath, he was not allowed visitation privileges in the hospitals and did tonsillectomies in his office. He could get rid of headaches by a special technique of rubbing the head. (Judy Minnis Lowe.)

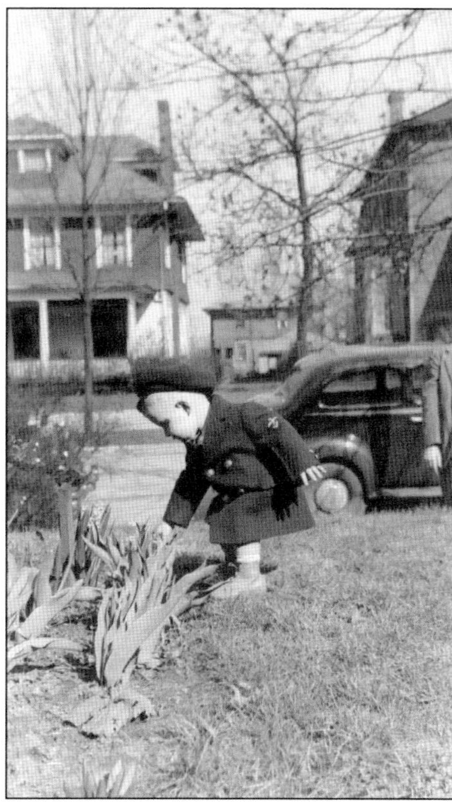

In front of the Minnis house at 1617 South Fifth Street, young Joseph C. Minnis III plays in his sailor suit in 1938. He and his sister Judy enjoyed sledding on Strawberry Hill in the winter. Like his father, he decided to go into dentistry. Father and son shared a dental office. (Joseph C. Minnis III.)

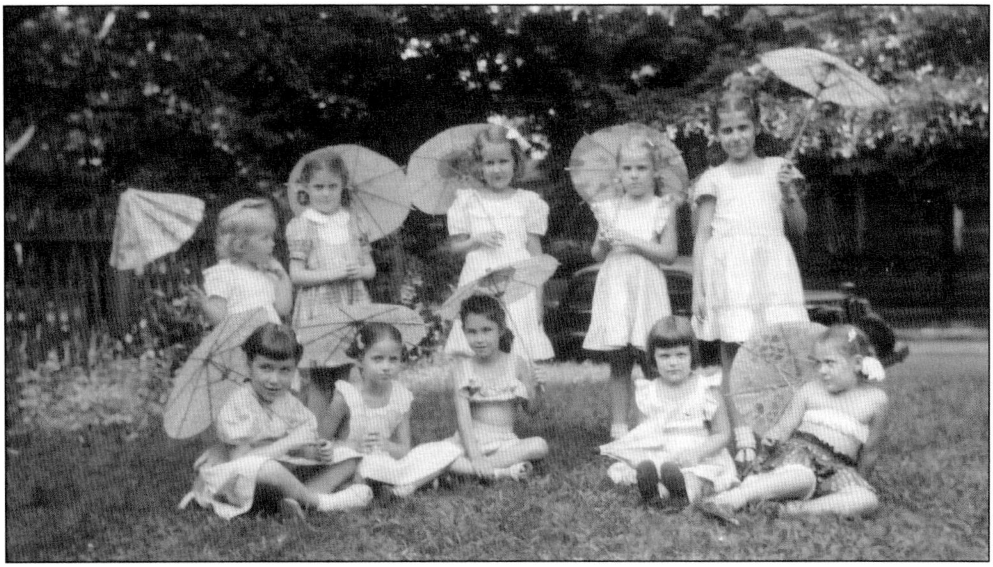

It was a perfect day for a little girls' party on the front lawn of the Minnis home at 1617 South Fifth Street in 1948. The parents of Judy Minnis had invited several little girls in the neighborhood, and they all dressed in their summer best with parasols. Judy is in the second row, second from left. (Judy Minnis Lowe.)

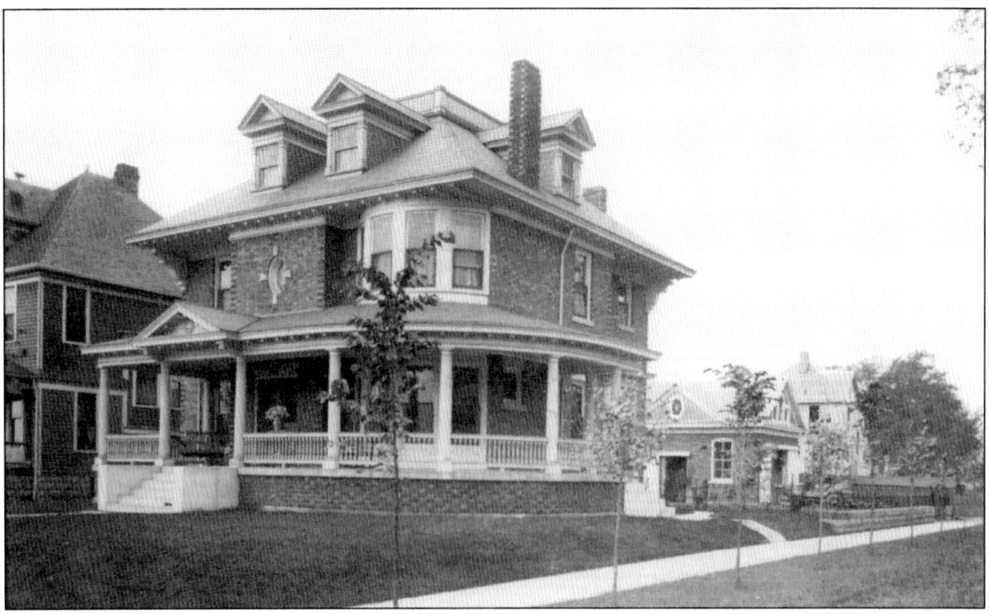

Another medical professional in the neighborhood was Dr. Charles Patton, who lived in this house at 1601 South Sixth Street in 1907. He was an eye, ear, nose, and throat specialist. The house was built around 1910 in Colonial Revival style and was designed by architect J.R. Vrydagh. (J. Richard Becker Jr.)

Four

Cattle Drives, Pottery, Businesspeople, and Fraternities

Hard to believe though it seems, cattle drives still took place in downtown Terre Haute in the early 1900s. Several slaughterhouses had sprung up along the Wabash River, with packinghouses and selling houses situated along Wabash Avenue, known as Main Street in pioneer days. Several of the business owners lived in Farrington's Grove.

Among them were Charles Ehrmann, brother of poet Max Ehrmann, and his neighbor Frank Hale. Though Hale was in the clay tile business, his house was filled with artistic pursuits, and the family enjoyed music. His daughter Mary Alice Hadley also took to the clay business, but she turned her talents to art, winning awards for her work and establishing the Hadley Pottery Company in 1945 in Louisville, Kentucky.

Living in Farrington's Grove made it easy for business owners to walk to work. Many built large two-story houses, particularly along Sixth Street. The neighborhood also contained small one-story homes. In the meat business were the Nagels, Wahlers, the Ehrmanns, and the Farringtons, to name a few. Among those in the coal business were the Talleys, the Atens, and the Richardses. The Potter and Zimmerman businesses specialized in hardware and metal products, respectively.

During the 1950s and 1960s, fraternities migrated from an area north of Indiana State Teachers College (now Indiana State University) to Farrington's Grove Historic District. Many large old homes formerly owned by wealthy families became homes for fraternities. Others were converted to apartment buildings.

Farrington's Grove was also home to Theodore Barhydt, an important figure who affected Terre Haute's entertainment history. He came to Terre Haute in 1897 to manage the new Grand Opera House, and his most enduring legacy is the Indiana Theater, an ornate example of Spanish Baroque architecture, which he funded through a stock company and which opened in 1922. Keeping pace with the times, he changed the Lyric Theater, which he also owned, into Terre Haute's first motion picture theater.

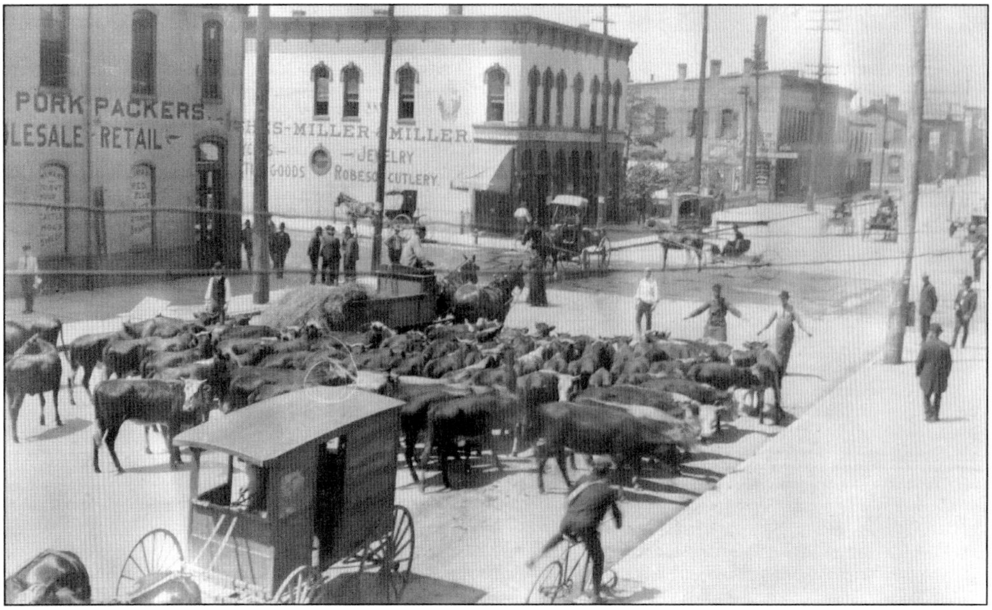

In this 1906 cattle drive down Ohio Street, well-dressed men herd cattle to Ehrmann and Company pork and beef packers at 100–102 South Fourth Street. The company had general offices at 411 Ohio Street. Nervous mothers kept children indoors during cattle drives down Ohio and Market Streets (known today as Third Street). Company owner Charles Ehrmann, his family, and his three brothers, including the young Max Ehrmann, lived in the house at 805 South Fifth Street (shown in the photograph below) in the early 1900s. The budding poet Max, a graduate of DePauw University, worked on his poetry while employed by his brother. Charles was successful in several businesses, including real estate. He loved photography and filled albums with pictures of the neighborhood. He also traveled widely. (Both photographs by Charles Ehrmann; courtesy of Special Collections Library, Pennsylvania State University Libraries.)

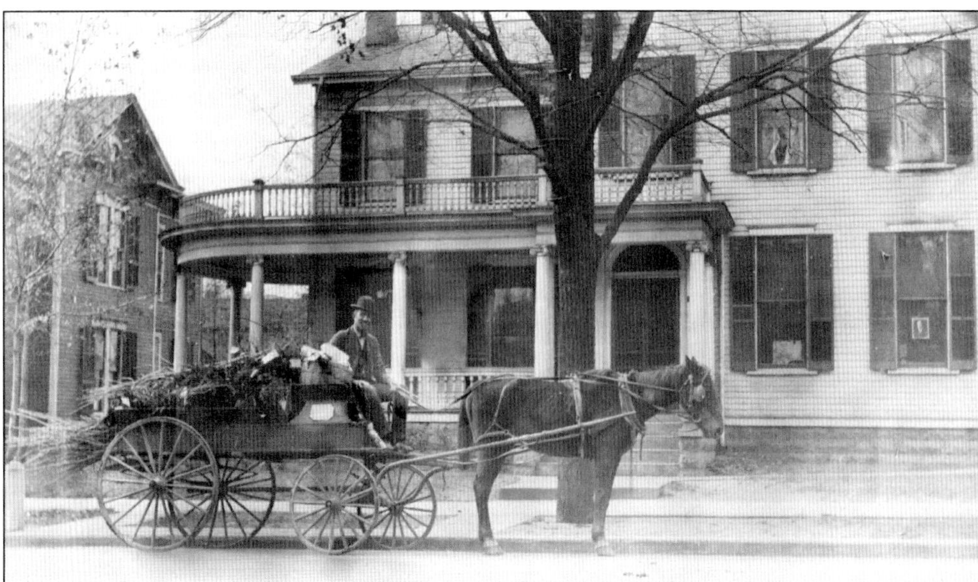

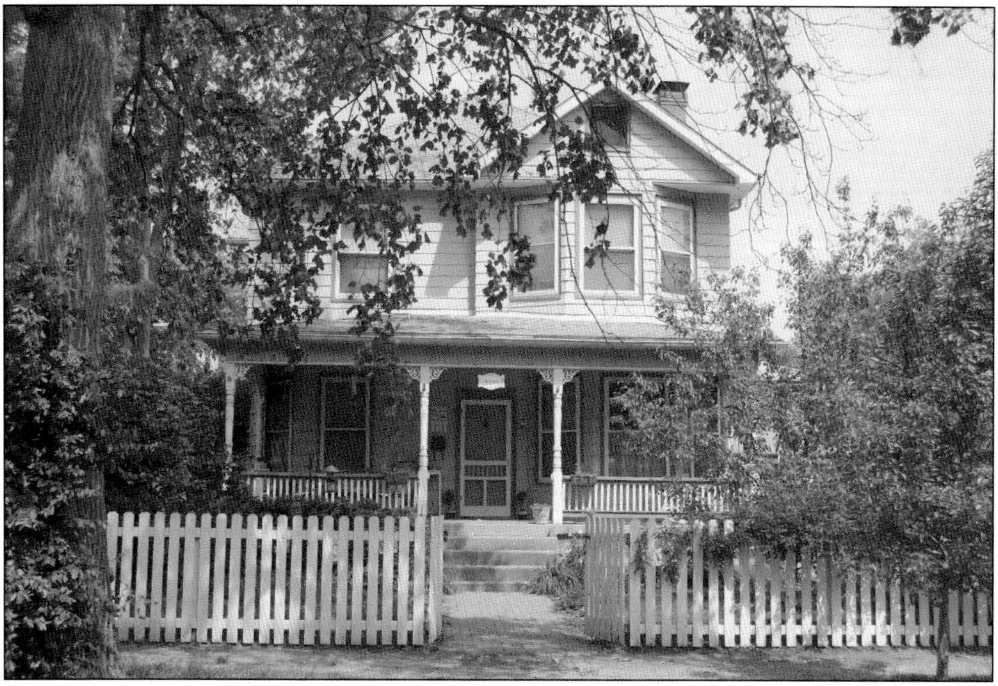

Frank Hale lived at 812 South Fifth Street across from Charles Ehrmann. Hale founded the American Clay Company and consolidated with Vigo-American Clay Company in 1915, becoming general manager of the country's largest manufacturer of hollow building tile. His family loved the arts and music. He reserved a private table for the Woman's Department Club lunch following the Terre Haute Symphony's first concert in 1926. (Photograph by Albert Christenberry.)

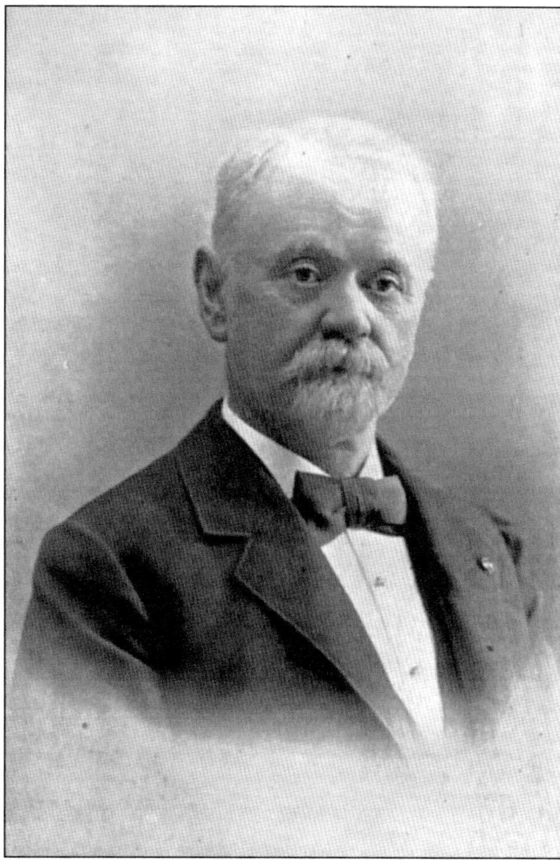

Before the Frank Hale house arose in 1906, a house stood at 812 South Fifth Street belonging to Col. William E. McLean, an attorney and deputy U.S. commissioner of pensions under Pres. Grover Cleveland. He persuaded the Indiana General Assembly to appropriate money to build Indiana State Normal. McLean was among the influential Big Five of Terre Haute, along with Daniel Voorhees and Col. Richard Thompson. (J. Richard Becker Jr.)

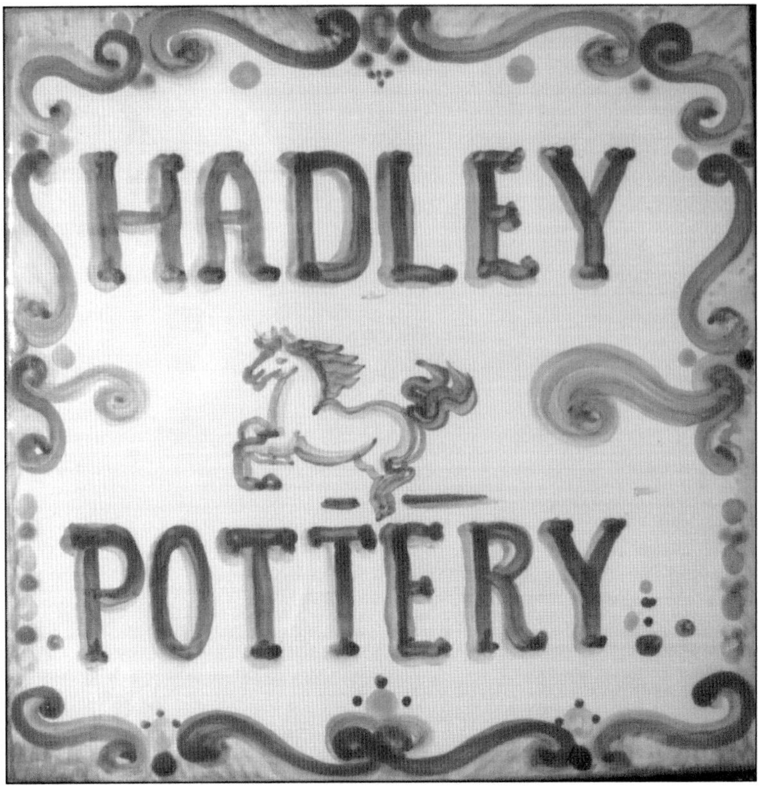

This tile is a symbol of Hadley Pottery in Louisville, Kentucky. Frank Hale's daughter Mary Alice Hadley could not find plates she liked for the Hadley Ohio River houseboat, so she created her own. The designs caught the fancy of friends, word spread, orders piled up, and eventually, her husband, George, bought his wife a factory that opened in 1945. (Rose-Hulman.)

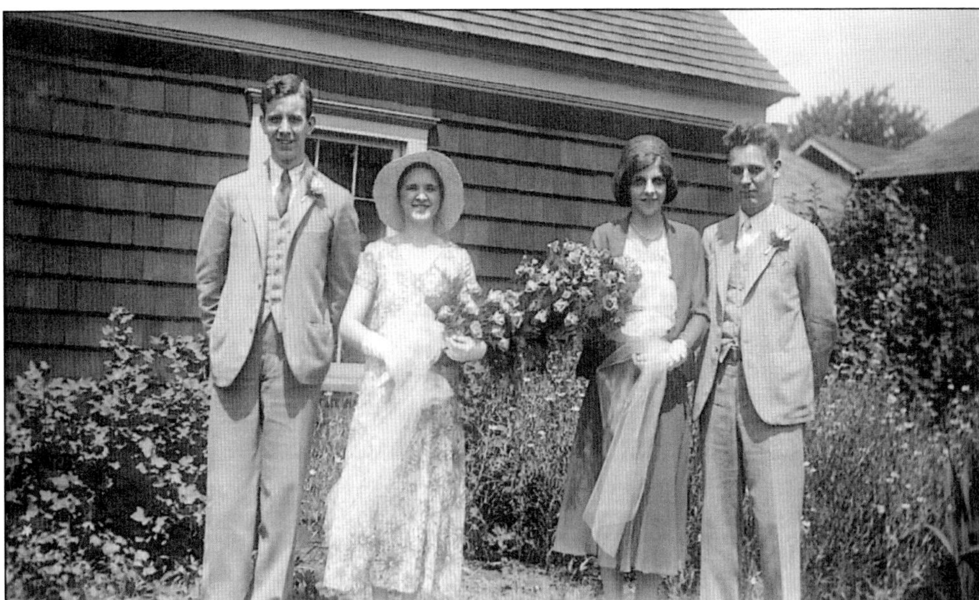

Frank Hale's daughter Mary Alice and her husband, George Hadley, were maid of honor and best man for their good friends Marion Watkins and Karl Richard "Dick" Garmong on June 14, 1931. From left to right are George, Mary Alice, Marion, and Dick. Mary Alice used her country style of horse, pig, cow, and farmer when Dick requested that she decorate ceramic tiles for the Garmong fireplace around 1950.

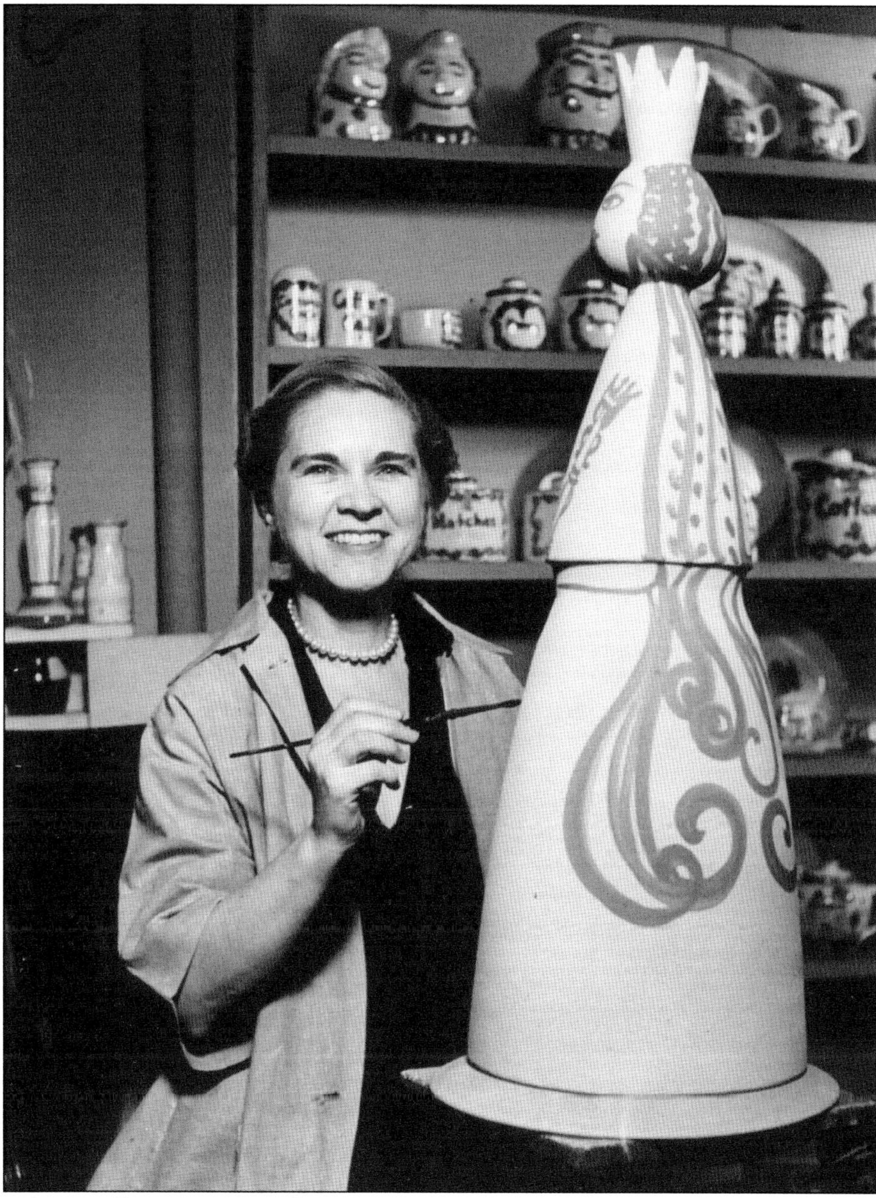

Mary Alice Hadley's interest in the arts began as she was growing up in the Hale home at 812 South Fifth Street in Farrington's Grove. The arts were important to the Hales. Her mother and sister painted china while she created plates; the family orchestra conducted weekly rehearsals. Later, this daughter of a clay manufacturer went into the pottery business. She created a variety of shapes and sizes for Hadley Pottery Company. They ranged from dinner plate sets to tabletop curios, to fountains, to this nearly three-foot-high statue of a queen. Hadley pottery goes through a high firing temperature; only certain colors, such as blue, green, and rust, work well on the white glaze used. Among traditional Hadley designs are country scenes, the blue horse, ship, whale, and pear and grape. However, she relished unusual projects, such as foot warmers and grinning-cat doorstop vases. MGM movie studio once ordered pins and cufflinks with blue horses as presents for employees. Hadley died at age 54 in 1965, but her company lives on, producing hand-painted pottery in the traditions she established. (Hadley Pottery Company.)

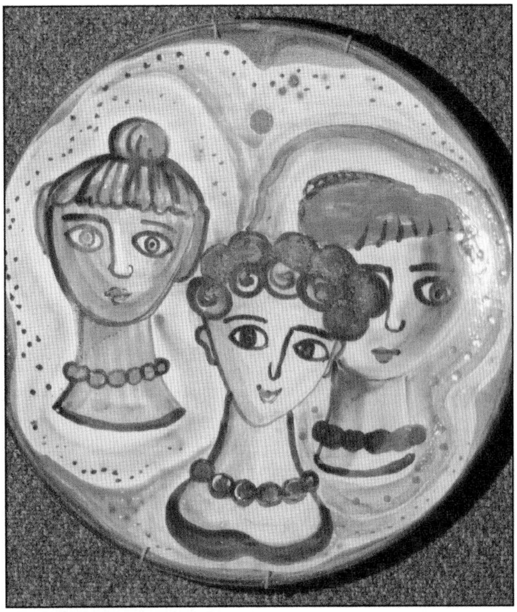

George Hadley donated a collection of more than 400 of his wife's pottery pieces to Rose-Hulman Institute of Technology, his alma mater. The collection shows Mary Alice Hadley's wide range, which extended far beyond the Americana designs popular in Hadley dinner plates. Trips to Europe and other parts of the world were influences. The dish with the three women is a 15-inch chop plate with colors of blue, green, and rust and a touch of Picasso. The seascape with the three fish is a 19-inch charger containing 16 three-dimensional seashells in blue and white. Mary Alice was a high-energy person with a sense of whimsy. On one visit to her friends the Garmongs, she arose at night with a flashlight and painted chickens and a rooster wearing tails, a top hat, and cane on their chicken coop. (Rose-Hulman.)

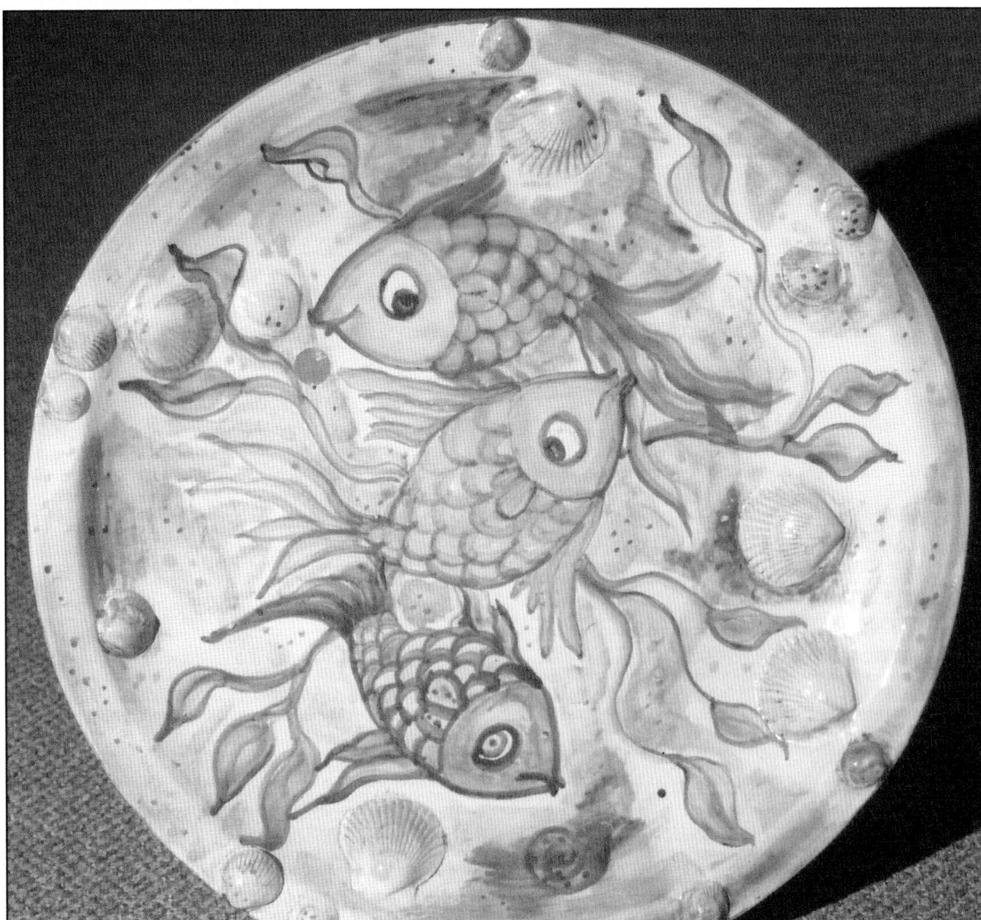

George Zimmerman, a worker in tin, lived two blocks away from the Frank Hale family. This 1880 picture shows the German native. His business specialized in galvanized iron cornices and metal roofing for prominent downtown buildings. It carried a line of warm air furnaces, stoves, and ranges, as well as a full line of tinware. Hale produced building materials in clay; Zimmerman produced materials in metal. (Robert Coppedge.)

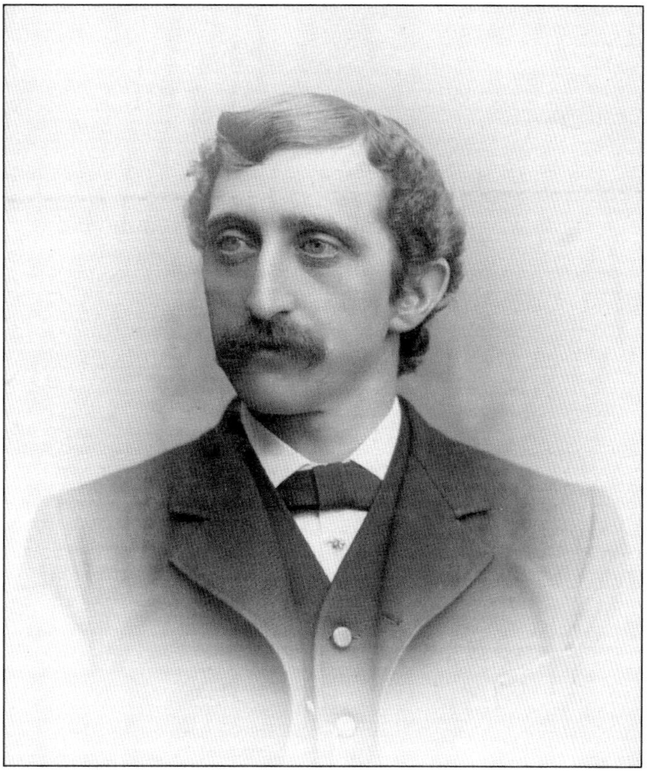

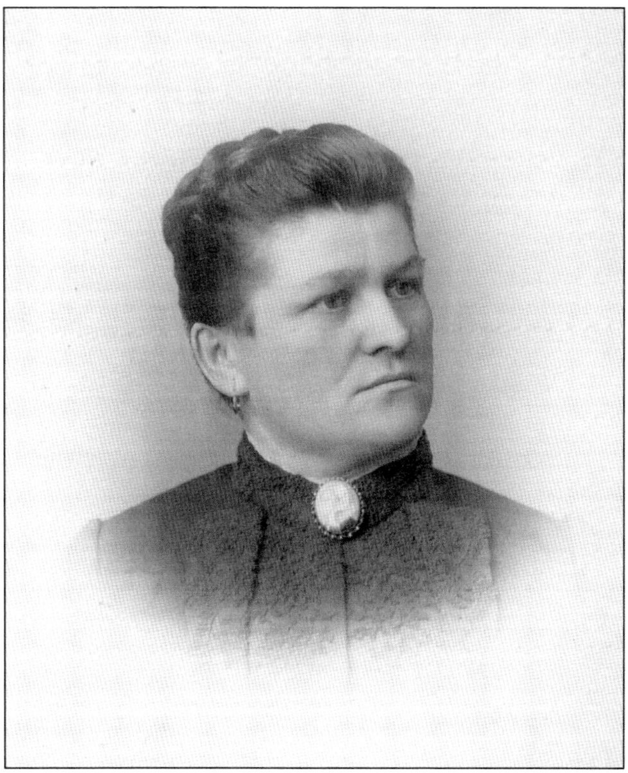

Salome Nagel Zimmerman (shown here) and husband George moved into 904 South Fourth Street in May 1889 at her aunt Caroline Layher Wahler's urging. George had to repair it. Salome told relatives it was "the ugliest house in Terre Haute . . . rundown, painted red, with rotted log front steps, and having heating stoves all over the place." The front window displayed Salome's body at her funeral. (Robert Coppedge.)

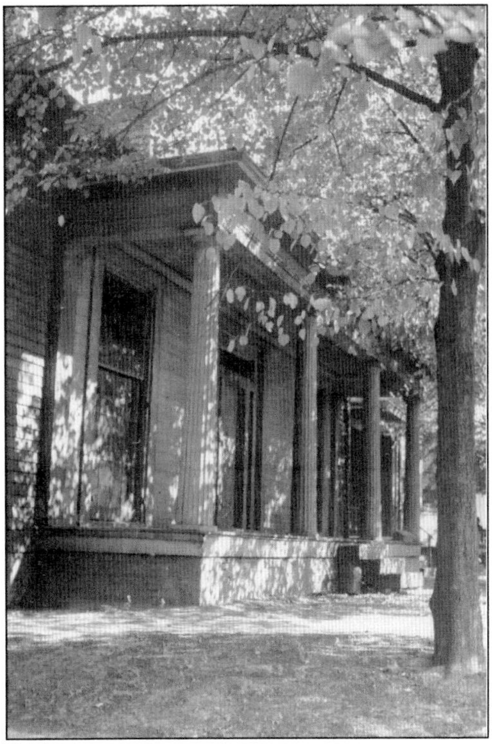

In 1894, George and Salome Nagel Zimmerman officially inherited 904 South Fourth Street from Salome's aunt Caroline Layher Wahler. Wahler had the extra house because a customer defaulted on a debt to the butcher business of her husband, Thomas Wahler. George installed a tin roof, the first such roof in town. It is probably the city's oldest residence, built about 1849 and moved to Fourth Street around 1873. (David Lewis.)

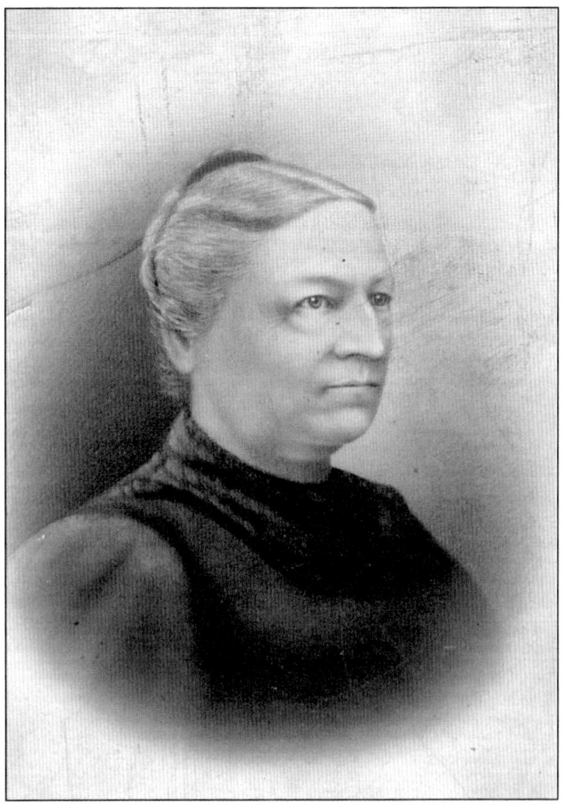

Caroline Layher Wahler (shown here) expertly ran her husband's butcher business after he died in 1883. Childless, she willed her property to her niece Salome Nagel Zimmerman and her nephew Clemens W. Nagel in 1894. She had supported the German Evangelical Lutheran Church, buying the old building at Fourth and Swan Streets in 1885 so the congregation could construct a new church at 645 Poplar Street. (Robert Coppedge.)

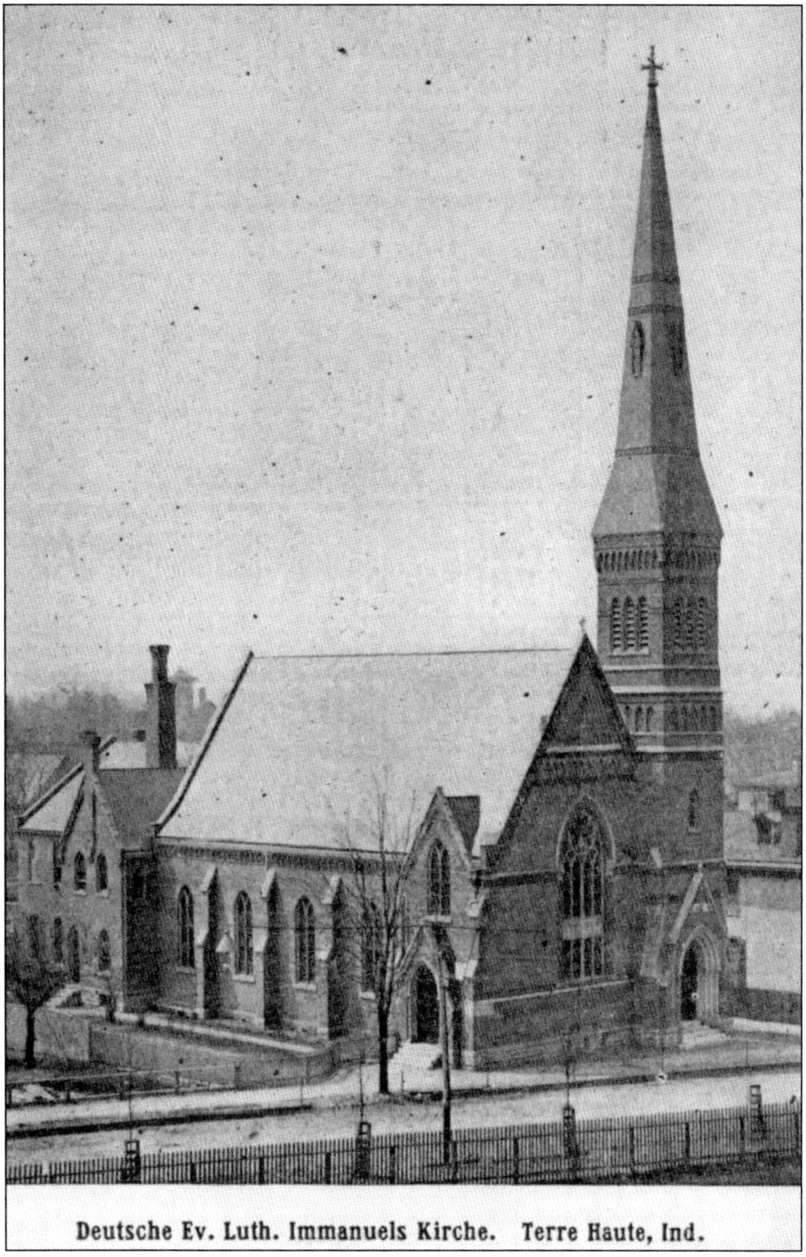

Deutsche Ev. Luth. Immanuels Kirche. Terre Haute, Ind.

Immanuel Lutheran Church emerged from a combined German Evangelical Lutheran and Reformed Church Congregation, which began in 1848 but split in 1857 into Lutheran and Reformed. The combined congregation first met in various places and then built a church between Oak and Swan Streets at 420 South Fourth Street. After the split, the Reformed group kept the building, paying the Lutheran group $750; later, the Reformed group sold it to the Jewish community in 1890. The Lutheran group became the German Evangelical Lutheran congregation and built its own church in 1858 at the corner of Fourth and Swan Streets. It outgrew the building and sold it to Caroline Layher Wahler in 1885. The funding aided in construction of this new, $25,000 church at 645 Poplar Street in 1885. Designed by well-known local architect J.A. Vrydagh, it is Victorian Gothic with German styling. (Ray Thomas.)

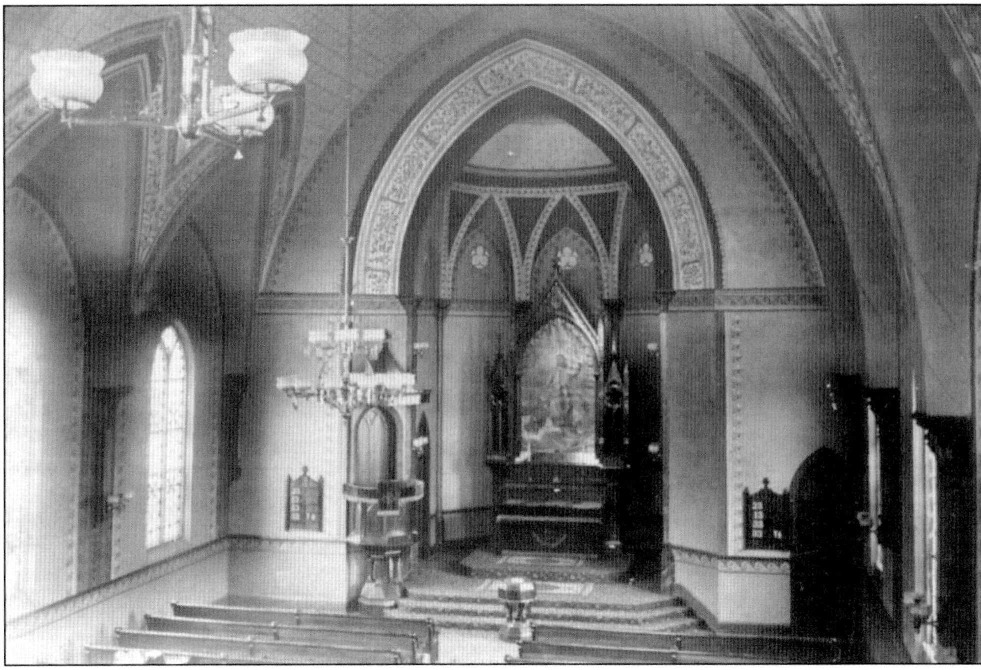

This postcard shows the interior of Immanuel Lutheran Church at 645 Poplar Street as it looked in 1890. The interior underwent extensive renovations in 1918 and again in 1954. The pipe organ was repaired and enlarged in 1921. In the beginning, services were conducted in German, although occasional services in English had begun by 1897. (Immanuel Lutheran Church.)

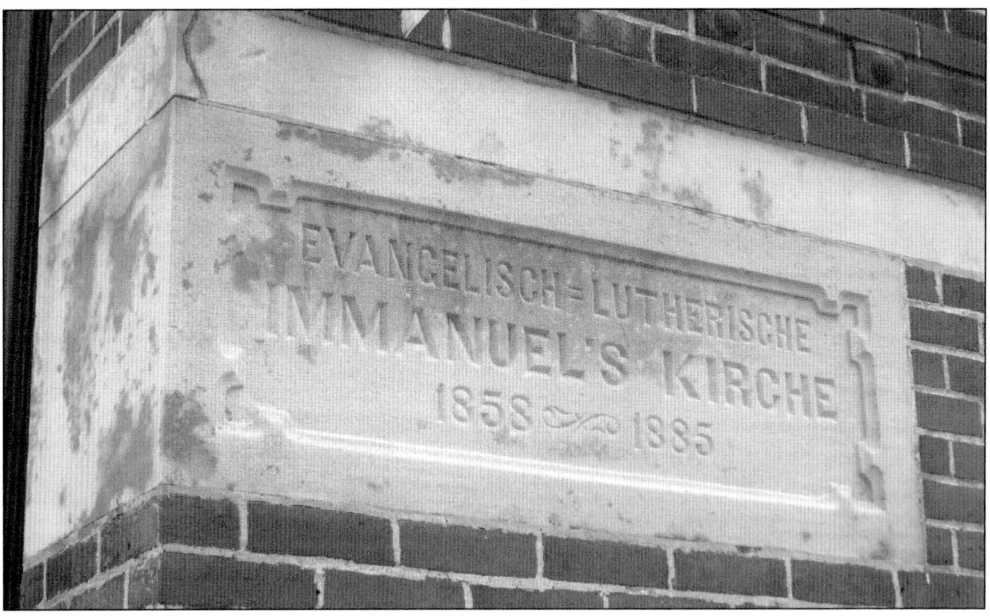

During World War I, anti-German feelings ran high in Terre Haute, and "Patriot Committees" sought to remove any evidence of German sympathies. A congregation member recalls the congregation had to cover the church's German-language cornerstone during the war. The bilingual Parochial School closed. In addition, in 1918, the Voters Assembly decided to change the church name to Immanuel Evangelical Lutheran Church, removing the word *German*.

Caroline Layher Wahler helped her nephew Clemens W. Nagel find a job. These photographs show him and his wife, Anna Held Nagel. At age 13, Clemens began working as an apprentice for his uncle Thomas Wahler in his prosperous butcher business. He moved from his parents' home in Clay County to work with his uncle and eventually managed the business. In 1890, he bought the business from his widowed aunt. In her will of 1894, she left her nephew the land and equipment. For a time, his family lived in the former Wahler house, which his sister and brother-in-law moved from 1039 South First Street to a lot next door to their South Fourth Street home. The vacant lot had been used by Immanuel Lutheran Church for ice cream socials. The Wahler house was demolished in the 1960s. (Robert Coppedge.)

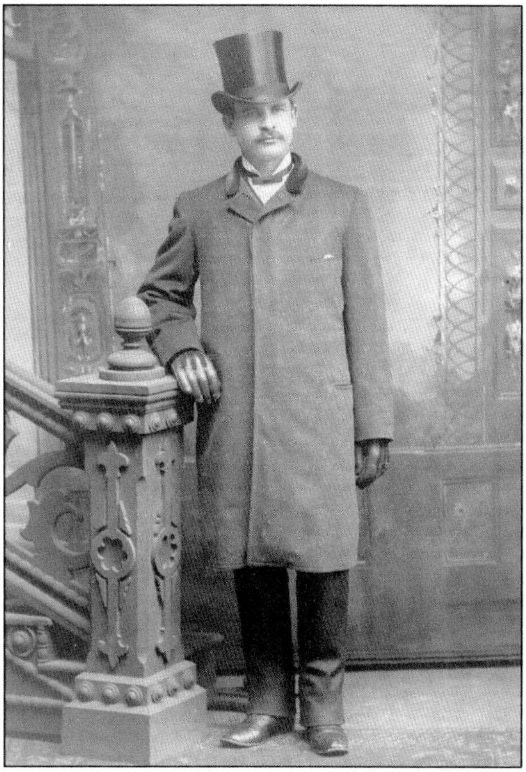

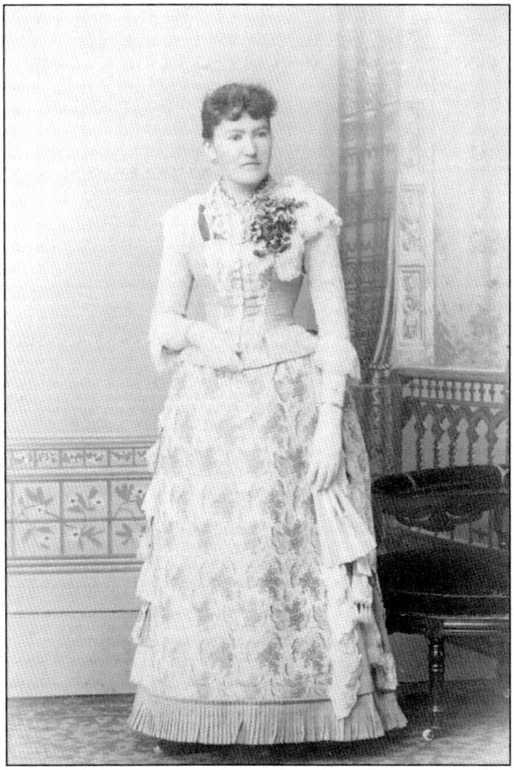

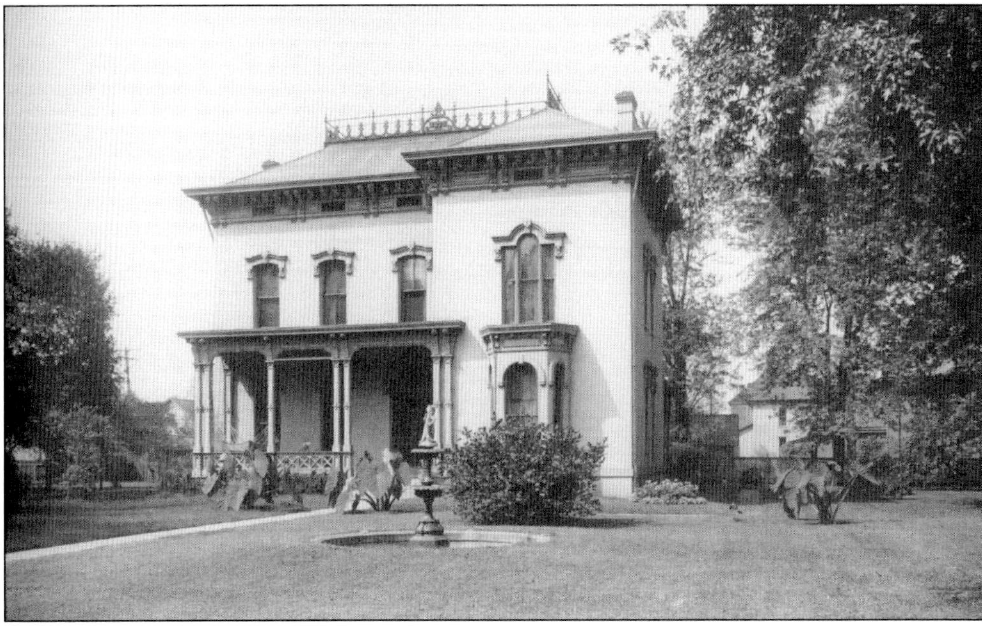

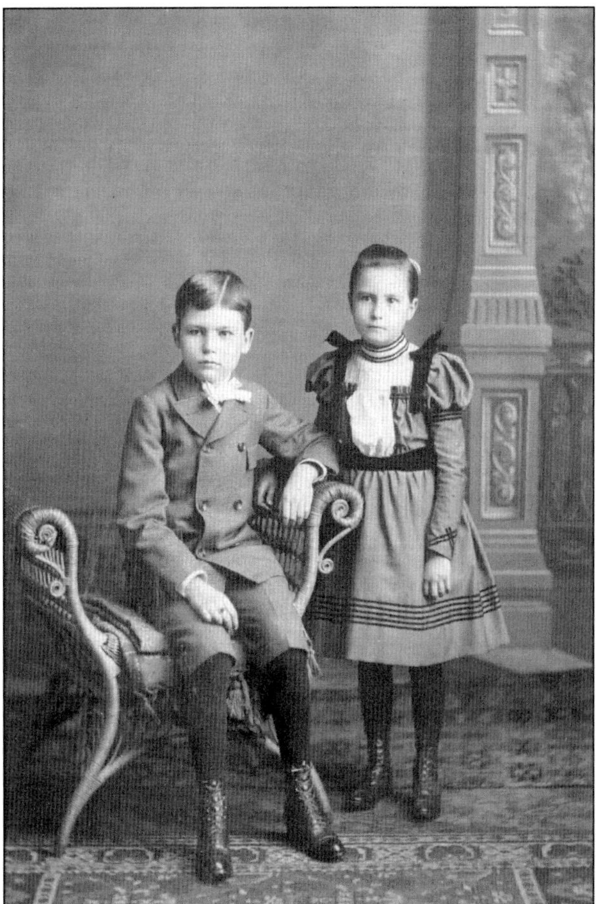

Clemens W. and Anna Held Nagel bought 1411 South Sixth Street in 1905. Under the roof by the eaves, their daughter Marcella discovered a peaceful hiding place to read. In 1957, the Vigo County Historical Society bought the house from Marcella Nagel Lundgren for its museum. The Italianate-style house was built in 1868 for William Sage, a baker and confectioner. (J. Richard Becker Jr.)

Clarence and Marcella Nagel grew up at 1411 South Sixth Street. As a girl, Marcella shared her secret reading spot with her friend Gwendolyn Volkers, daughter of John and Alice Yeakle Volkers. Marcella moved away and married Fred Lundgren, whom she met at the University of Illinois, but later returned to the family home. She used part of the house as a convalescent home for elderly men discharged from St. Anthony's Hospital. (Robert Coppedge.)

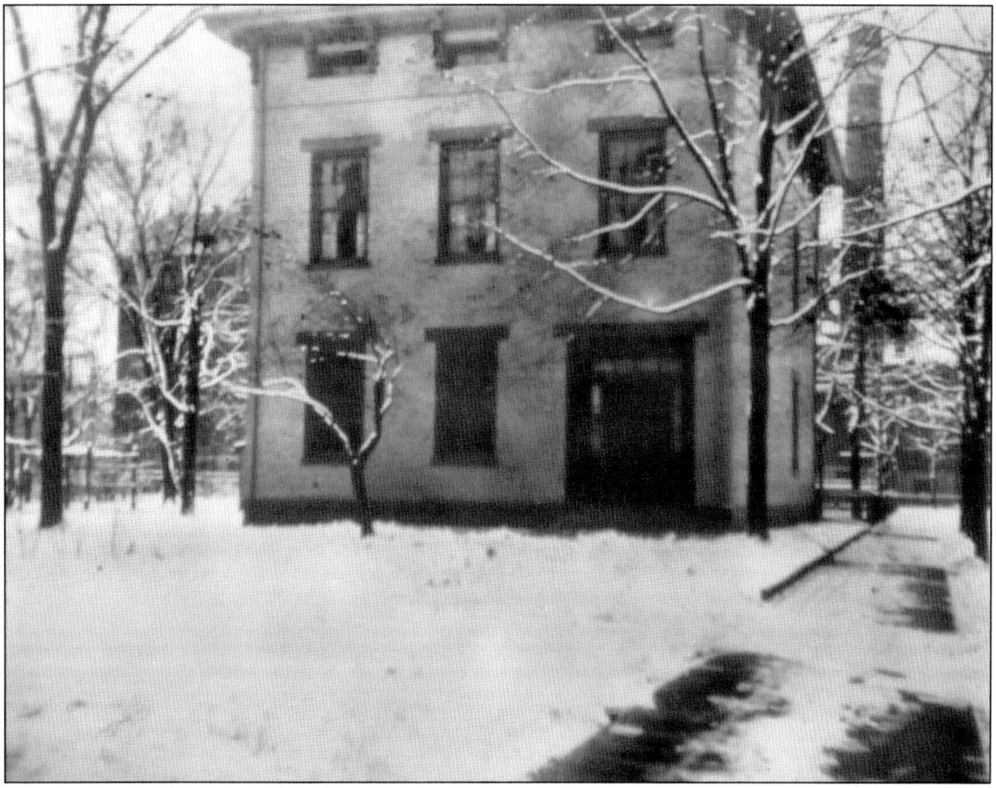

In 1831, James Farrington bought 47.76 acres; in 1841, he built Woodlawn, shown here at 920 South Fifth Street in the early 1900s. Farrington's Grove derives its name from Farrington. He was an attorney, bank president, and partner in H.D. Williams and Company, major hog exporters. At Woodlawn, he hosted celebrations, speeches by notables (such as Stephen A. Douglas on Sept. 30, 1856), and community picnics with treats such as a gigantic sea turtle. (VCHS.)

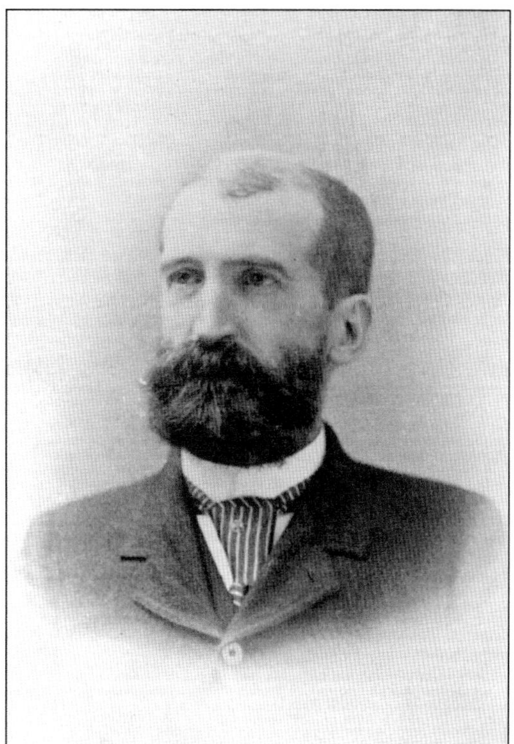

Until he died in 1920, George E. Farrington kept his father's home Woodlawn, located between Park and Farrington Streets on Fifth Street. It was demolished around 1922. His father rebuilt Woodlawn at half its original size after a major fire in 1855. George was an official of the Terre Haute & Indianapolis Railroad and a member of the Rose Orphans Home board. (Photograph from Tribune-Star; J. Richard Becker Jr.)

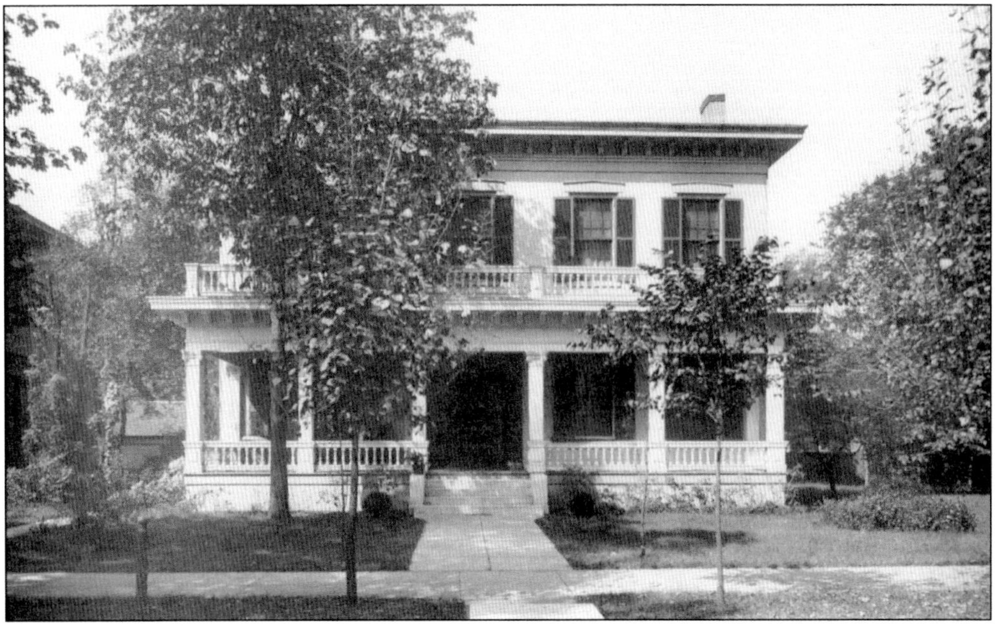

Samuel H. Potter said Farrington and Williams packed several thousand beef a season. On an 1844 stop in Terre Haute, he was "charmed and delighted" by the old courthouse, park-like square, and blossoming locusts. He stayed, opened the city's first hardware store, and built this house at 823 South Sixth Street around 1870. Potter traveled Europe, describing Ireland, Scotland, Germany, Holland, and Rome in newspaper articles. (J. Richard Becker Jr.)

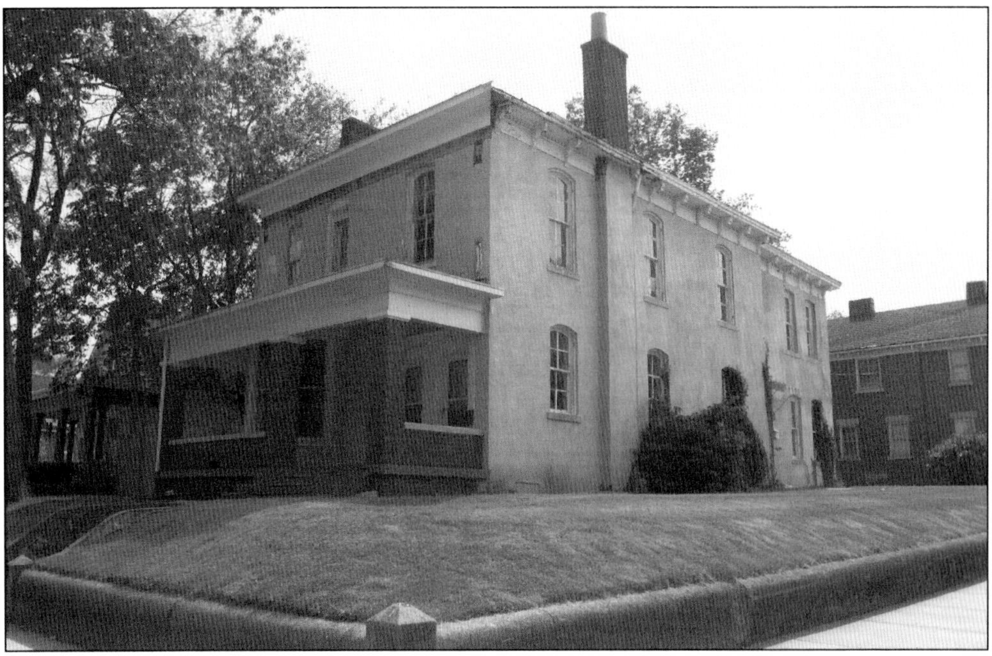

Samuel H. Potter sold hardware; Richards and Sons sold coal. In a disaster reminiscent of the *Titanic*, founder George C. Richards and his wife, daughter, and niece died when the *Empress of Ireland* sank in the St. Lawrence River on May 29, 1914. They were journeying back home to England. The Richards family lived at 1403 South Center Street.

Nellie Talley stayed single and had this house built at 1304 South Sixth Street in 1917. Her brother, Homer Talley of Talley Coal Company, lived at 1200 South Sixth Street. In 1963, the first sign went up for Alpha Tau Omega (ATO) fraternity. Charter member Alan Tehan made the sign over the door. Fraternity members stripped and repaired two front porch columns, gluing the shattered wood together. (John Woelfle.)

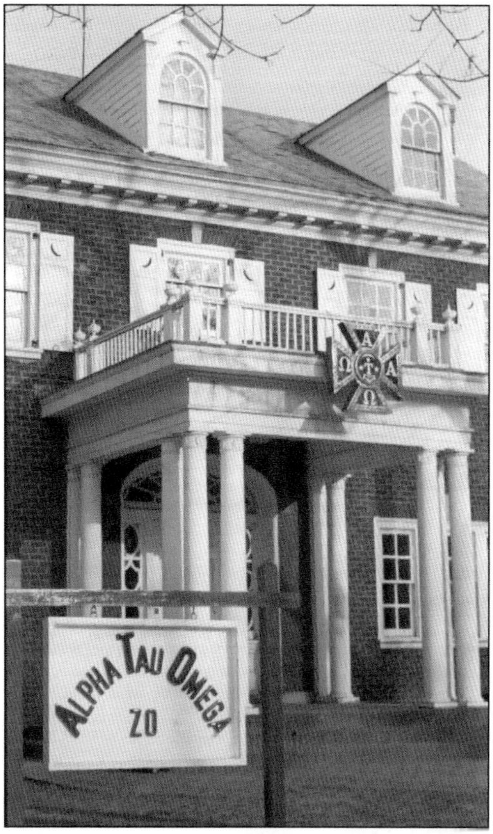

Fraternity brothers of Alpha Tau Omega pose in front of the home at 1304 South Sixth Street. John Newton, first row, left, was an ATO member and served as an adviser to the fraternity in later years. Newton worked for Indiana State University (ISU) for many years, helping organize the first Donaghy Day campus cleanup and working for the ISU Alumni Association and the ISU Foundation. (ISU.)

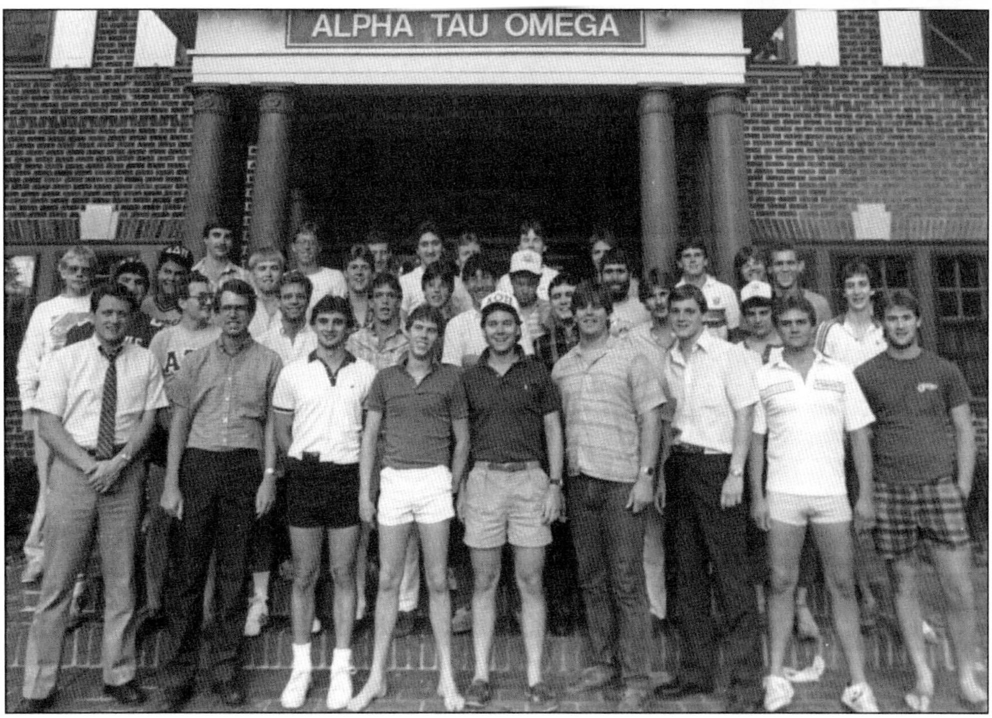

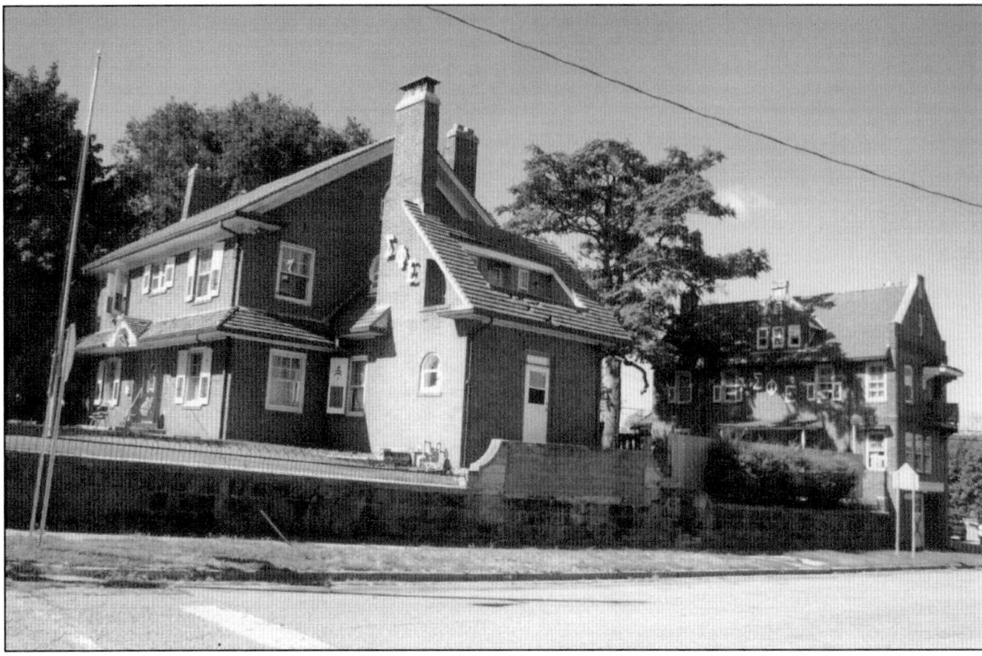

Several fraternities from Indiana State University and Rose-Hulman Institute of Technology moved into the spacious homes in Farrington's Grove in the 1950s and 1960s, creating fraternity houses. Sigma Phi Epsilon members lived in this massive English Cottage–style house at 801 South Fourth Street for many years. It was built around 1915. (J. Richard Becker Jr.)

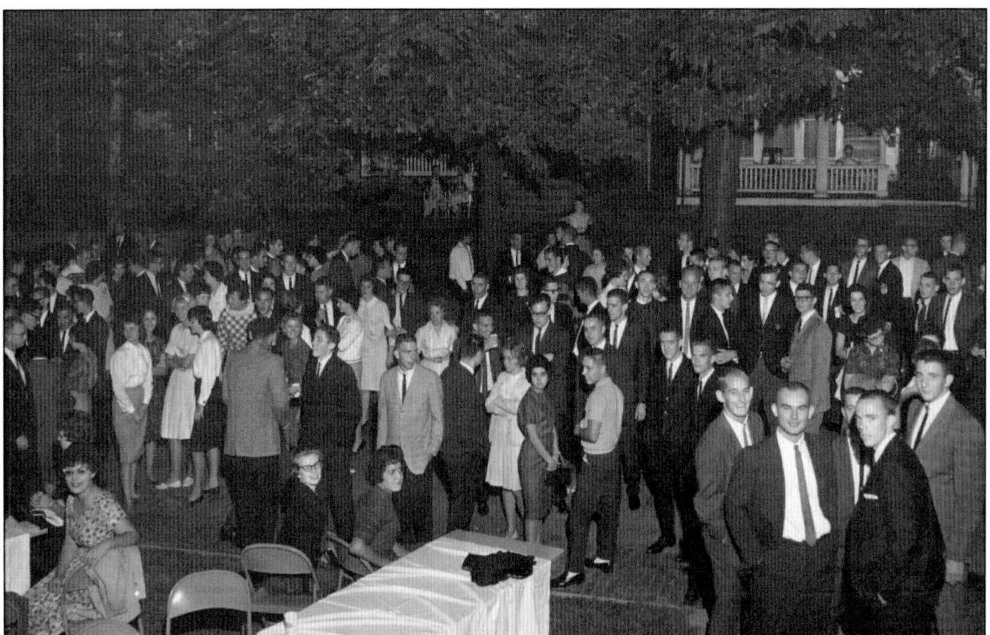

The Sigma Phi Epsilon fraternity members had an active chapter. In the 1950s, the members sponsored this formal street dance in a residential neighborhood of Terre Haute, generating interest among onlookers from the porches of nearby homes. The crew cuts, narrow ties, and horn-rimmed glasses make a fashion statement from the 1950s. (Photograph by Martin's Photo Shop; ISU.)

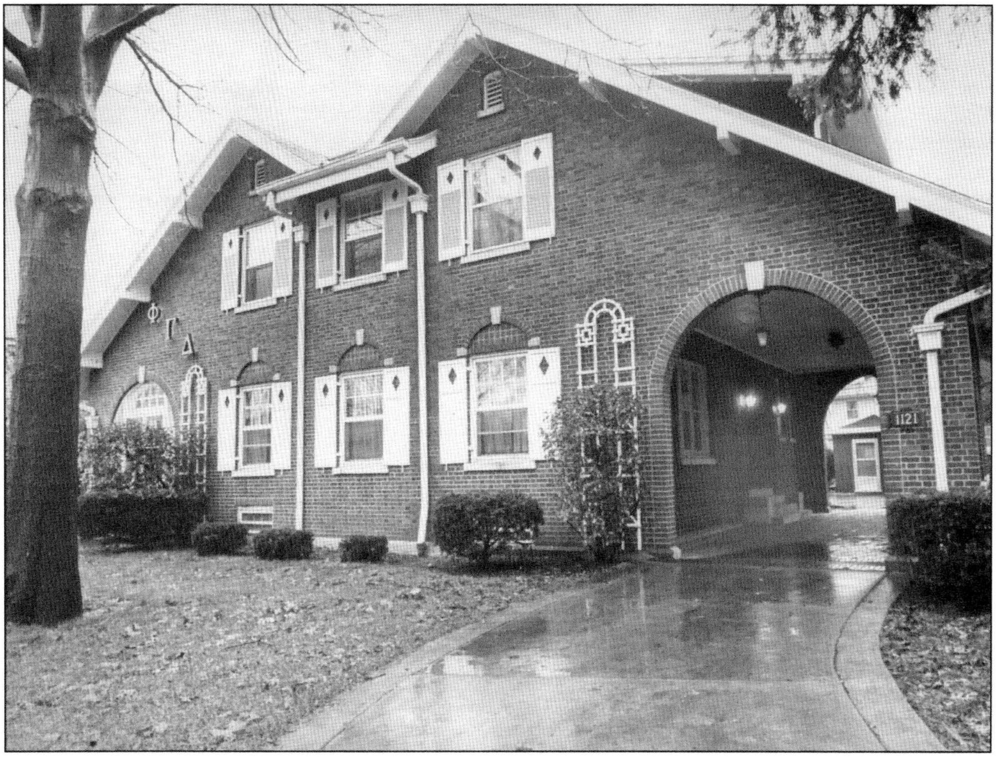

Today the home of Phi Gamma Delta fraternity, in 1921 this English Cottage–style house at 1121 South Sixth Street was built for Theodore Barhydt. His greatest legacy to Terre Haute is the Indiana Theater, built in 1921 and opened in January 1922. Peacocks strolled around the theater lobby's mosaic floor at the grand opening. The $750,000 Spanish Baroque–style theater is one of the city's architectural treasures. (Photograph by Tribune-Star; VCHS.)

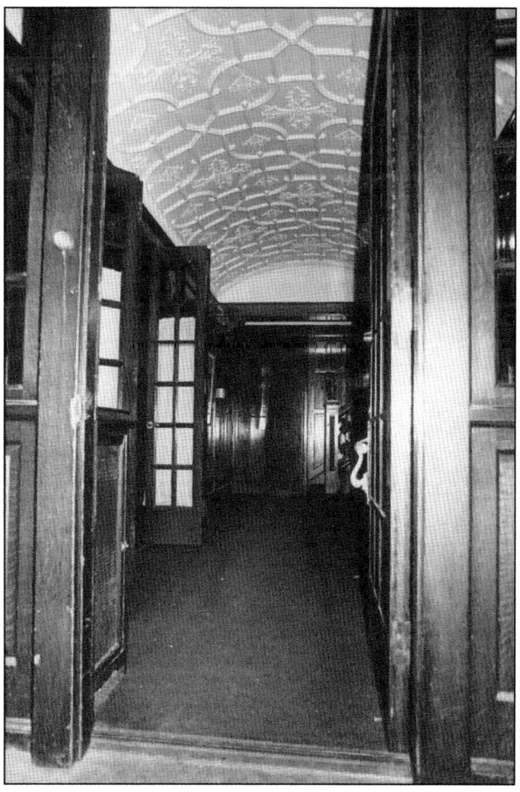

The ceiling tiles shown in the home at 1121 South Sixth Street are like ones in the Indiana Theater; some of the same building materials were used in the house. Architect John Eberson, of Chicago, designed this house for Theodore Barhydt. He also designed the Indiana Theater, which used a $50,000 Wurlitzer pipe organ to accompany early silent films. (Photograph by Tribune-Star; VCHS.)

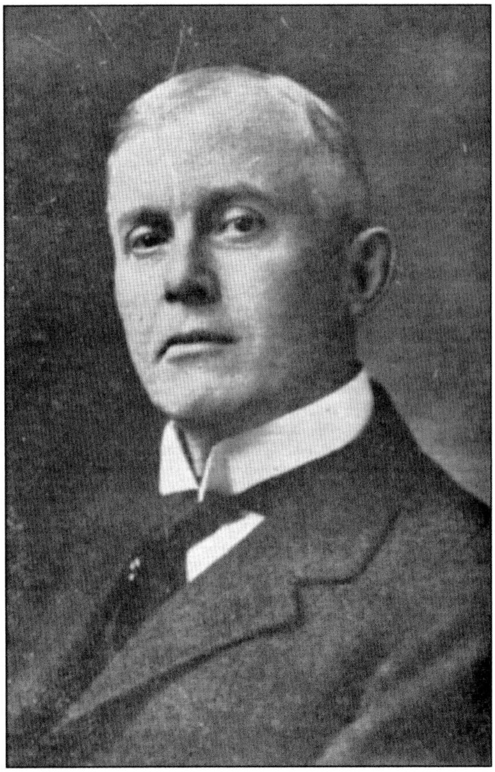

Theodore Barhydt came to Terre Haute in 1897, already experienced in the theater business, to manage the Grand Opera House. With another investor, he founded two vaudeville houses, the Lyric and Variety. Next came the Hippodrome in 1914 at Eighth and Ohio Streets, also designed by John Eberson. The Hippodrome, previously the home of Community Theatre and now owned by Scottish Rite, is notable for its *Ben-Hur* chariot race mural. (VCHS.)

Although hotels accommodated visitors downtown, in this postcard, Charles Gose advertised this Queen Anne–Victorian-style home at 825 South Seventh Street as "The Gose / Home for Tourists." It served as a guesthouse in the late 1930s and early 1940s. The house was built in 1894; an early owner was Henry Miller, president of Miller-Parrott Baking Company, wholesalers of crackers and bread. (Ray Thomas.)

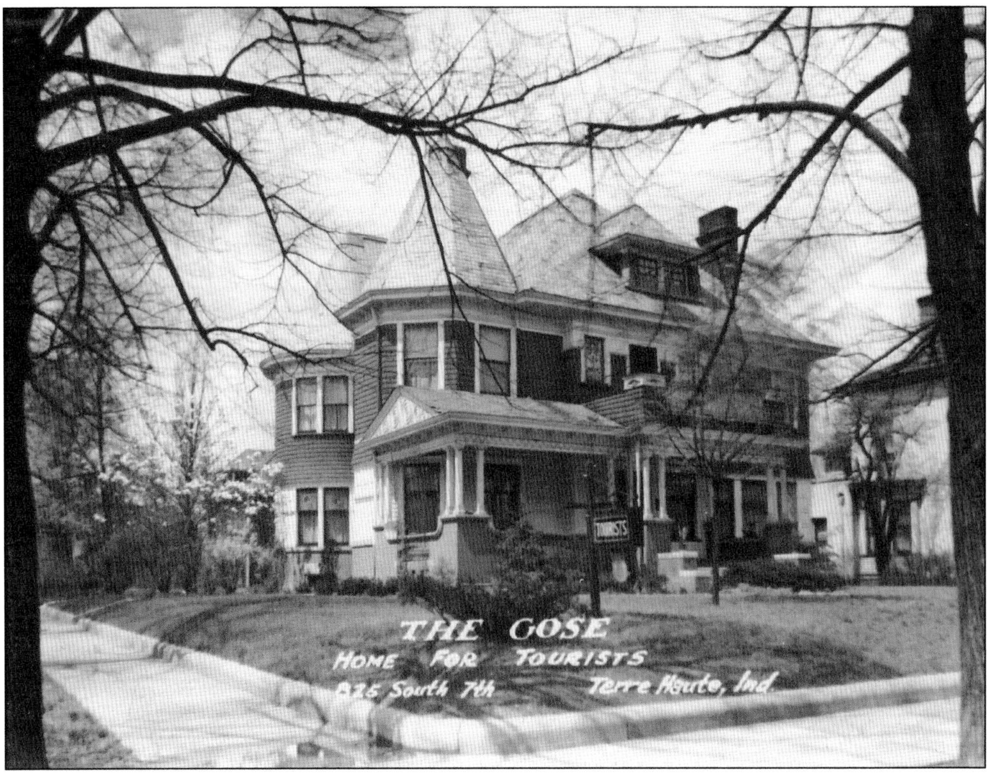

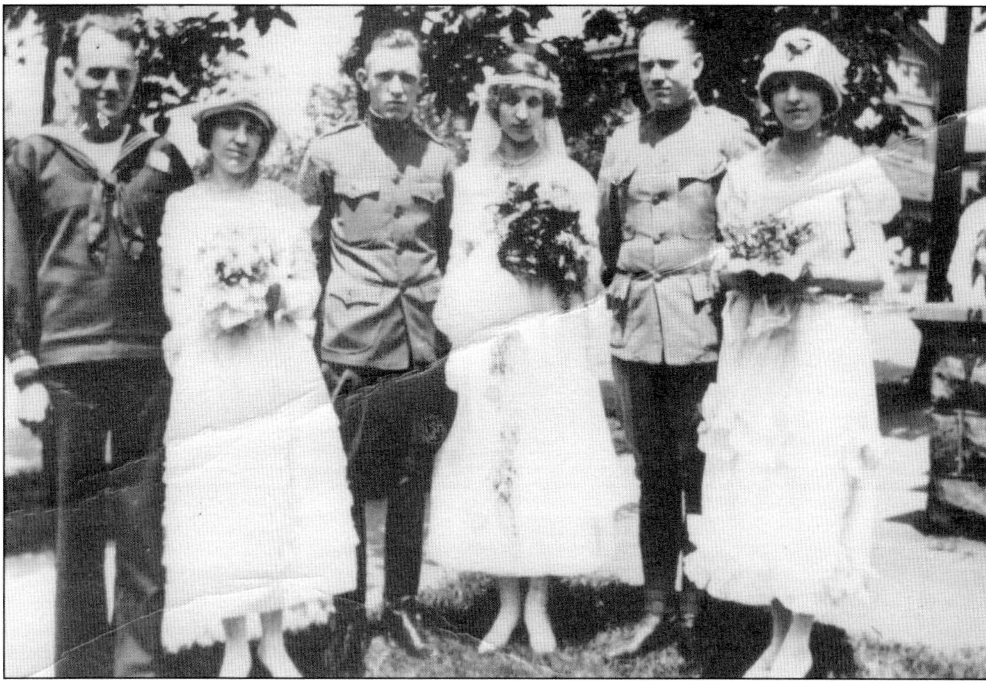

John Kelly and Katharine Walsh, third and fourth from left, were wed on July 6, 1918, while John was home on leave from camp in South Carolina. He was originally assigned to the 309th Ammunition Train, 84th Division. Shortly before the wedding, he had completed Officers Training School and received a promotion to second lieutenant. After returning to Terre Haute, he became influential in road construction work. (Anne Burkett.)

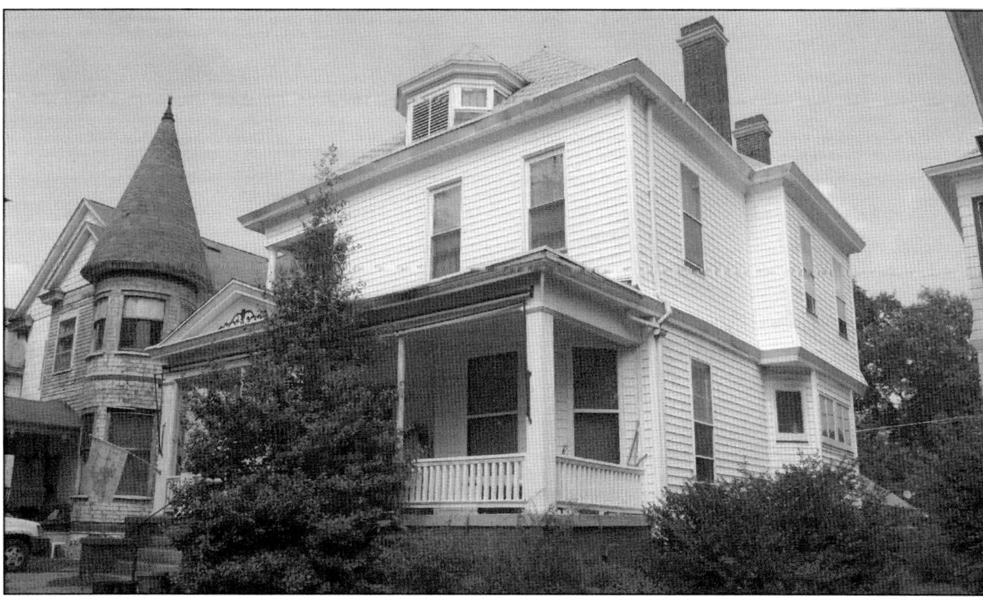

John and Katharine Kelly raised five sons—Richard, James, Thomas, Joseph, and William—in this house at 718 South Fifth Street. Before he went into the armed forces, John got his grounding as a salesman for the Nattkemper-Connelly Company, dealers in coal and gravel as well as road builders. The house is a Queen Anne Classic Free style built in 1895.

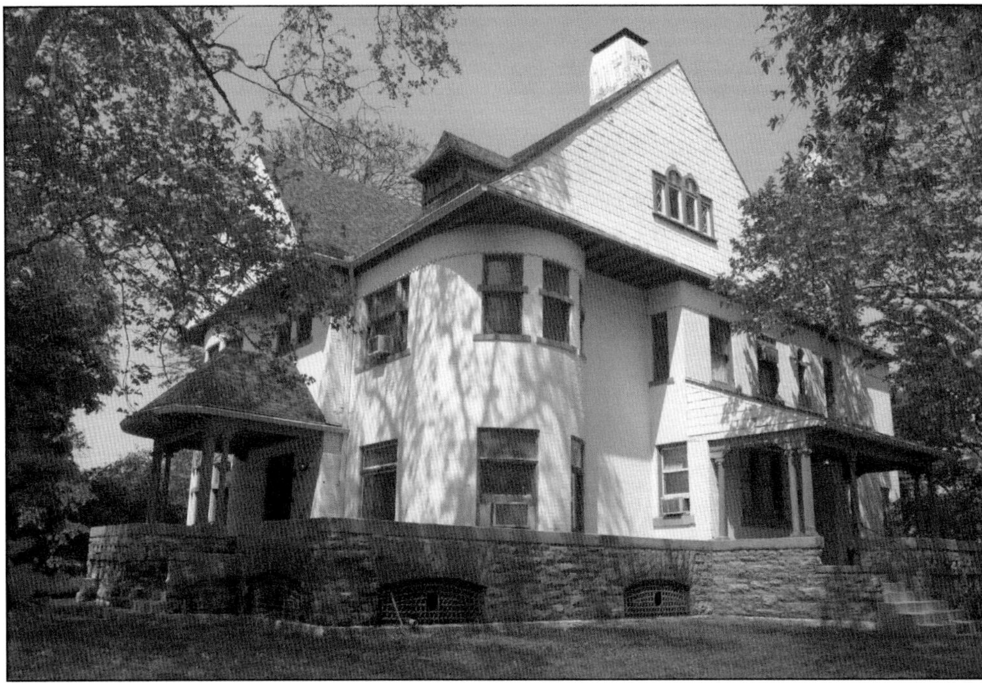

So his sons could walk to work from home, John Kelly purchased 444 South Sixth Street. It served as headquarters for his Bituminous Materials Company, which he started in the 1930s, and for Wabash Valley Asphalt, started in 1929. The companies specialized in road construction. He installed an elevator for his niece's husband, a paraplegic from the Korean War. The house contains 11 fireplaces.

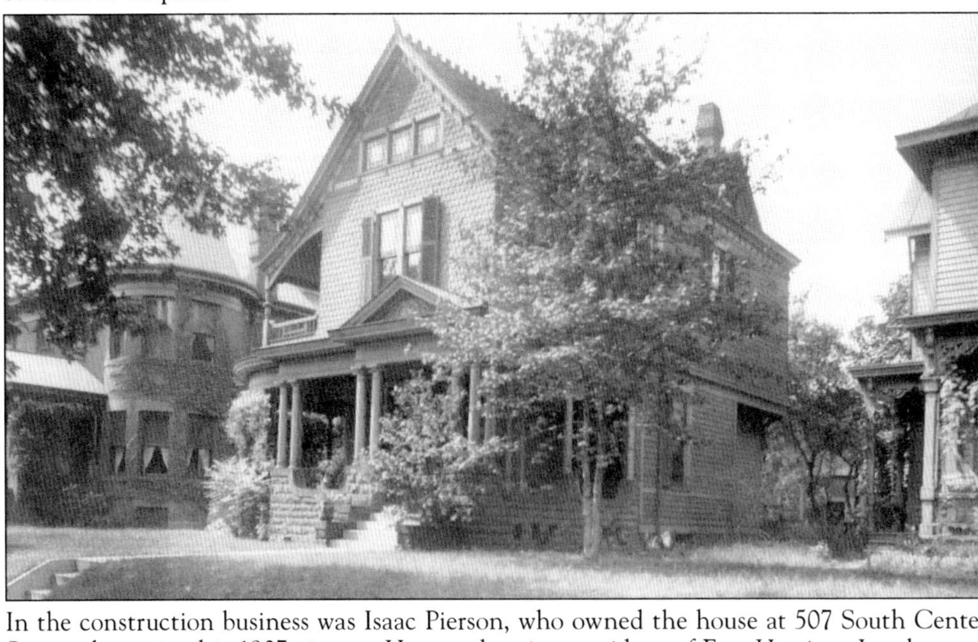

In the construction business was Isaac Pierson, who owned the house at 507 South Center Street, shown in this 1907 picture. He was the vice president of Fort Harrison Lumber and founder of Pierson and Brothers. The house, a Queen Anne style, was built around 1890. (J. Richard Becker Jr.)

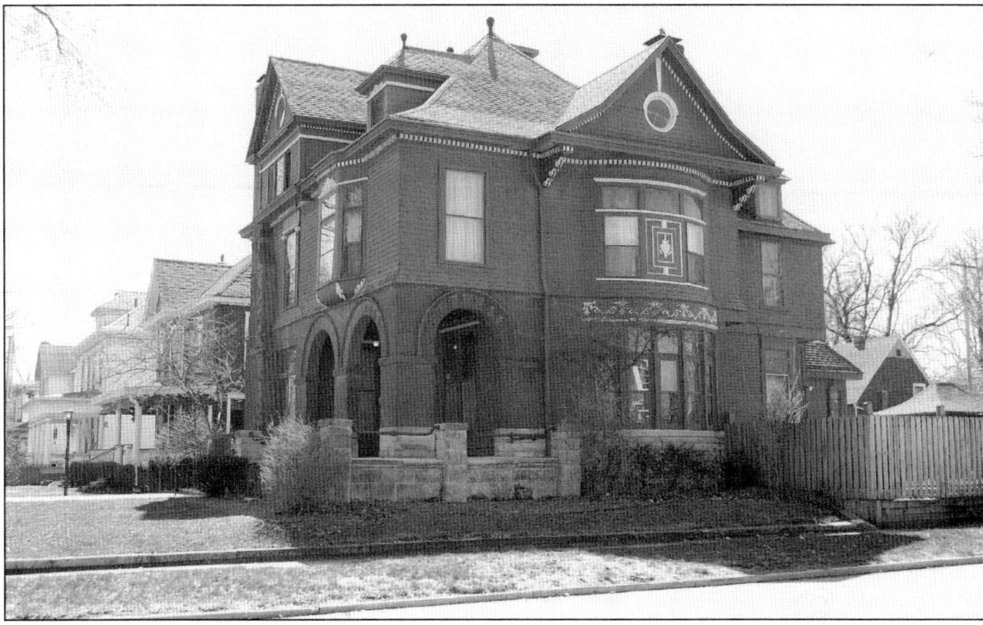

The large arches on the veranda of this Queen Anne–Romanesque Revival house at 903 South Center Street give it a distinctive appearance. Owner Ira Aten was another Farrington's Grove resident involved in coal. He was a pioneer in Ohio's coal industry before moving to Terre Haute in 1912. He was assistant treasurer of the Maumee Collieries in 1927; by 1947, he was director and department manager.

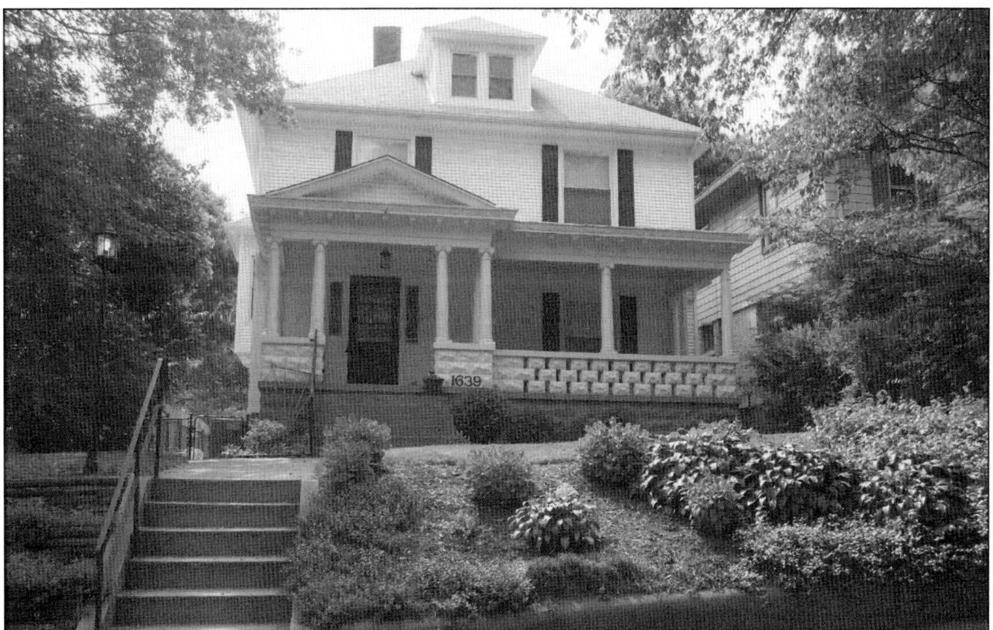

Ira Aten's son Charles W. Aten owned this house at 1639 South Fifth Street and also worked at the Maumee Collieries. In 1947, he was a clerk, and by 1955, he had risen to personnel manager. Among Maumee mines in the area were the Chieftain Fifth Vein, Old Glory Brazil Block, Antioch Fifth Vein, and Linton Supreme Fourth Vein. (Photograph by Albert Christenberry.)

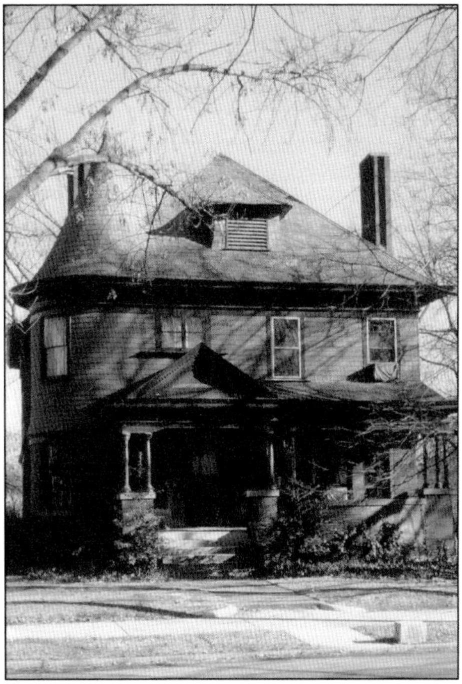

James A. Crawford, second owner of this house at 800 South Sixth Street, was born into a family that established the first iron blasting firm in Terre Haute—the Vigo Blast Furnace Company—and the Wabash Iron Works. His daughter Helen Crawford Hughes loved to show her spaniels, drive a bright yellow Cadillac around town, and share strong opinions on many subjects. (Daniel and Kaylynn Sanders.)

Indoor plumbing was new when 800 South Sixth Street was built in 1894, and pipes were not hidden behind walls. The kitchen showcases the original lead pipes, now a curiosity and no longer used. Two pipes governed by a foot valve released rainwater to the kitchen and basement from a collection tank in the attic. Other pipes brought well water, hot and cold, to the kitchen and bathroom. (Daniel and Kaylynn Sanders.)

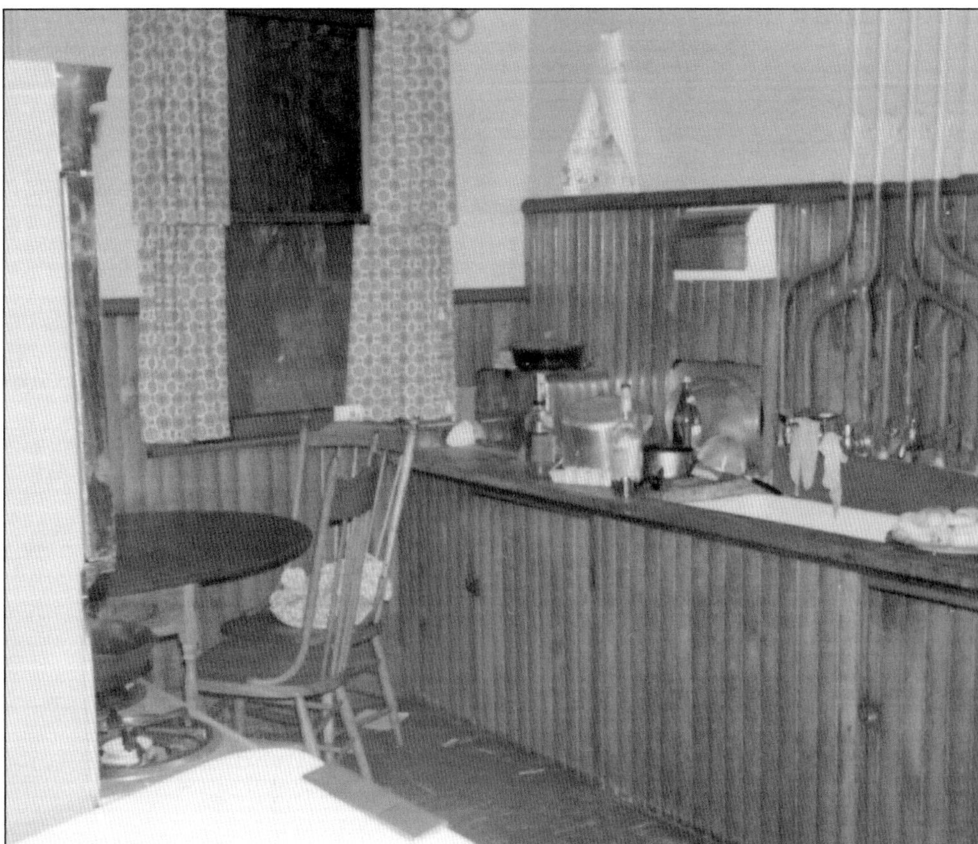

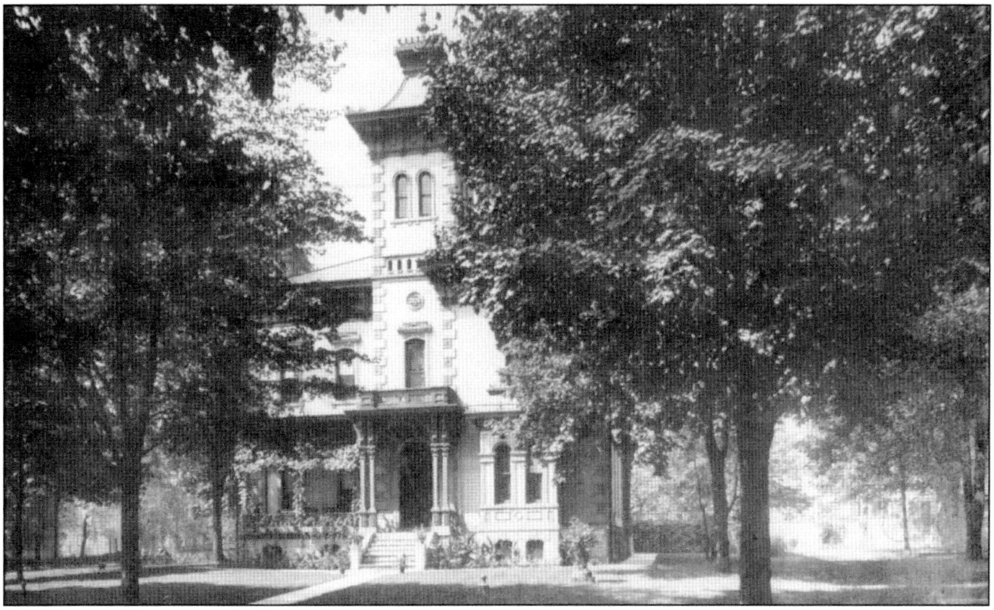

The Crawford family business was metals; the Keyes business was wood and carriages. Jay Keyes owned a Kentucky lumber company; his house formerly stood at 723 South Sixth Street. Keyes established the city's first golf course at Fourteenth and Beech Streets in 1898. Later, he moved it east of Highland Lawn Cemetery, leasing land from Virginia Jenckes's husband, Ray; in 1900, it became the Country Club of Terre Haute. (J. Richard Becker Jr.)

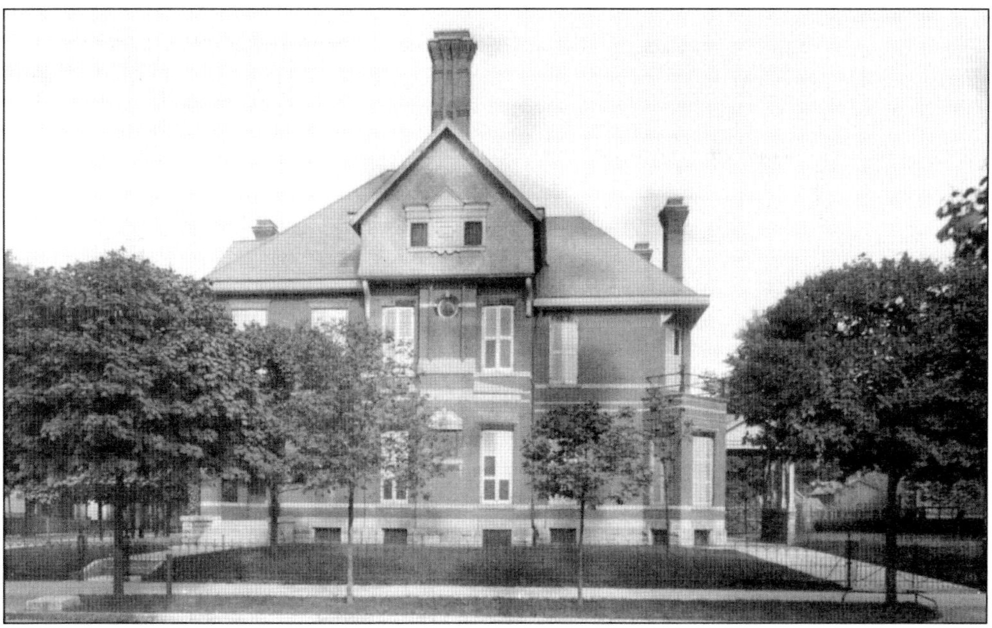

Crawford Fairbanks's home at 402 South Sixth Street no longer stands, but his impact has lasted. He and his brother donated land for Fairbanks Park. He gave $50,000 to build Emeline Fairbanks Library in 1906. He built the Tribune Building in 1912 and owned or partly owned the world's largest distillery in 1880, the *Terre Haute Tribune*, and French Lick Springs Hotel, among other holdings. (J. Richard Becker Jr.)

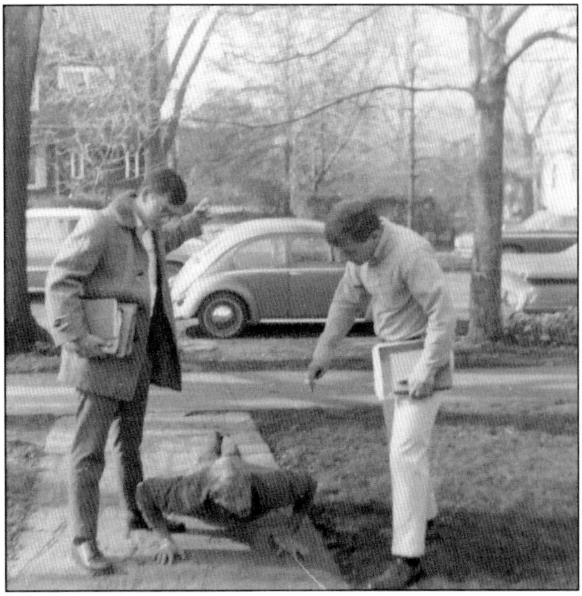

Although Homer Talley, of Talley Coal Company, originally owned the home at 1200 South Sixth Street, the house later became one of several large houses on Sixth Street used by fraternities. Here, some members of Lambda Chi Alpha put a pledge through his paces with some pushups on the front sidewalk. (ISU.)

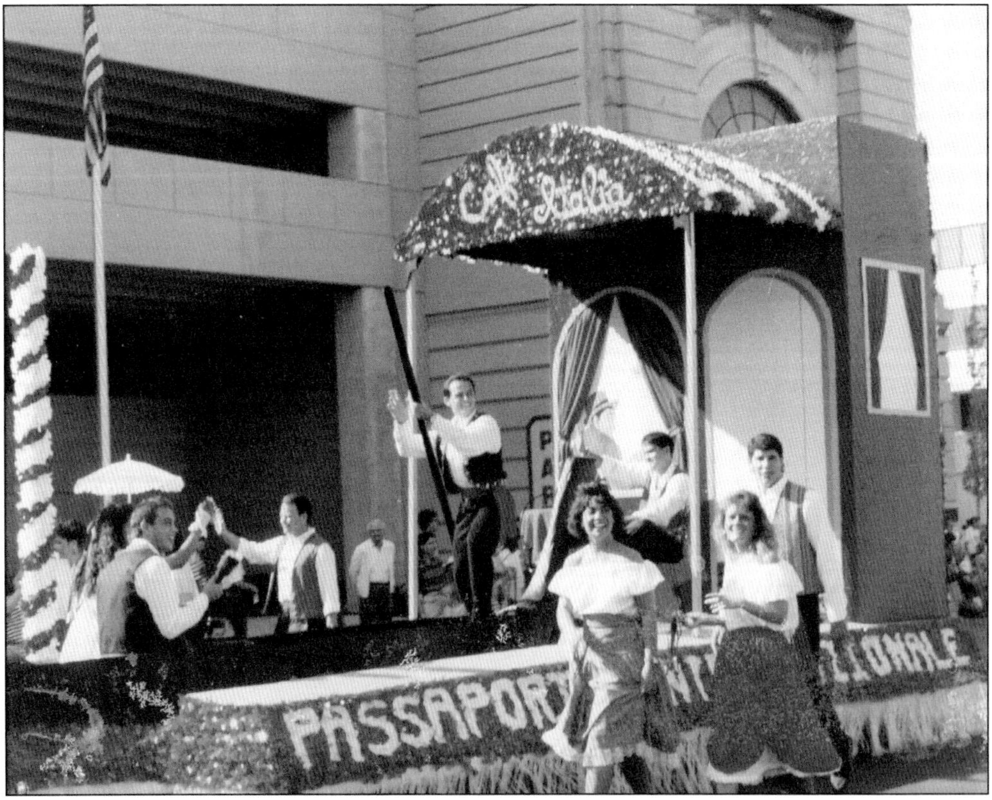

Tau Kappa Epsilon, like many other fraternities and sororities at Indiana State University, built floats each year for the ISU Homecoming Parade, the largest such student-run parade in the nation. This float with an Italian theme was named Passaporte Internationale. The floats were built in secret. After the parade, fraternities in Farrington's Grove often displayed the floats on their lawns. (Tau Kappa Epsilon.)

Tau Kappa Epsilon fraternity at 1308 South Sixth Street was known as Forum in its earlier years. In the photograph below, three members engage in a pie-eating contest. Apparently, the contest involved some wagering, as two members eagerly wave money in their hands. At right, Tau Kappa Epsilon members indulge in a game of poker and some smokes. Blue jeans were not yet the norm for college students; members wore dress slacks. At this time in the 1950s and later, it was common for fraternities to have "smokers" during Rush Week. Prospective pledges would drop by the fraternity houses, visit, and have a smoke so the students and fraternity could size up each other. (Both, ISU.)

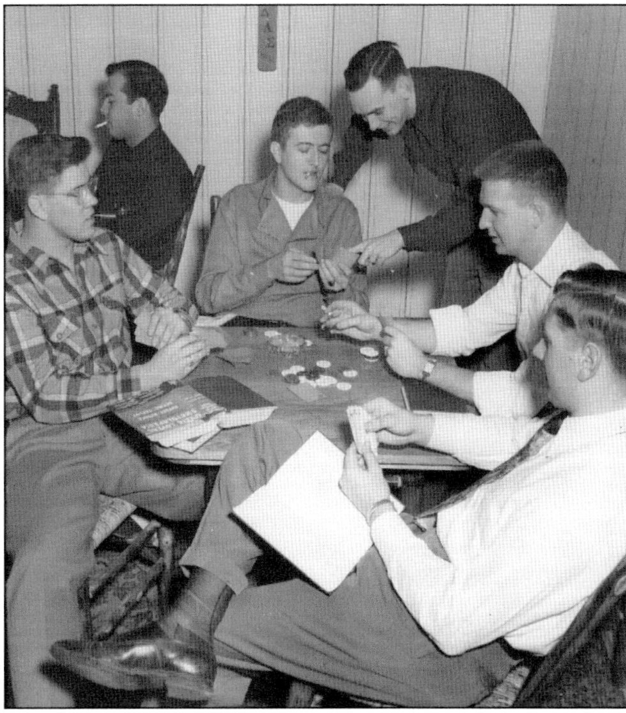

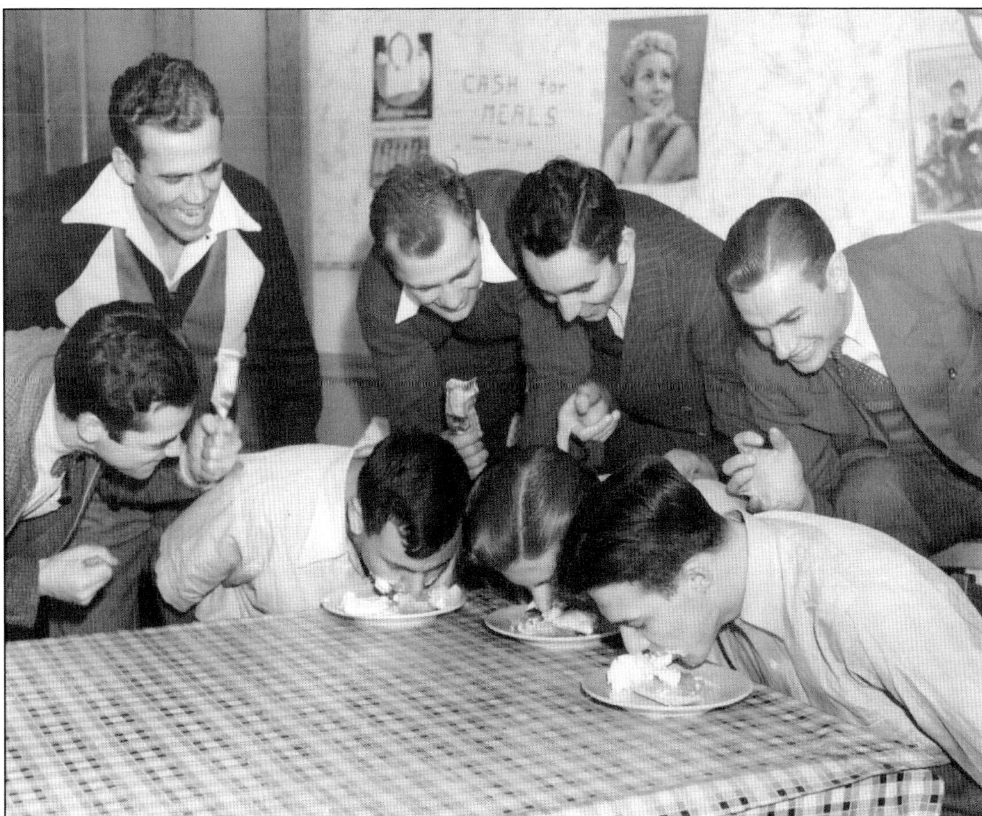

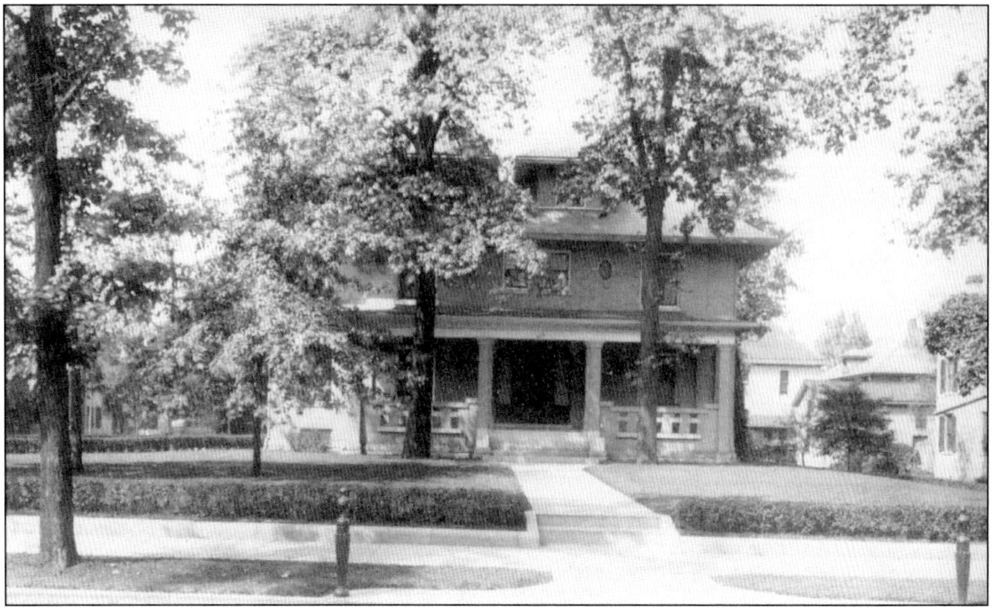

This house at 429 South Sixth Street was the home of E.P. Fairbanks, who paid $10,000 for the lot from the Warren estate and built a $20,000 Colonial Revival–style residence in 1905. He was the vice president of Terre Haute Brewing Company. Perhaps that history was a happy coincidence for the fraternity that moved in later. (J. Richard Becker Jr.)

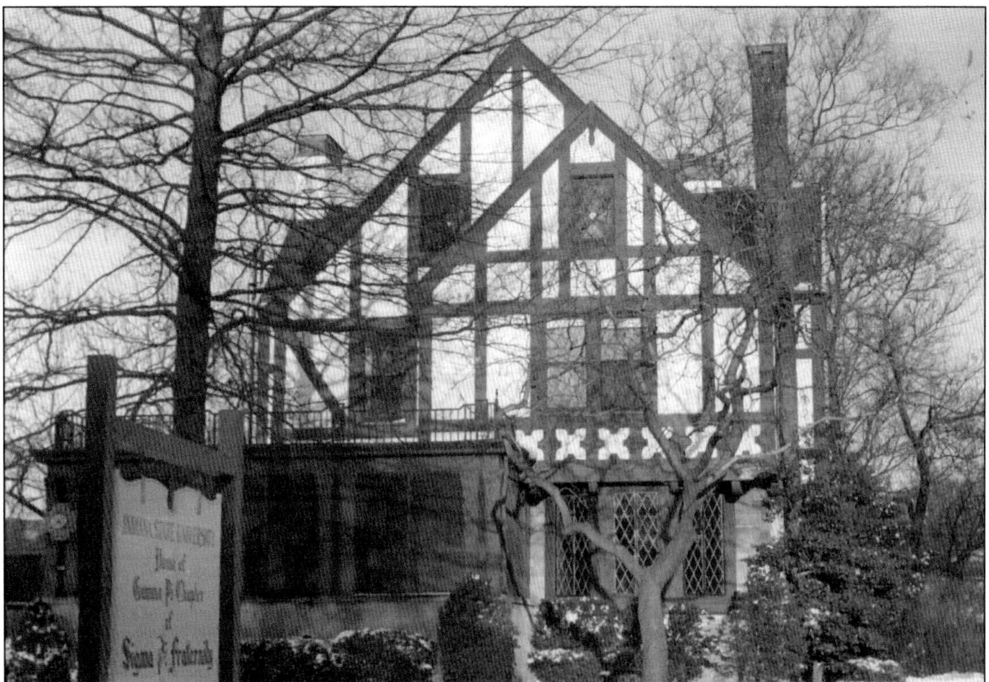

The Tudor Revival–style home at 1130 South Sixth Street differs from other houses along its block in Farrington's Grove. It was built around 1890. In 1939, Stewart Rose, president of Louden Packing Company and vice president of American Packing Corporation, owned the house. Sigma Pi fraternity later occupied the house; Sigma Tau Gamma occupies it now. (ISU.)

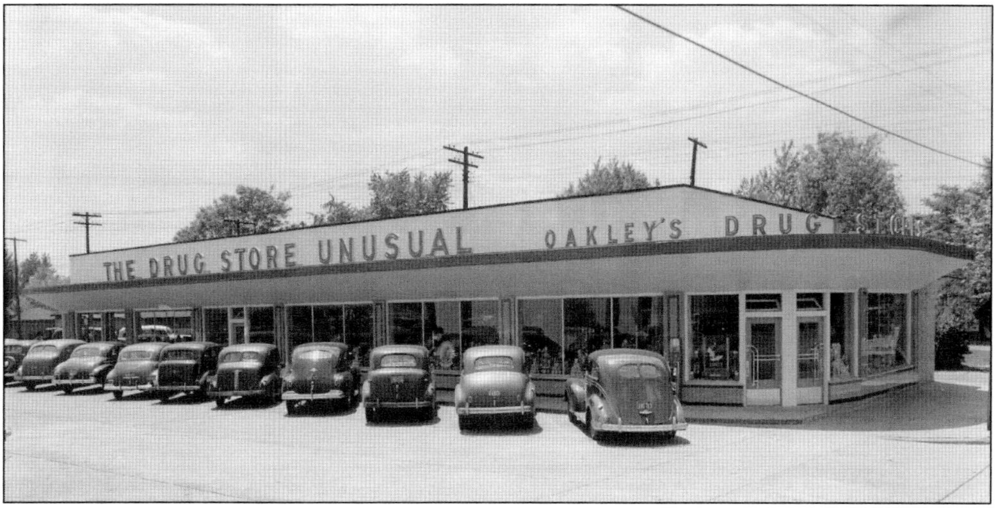

Oakley's Drug Store—the Drug Store Unusual in the upper photograph—caused quite a stir when it opened at the southwest corner of Seventh and Hulman Streets in 1941. It was the first super drugstore in Terre Haute. Part of the structure still exists today in a gas station and convenience store. In the photograph below, the menu shows the prices of the day, regulated by the US Office of Price Administration during World War II. The Oakley family previously owned a chain of corner grocery stores in Terre Haute and the Wabash Valley. In 1932, they owned 34 city grocery stores, including those at 500 and 1524 South Seventh Street in Farrington's Grove. The Oakley family sold their stores to the Kroger Company before opening the drugstore. (Above, photograph by Martin's Photo Shop, Oakley Corporation; below, Oakley Corporation.)

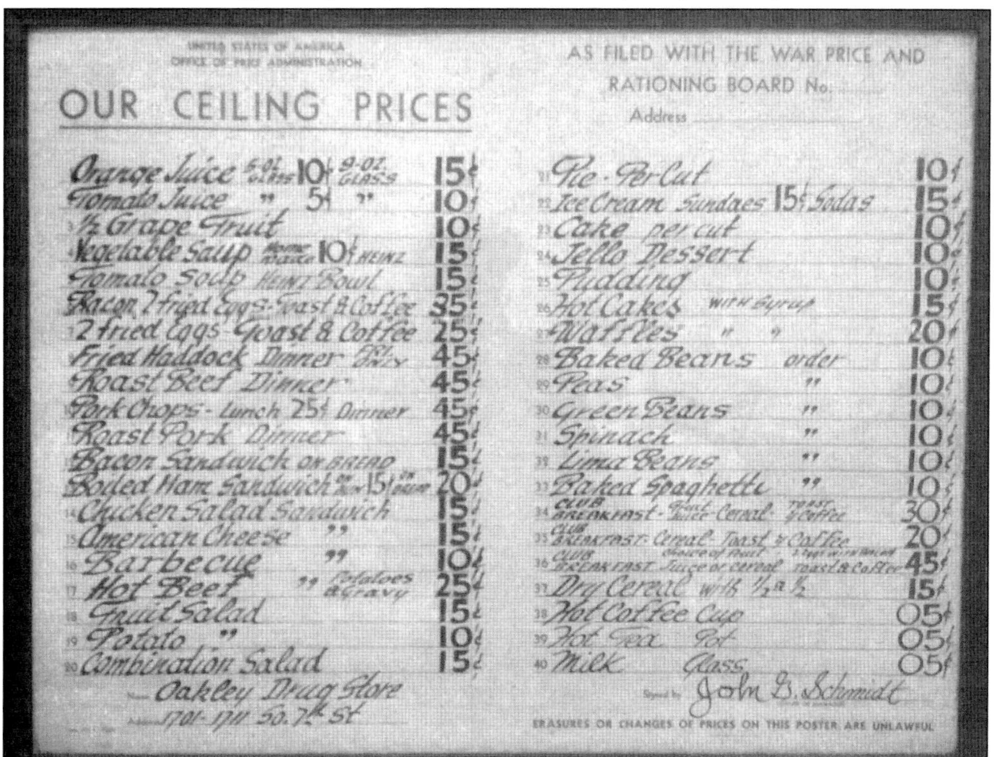

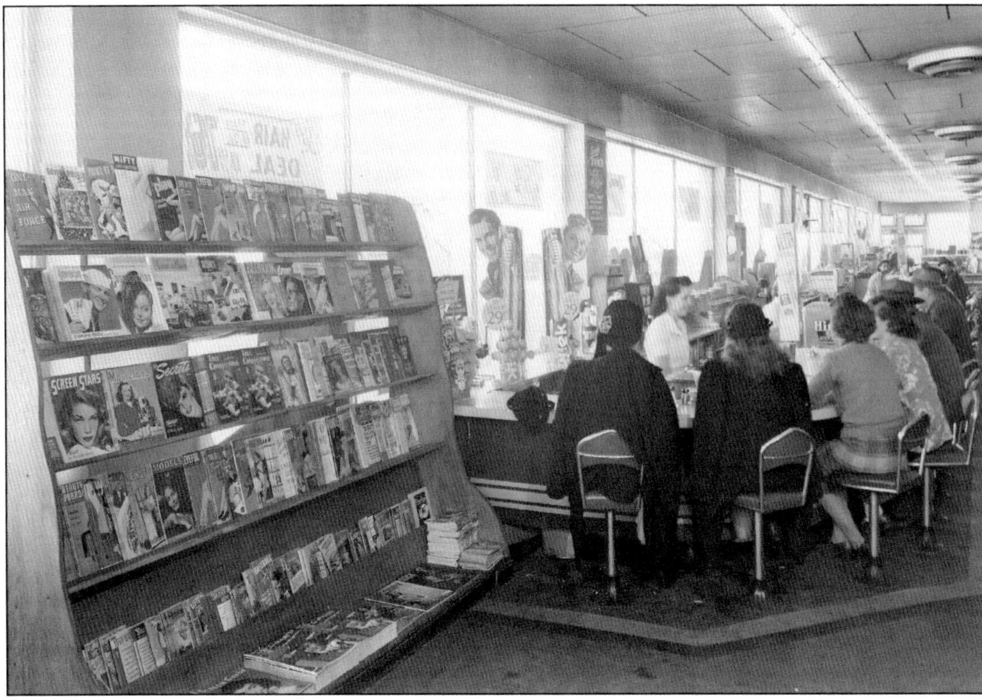

The lunch counter at Oakley's Drug Store at the southwest corner of Seventh and Hulman Streets was busy during opening week in 1941. People could buy a roast pork chop dinner for 45¢ and a slice of pie for 10¢. Like many other businesses, Oakley's had to file a list of prices with the War Price and Rationing Board. (Photograph by Martin's Photo Shop; Oakley Corporation.)

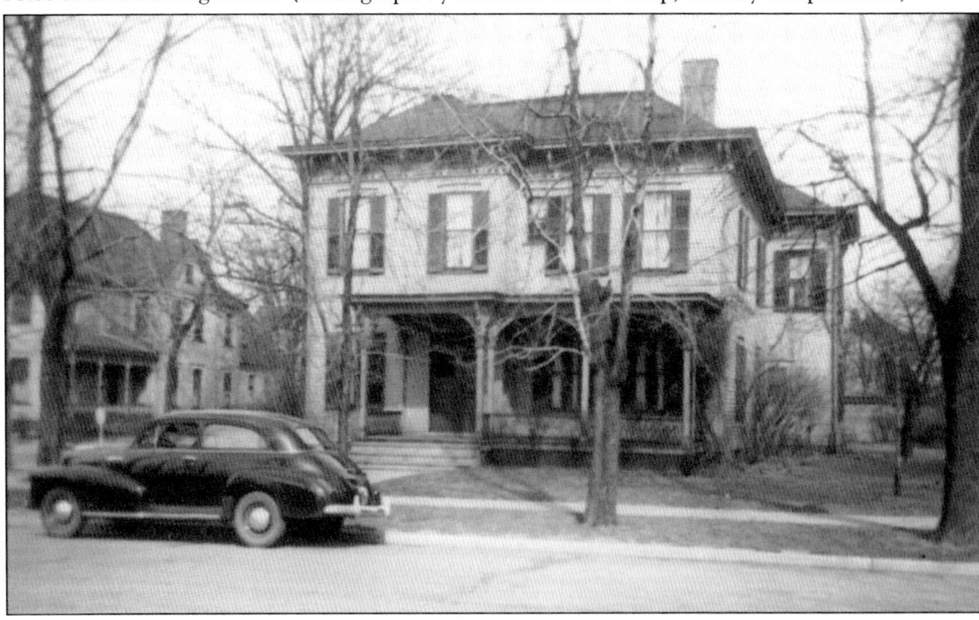

Besides drugstores, the Farrington's Grove area also has been home to several medical professionals. This home at 800 South Center Street is an Italianate-style house built in the 1870s for Dr. Samuel Humphrey and later owned by Anthony Blake, who was associated with the Joseph Strong and Company wholesale firm. (VCPL.)

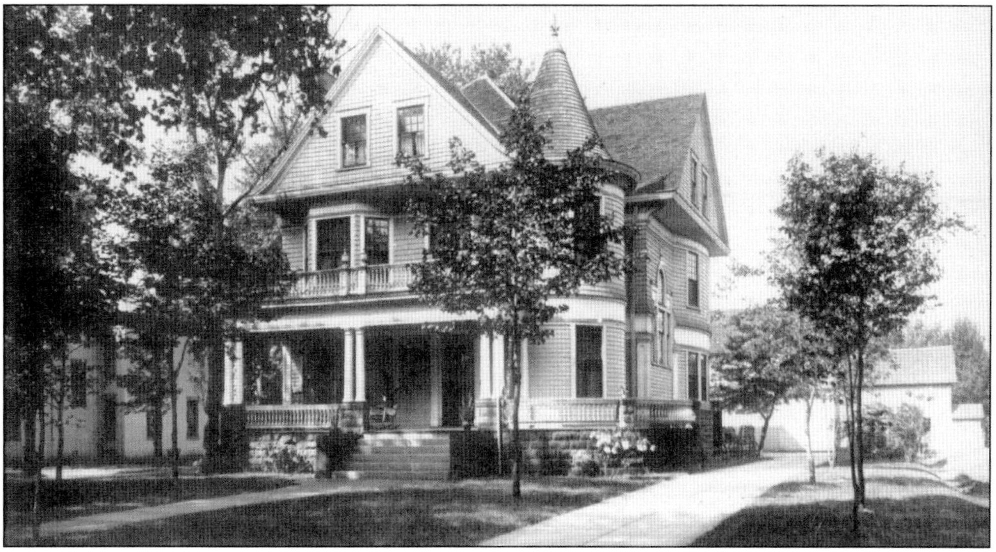

If there are doctors and pharmacies, then there must also be insurance agents. W.A. Hamilton owned this house at 1227 South Sixth Street in 1907; he was a manager for Mutual Life Insurance Company. The massive Free Classic–style house was built about 1898. A one-story solarium was added in 1924. (J. Richard Becker Jr.)

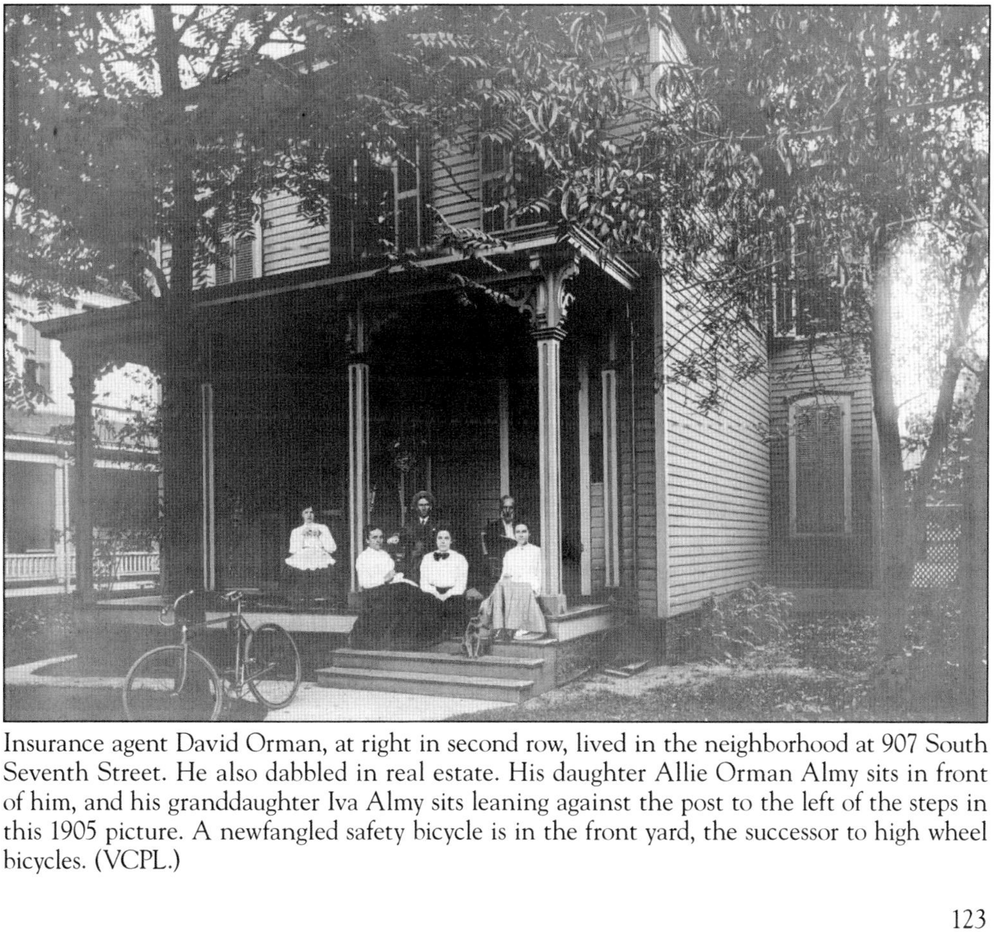

Insurance agent David Orman, at right in second row, lived in the neighborhood at 907 South Seventh Street. He also dabbled in real estate. His daughter Allie Orman Almy sits in front of him, and his granddaughter Iva Almy sits leaning against the post to the left of the steps in this 1905 picture. A newfangled safety bicycle is in the front yard, the successor to high wheel bicycles. (VCPL.)

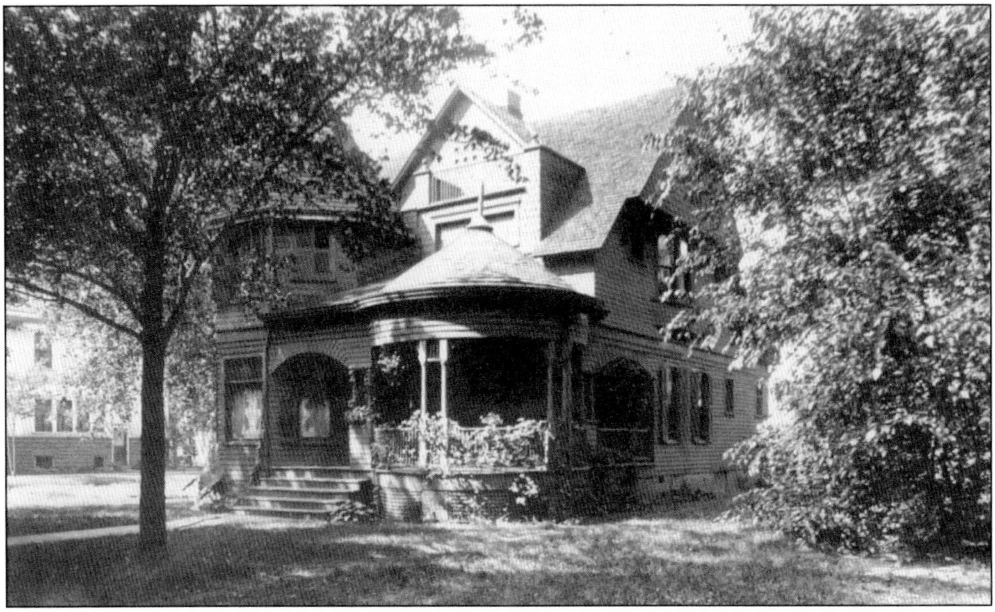

Attorney James Swango owned this home at 1205 South Sixth Street, a few houses north of W.A. Hamilton, in 1907. Swango later served as a judge in the city. The house is a Queen Anne and was built about 1892. The architecture looks much the same today compared to this 1907 photograph. The tower on the house has fish-scale skirting, and it is flanked by a one-story, flat-roofed sunroom. (J. Richard Becker Jr.)

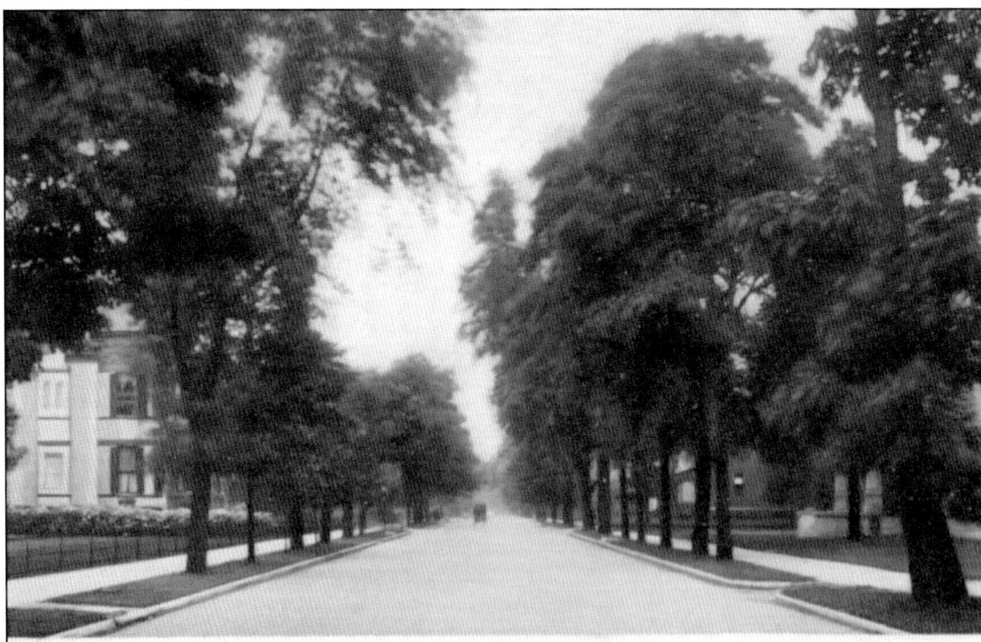

James Swango, Col. Richard Thompson, Chapman J. Root, and many others owned homes on South Sixth Street in Farrington's Grove. This view looks south on Sixth Street in the early 1900s, in the direction of their homes. Many wealthy and upper-middle-class families built homes on Sixth Street. Around 1871, Samuel McDonald raced chariots down this stretch. (Ray Thomas.)

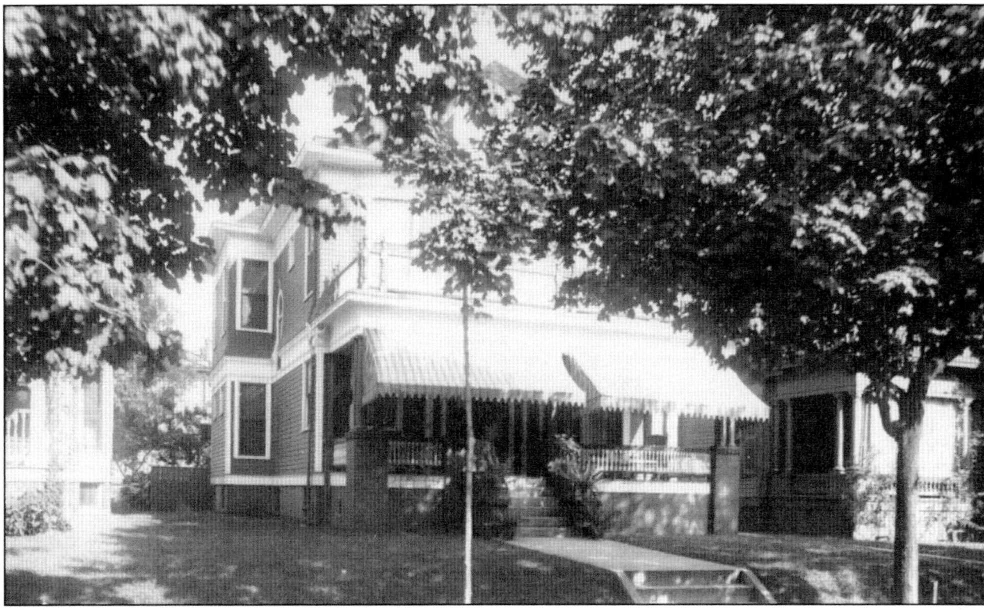

Lee R. Whitney, of 722 South Fifth Street, kept busy in the business community. He worked with Frank Hale, serving as general manager of National Drain Tile Company after its incorporation and as president of Vigo-American Clay Company. He was also president of the State Bank of West Terre Haute. This picture shows his house in 1907. (J. Richard Becker Jr.)

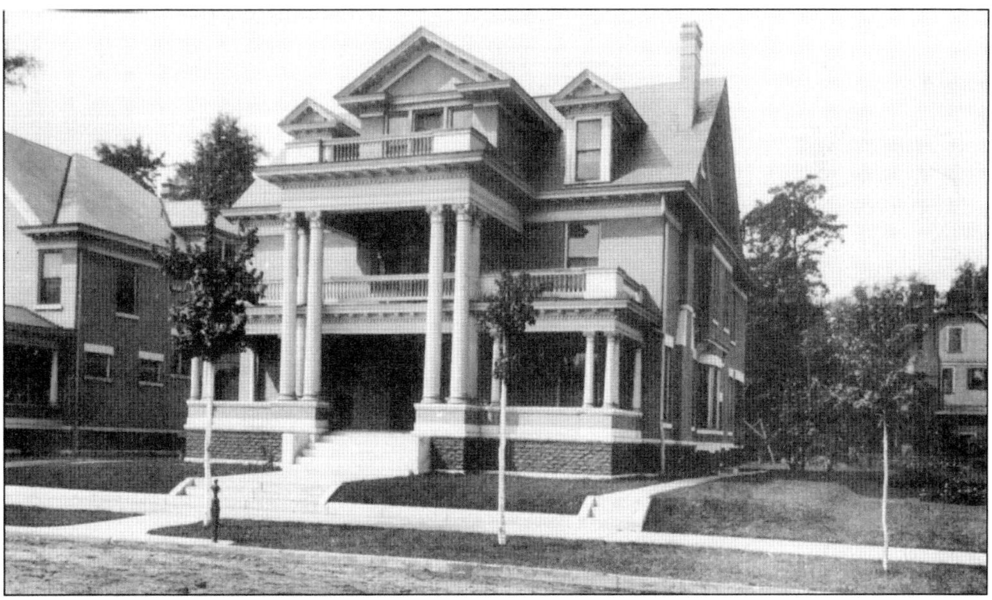

This Colonial Revival house at 1139 South Center Street looks quite different today compared to this 1907 photograph; the two-story columns are no longer there, and the front porch has been changed. George Foulkes was the original owner. He was involved in many businesses, including Foulkes-Forbes paving contractors, Foulkes Brothers Hatters and other men's clothing, and real estate and loans. (J. Richard Becker Jr.)

INDEX

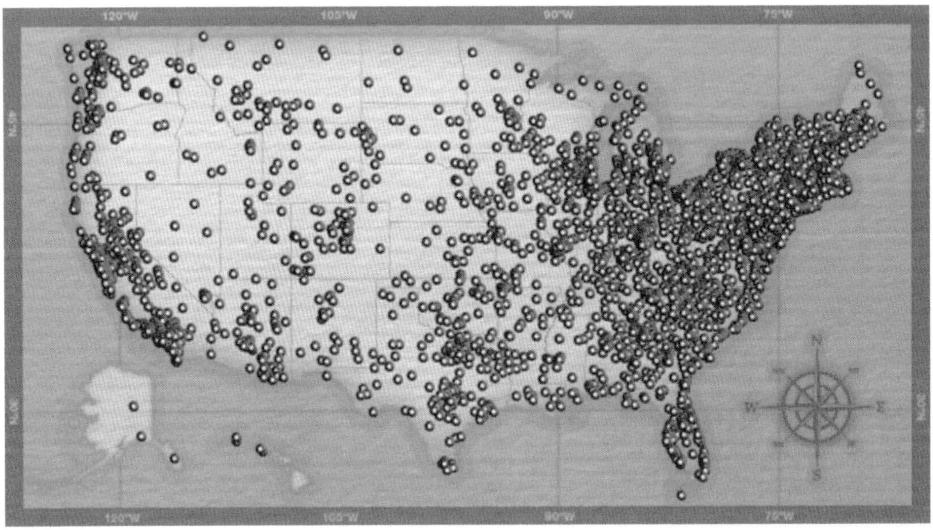